GIBBY

GIBBY

TALES OF A
BASEBALL LIFER

JOHN GIBBONS
AND GREG OLIVER

For Jordan, Troy and Kyle

CONTENTS

FOREWORD

You probably hear a little bit too often about a manager that's a player's manager, but that was Gibby.

Like any manager, Gibby had his own methods of making his line-ups, doing the bullpen changes and looking for talent when the roster positions were up for grabs.

But when it came down to it, no matter what, you knew as a player that Gibby always had your back. That included handling situations with umpires or the media — and Gibby was a true media darling.

Now, we would jab at each other all the time, just kind of bantering back and forth. He would give it to me, and I'd give it back to him. I'm often asked about our one confrontation in the dugout at Yankees Stadium. We were into our third game in two days, and I didn't think that I was going to be in the lineup that day — but I was. Yankees pitcher CC Sabathia was just blowing my doors off. I didn't even know why (or how) I was playing, since I had zero in the tank.

CC struck me out again in my second at-bat and I broke my bat on the side of the rail in our dugout, right beside Gibby. He started at me:

"Are you directing that towards me?"

"No, Gibby, I'm pissed off that I struck out for the second time against a guy who I shouldn't be striking out against."

Gibby got a little too close, so that's where the whole quote about smelling my Tom Ford cologne came from.

The fact is that Gibby was looking out for me, trying to get me back into a good mental spot. As the guy who was one of the main pieces of those Blue Jays teams he managed, I took a lot of responsibility in a lot of areas. So, I was always just trying to see how we could get better, how I could get better. Sometimes Gibby would say, "Hey, relax, calm down." He'd tell me to just go out there and take care of my own business.

Our Jays teams had a lot of big personalities and he had to be able to manage that. He's just a good ol' southern boy up in Toronto, to where you wouldn't necessarily always think that would be a good fit because of different mindsets and mentalities. I thought he did a great job there.

Gibby was one of my favorite managers that I've had during my many years in baseball.

He grew on me, and he grew on Canada too, because he was authentic to who he was.

— JOSH DONALDSON

INTRODUCTION

Y ou've got to be kidding. You want to read about me?

Didn't you get enough of me when I was mumbling my way through all those interviews when I managed the Blue Jays? That Toronto media was non-stop and couldn't get enough of me. Pretty sure I was on TV more than the prime minister.

And I *know* I was better liked, at least when the Jays were winning.

People always told me that if the team was relevant in August and September, by which time the fans knew the team was legit, they'd come out in droves — but they wanted evidence. They were wary — tired of being fooled for decades. I never saw it as a player, since I was in the National League, with the Mets, well before interleague play was a thing. Or I was stuck in the minors.

Sure enough, when we were in it and we had something to play for, the SkyDome, or Rogers Centre, whatever you want to call it, absolutely rocked. I'd be sitting there in the dugout, and you could *feel* the place shaking. It was pretty special.

So was my time in baseball.

I guess since you bought a book, I'd better get to spinning some stories, huh? Or maybe I should say "eh"? Like all those Canadians do.

1.

GROWING UP

My first swing of a bat in a competitive baseball game happened in Goose Bay, Newfoundland and Labrador, of all places. If you don't want to get out an atlas, let me tell you where that is. Think top-right on a map of North America, and you're close. Labrador is attached to the rest of Canada, while Newfoundland is an island further east in the Atlantic Ocean.

Canadian Forces Base Goose Bay was established during the Second World War. It's since grown into the largest military base in northeastern North America, and it has the longest runways in the world.

It's three thousand miles to Great Falls, Montana, where I was born — on June 8, 1962, in case you don't have my baseball card handy — or thirteen hundred miles to Boston, which is really home, since that's where both my parents were from.

How'd we end up in Goose Bay? My father, Bill Gibbons, rebelled against his optometrist roots and joined the military in research and development. That far north, the summer lasts only about a month. And the blackflies were everywhere.

So there was my dad, making the most of a short season, taking his youngest child to the local baseball field to try out for the team. I was only seven and scared to death. I wouldn't get out of the car. Luckily, one of the guys my dad worked with was coaching one of the teams, so Dad talked to the guy, and the guy put me on his team — I didn't have to try out. If he hadn't known the coach, I probably never would have played.

Like all kids, I enjoyed those early games but was not obsessed with baseball. Not yet. That wouldn't happen for a couple more moves.

Our father was co-captain of the 1954 Beverly High football team in Beverly, Massachusetts. He didn't play competitive baseball, just in the sandlot with buddies.

Our mother, Sallie Boyson, was a cheerleader at the same school, a year younger, and she was good friends with Dad's sister, Janet. As Mom tells it, it was a "beautiful little story." The athletic genes got transferred to all three Gibbons kids. Billy, named for Dad and born in 1959, played college football on a scholarship; Kristen, born in 1961, loved to ride horses and played basketball; and then there's me. If any baseball roots got passed down to me, it was through my grandfather on my mother's side, Dutchie Boyson, who was a semi-pro catcher in Beverly.

Raised in a very structured household, Dad was the perfect child, always doing the right thing. But instead of joining the family optometry business in nearby Marblehead, he joined the U.S. Air Force. He started out checking eyes, which he didn't want to do, with the intent of branching out. My dad was way too smart to pigeonhole himself. He eventually got into researching the use of lasers on the eyes, a precursor of LASIK. He also looked at ways to protect fighter pilots from radiation. It turned into a fascinating career. He traveled the world as the research and development representative for the Air Force in NATO. Mom went to dental hygiene school at Tufts in Boston. Thanks for the smile, Mom. She wore me out complaining about my tobacco use.

Mom's upbringing was quite different. My grandfather had a window blinds business, but it was actually a front. He was a small-time bookmaker. If you catch her in the right mood, she'll tell stories about being a Mafia princess and how the mob guys used to scare her. My mom is an angel on earth, so she figured it all out.

We got shuffled around as a military family. Billy was born in Boston, and Kristen and I in Montana. From there, we went to Loring Air Force

Base in Limestone, Maine, on the Canadian border. After that rugged winter, my dad was going to resign his commission, but they enticed him with a stint in Puerto Rico for three years.

After Puerto Rico, Dad left the military to help his father out and decide, once and for all, his future. After a year in optometry, he was convinced that it still wasn't for him. So he got back in the Air Force and headed to Goose Bay. What's funny, my mom tells me, is everyone asked them, "What did you do wrong to get sent up to Goose Bay?" But she says they loved it, one of their favorite assignments. (I learned to move regularly, so pro ball was easy for me.) After the Goose, the military paid for my father to get his doctorate down at the University of Houston. Then on to San Antonio, where I call home. His final assignment was in Washington, DC, in the surgeon general's office, but it was just him and Mom by then.

There are a number of military bases in and around San Antonio, and Brooks Air Force Base was a big, big research and development base in the military, and so my dad was stationed there for an unheard of 13 years — very rare in the military, but Dad had a unique job to do. When we moved to San Antonio, I was going into the fifth grade, and I graduated in 1980. My siblings and I, we all did our schooling in San Antonio. You're not going to get rich in the military, but with my dad advancing through the ranks and my mom being a hygienist, we had everything we needed and more. But I did learn the value of a buck.

Our favorite stop had to have been Puerto Rico. My mom called it paradise. Even though I was very young, I remember a lot. The not-so-fun I remember was that I was allergic to a lot of tropical plants, especially hibiscus, so I had to get shots a couple of times a week to help with my asthma. The one story that probably gave an indication that I would carry a stick or a bat my whole life happened one day when I put a cape on, grabbed a stick and went to my buddy's house to see if he could come out. When his mom said he wasn't in, she also told me not to play with sticks. So, I went home and climbed one of our trees and, like Superman, jumped. When I landed, the stick punctured the roof of my mouth. My mom ran me to the hospital down the street. When they stitched me up, the doctor told us that if it had gone in another eighth of an inch, I'd have been in big trouble. Kids, when parents tell you, "Don't play with sticks" — don't play with sticks!

My first brush with professional sports stardom happened in Puerto Rico too. We lived on base, and our next-door neighbor's brother was Mick Tingelhoff, center for the Minnesota Vikings. Mick would come down to visit his sister during their offseason. I was really young, but I do remember meeting him. The Vikings became *my team* because I met Mick Tingelhoff. I started writing letters to all the players on the Vikings to see if I could get an autographed picture. You'd be amazed how many I got back. This was the days of the Purple People Eaters. Bill Brown, the running back, Joe Kapp . . . what a thrill for a young kid. When I got into baseball, in the big leagues, it was always important to me to sign autographs. People would send you pictures or baseball cards. Of course, there were times when you thought, *Damn, how many of these do I have to sign?* But then I'd think back to being a little kid and getting stuff back from the Vikings. This is what it's about.

But most of my early memories come from Texas, when I was a little bit older.

My mom always loved horses growing up, and she started riding when we were in Houston and never stopped. Well, she actually just stopped, at age 83, after she broke her tailbone dismounting. She's one tough gal — sure she's not Canadian? My sister started riding as well and became very good. Me? No chance. My mom would always try to get me to go on trail rides where she boarded her horse. One day, I relented and went. She put me on a quiet stable rental horse and off we went. I was the last horse and we were trotting down this trail, and all of a sudden my horse took off, heading for home: I'm yelling for my mom, the horse expert, and my horse starts heading down a hill and I'm ducking tree limbs and scared to death. Finally, he stops because there's a big drop-off. We eventually made it home, but that was the last of my horseback-riding career. The reason I'm telling you this story is because horses were always part of our lives. For the women anyway. From there on out, I just mucked the stalls.

Being closest in age, Kristen and I were often together, playing, fighting or doing something as a duo. One of the fun things our family liked to do was head down to Nuevo Laredo, across the Mexican border, for some shopping. I'm not too sure if it's safe to do now, but everybody did it back then. One year, I got a bullwhip, and back home, any time Kristen annoyed me, I'd get the bullwhip out and try to whip her. But she'd take it from me and pound on me pretty good.

On another trip to Nuevo Laredo, I talked my mom into letting me get a big ol' set of bull horns, the kind you sometimes see on someone's low-rider car. I also bought a mask of my favorite pro wrestler — Mil Máscaras — and wore that dragging these horns across the international bridge. I can remember goring a couple of people along the way. Well, Mexico is known for its bull fighting, isn't it?

Billy was very much like Dad. He was a go-getter, an achiever, things came easy to him. I was the youngest and hyperactive, which tested my parents' patience. My sister was the smartest of us three and could have done anything she wanted. She ran into some problems at home and ended up going to live with my aunt in Boston. It was the right decision for her to move away out east because she finished high school. But it was tough on us, especially Mom. Kris and Dad butted heads all the time — that was our dysfunction.

After she moved out, I didn't see a whole lot of her, and I regret that. She and Billy were diagnosed with different kinds of cancer on the same day. Bill has been fighting it ever since, and his stubbornness and faith have been an inspiration to me. Kristen lost her battle in 2021, passing away in Reno; she had breast cancer, multiple sclerosis and then melanoma. She was dealt a bad hand health-wise. She was a strong, tough gal and never complained. I wish I had been a better brother and been there for her more. I'll see her again someday in heaven.

Faith has always been an important part of my life. I grew up in the church, and Mom taught religious education. It doesn't mean I've done everything right — no chance. I've never gone out and preached or judged or pushed it on anybody, because I don't think you're supposed to do that. But I wanted to be known as a good guy with good morals. Right from my early days in baseball, I was a part of the Fellowship of Christian Athletes.

Our parents were supportive of whatever our interests were. For me, that became sports. I played baseball and basketball, and I took up football when I got to middle school.

During the two years in Houston before we moved to San Antonio, we went to a few Astros games at the Astrodome — that was my introduction to professional baseball. These guys were like gods, and I was in awe. My mom signed me up for a club called the Astro Buddies. You got an Astros T-shirt and cap and got to attend a couple of clinics as well as go on the field to meet a few players — my destiny. I was getting hooked.

I mentioned basketball earlier, but that didn't last too long. My first year, an opposing team's player was at the free throw line, and I was in my spot on the key, but up top, near him. Right as he took his shot, just as he was releasing the ball, I would stomp my foot. Finally, the ref told me to stop or I'd be ejected. In the car after the game, my dad jumped my butt about sportsmanship and playing the game right. I was only trying to win, but I learned my lesson, finished out the season and was done with the game. Too much running anyway.

We only went to one Rangers game at the old Arlington Stadium. Fergie Jenkins was pitching that day and threw a one-hit shutout. Another great Canadian athlete. Who knew that he'd one day be one of my coaches . . .

2.

A CATCHING PROSPECT

There's no way that I'd have made the major leagues, taken in the first round of the 1980 Draft by the New York Mets, without my high school coach Syl Perez. He pushed me and really helped open some baseball doors.

I was blessed with athletic genes, but what I really needed was someone who understood highly competitive athletics and would push me to my limits but wouldn't treat me any differently than anyone else on the team. That was a lesson I took with me when I started managing — some players will be more talented than others, but you need to be fair to everyone.

Perez was a great coach and came along at the right time in my life. I didn't need a disciplinarian — with my old man, I wasn't going to step out of line. Instead, Perez taught me what it takes, the work ethic that you need in the sports arena. And he was a fighter — you knew he'd have your back, and in return, you wanted to deliver for him.

Based on where we lived in San Antonio, MacArthur High was not the high school that I should have attended. But since my older brother and sister had gone there, I was grandfathered in, instead of going to the new school, James Madison High. My brother was a beloved figure at MacArthur. The girls loved Bill, and things just came naturally to him.

It wasn't like he was a real outgoing guy, but he was into having fun and would bend the rules when our dad traveled on TDY (temporary duty).

Bill was a natural at everything and a really good baseball player, but during spring break, he also wanted to party with his buddies, so they'd go to Padre Island, on the Gulf of Mexico (a big spring break spot). The baseball coach had warned if anyone went there, they'd be kicked off the team — he got the boot and just played football, which he excelled at.

I played my first football in middle school, in the seventh and eighth grades. I'd enjoyed it, but I hadn't had a growth spurt so was considering just playing baseball in high school. There was too much running in basketball, and football was for guys with size. Bill kept prodding me to play, though, so one day during their summer preseason workouts, he took me to the school to show me around and meet some coaches. The first coach I met was their great linebacker coach and a true redneck. Bill said, "Coach, this is my brother, John; he's not gonna play football this year." The coach said, "What, you're going to be in gym class with all the sissies? Then you might as well play that communist sport, soccer!"

Boy, did I change my mind quick. "No, Sir." (Red, white and blue, baby!) That's what swayed me. Football in Texas is like hockey in Canada, it's almost like you have to play it or you're an outcast. I'm glad I played. It toughened me up and physically helped me quite a bit, even though it's a sport you really need to be bigger and faster for than I was at the start. I was actually a running back, or more appropriately, a blocking back. My brother got the speed gene in our family.

Then I fell in love with football because I grew a little bit and I liked the contact. Coach Frank Arnold was a great leader too. Given the opportunity, if I'd been bigger and faster, I would probably have stuck with football. I was a decent blocking back. But I didn't have Bill's speed or natural ability. Football took precedence over all else: When the season ended, you'd get a measly couple of weeks off before offseason football started. It was brutal. They worked us hard, military-style, teaching with discipline to weed out the guys that weren't going to sacrifice. I think it was harder than the regular season.

Our baseball team was in the playoffs, and even on the day of a big game, the guys that played both sports had to go through offseason football in the morning. Baseball was extracurricular, and football was your job. Boy, am I glad I sucked it up.

Bill ended up going to Southwest Texas, which is now Texas State, on a football scholarship. He quit because he got tired of the beating players took. But he could fly.

With Bill gone from MacArthur, there was less comparison to him for me. My high school was like any other, with the jocks, the socials and the dopers. We had a great class, and I made some really good friends. I had a couple of girlfriends in high school — young love — but nothing too serious. I guess I was kind of shy. I was selected king of the homecoming court one year and didn't even go — what a dud. They had to find a replacement to walk my co-winner down the line. Like I said, what a dud. Sorry, Shelly. I was just as happy hitting a fishing pond.

I was a good student, making As and Bs, and I never acted up in class. My dad demanded that. I even received a student-athlete award my senior year. Go figure.

Report card day could be a good or bad day if you were in football. When we got to the fieldhouse (which is what we called our athletic center) for practice, they would line us up and check our grades and conduct marks. If you had a failing grade or a note about disrupting the class, the coaches would send you to a different line. The students in shop class had made a giant paddle that had a bat handle and widened out at the other end, with some holes drilled in to lessen friction. The executioner coach would tell you to grab your ankles, then you got smoked, and the number of bad marks on your report card determined the number of licks. Some guys were really hurting. They never got me. I could study a little and keep my mouth shut in class. Parents loved the paddling: less work for them to do at home.

In my sophomore year, I made the baseball team and played right field. It wasn't much different than little league for me, where they stick the kid that's just learning out in right to get him out of the way. Perfect spot for a sophomore on varsity — not your major league right fielder stud. And I hit so-so.

But I always wanted to be a catcher.

In my junior year, I finally got to be. It didn't hurt that my good friend and fellow catcher James Kleinfelder was such a great third baseman that Coach Perez moved him. We had great infielders, with every one being named All-District at their positions: Kleiny at third, Gino Martinez at shortstop, Matt Foley (best man at my wedding) at second, Brian Rosenbloom at first.

I had a good year defensively but hit about a buck-eighty (.180) — not good for high school, or in any league for that matter.

Coach Perez knew a scout with the Cincinnati Reds: Joe Caputo. Coach started talking me up, and Caputo showed some interest. Scouts always grade your tools — arm strength, hitting ability, power, running speed. They are mostly subjective, but the running time is absolute.

Caputo watched me play and told Coach Perez that I needed a good running time in the 60-yard dash to get the invite. Coach measured off 60 in the outfield to time me while Caputo watched. I ran a couple of sprints. Caputo said, "Kid, you can really run." Coach told him, "Yeah, he plays running back in a good football program." After the scout left, Coach told me he marked it at 55 yards, not 60. Now that's my man, always looking out for me.

So, Caputo invited me to an annual Reds tryout camp at San Jacinto Junior College. The tryout camp was a huge boost of confidence. I saw all the other players that they brought in, and I thought, *I can do this, I'm as good as these guys.* That's when I really started taking baseball seriously.

The big change, though, was Coach Perez coming in to coach the team my junior year. He had me believing in myself, and I started to share that dream with others. That year, my desire for baseball caught fire. When a teacher asked us to write about our ideal job, I put down professional baseball player — and I wasn't joking.

I started to fill out too. In the football program, we would go up to the school during the summer to lift weights and run. But I had to have a summer job. I worked with a construction company digging ditches and filling sandbags for the foundations on new homes. Man, was it hot. South Texas summers are brutal. There were probably about 10 American kids, and the rest of the workers came over from Mexico. (Boy, did they outwork us.) To get to the construction site, we'd all jump on the back of these big flatbed trucks and off we'd go. A couple of times, we were heading down the road and here comes these flashing lights. It was immigration. They'd pull us over, and half our crew would scatter. Problem was, now there were only a few of us left to do the work. That was rough. The next day, there'd be a whole new crew. These guys came to the U.S. to try to make a better life and worked hard. The American kids would make minimum wage, which wasn't much, and I heard they paid the Mexican workers half of that. It's actually sad. But I'd never seen men work so hard. That job taught me you don't want to dig ditches in the South Texas sun your whole life, but it sure got me in shape for sports. Maybe this is also why my dad always preached education.

Between our legendary football coach, Frank Arnold, and Coach Perez, I really learned the meaning of team first. You can have great individual performances, but it's the team that wins. Successful teams also have to have leaders, and I think I was one of them. I was never looking for a pat on the back; as a matter of fact, I felt uncomfortable in the spotlight.

But the spotlight comes with the territory when scouts are considering drafting you in June for the major league. San Antonio always had good high school baseball, but not a lot of guys were drafted. Most went to play in college, but they had the same dream I had. Now with scouts coming around to watch me, here was everyone's chance to show their skill. Scouts came not only to games but also practices.

Nowadays, you've got everything — the scouting reports, the statistics, the websites, the videos — and nobody is sneaking into the Draft. Back then, the scouts had a territory, an area they watched for their pro team. One of the first scouts I remember meeting was from the Blue Jays, Al LaMacchia, who was from San Antonio. One day in practice, I'm catching a pitcher and I see this older guy standing off to the side where he probably shouldn't be. He was just watching me. A little strange, maybe even a little unnerving. I finished catching the pitcher, and as I was walking off, he said, "Son, can I talk to you a second?" I was supposed to go hit, but I stopped. Al said, "Do you know how many balls you dropped there?" I admitted it hadn't occurred to me to count. He told me it was six. "That's too many." I sort of scoffed, but didn't say anything except thank you. When I went to go hit, Coach Perez asked me what that was about and I told him. He went and chewed Al out: we were practicing, and he's the coach.

Then a Dodgers scout called me on the phone one night — I had no idea how he even got my number. He was talking about my hitting, and I tuned him out. The next day, I told Coach about it, and being my protector, he found the number for the Dodgers scout and called and ripped that guy's ass too. Coach had my back.

We were playing a rival high school one night, and I was catching and one of their hitters was in the box and said something stupid to me. He was a pretty good player, but nobody was looking at him — the scouts were there for me. We were jawing back and forth, and the umpire stepped in between us.

After that game, Coach Perez told me he'd give me a ride home, which he'd never done before. He laid into me in the car: "You've got people on other teams that see everybody's coming out here to look at you. There's some envy there, and they're trying to distract you. Don't let them do it to you. Try to ignore them, don't jaw back and forth with them and don't get carried away." He was reminding me to be humble but also to keep the pressure off myself. I'm sure he also said, during the game, "If you get a chance, slide hard at second base and knock him on his ass." That's Perez.

Coach Perez didn't treat me any differently than he treated the other guys on the team. But when I do get together with old teammates over a beer, they joke that when scouts were around at batting practice (BP) and it was my turn to hit, Perez always had brand new baseballs for me. I didn't mind. But as far as treatment or discipline, everyone got treated the same. He wasn't afraid to jump your ass either. (Back in those days, coaches were allowed to use physical punishment to keep you on the straight and narrow, and, like I said earlier, parents loved it.) What I learned from him and carried with me to managing is to treat all your players the same. It's easy to get on the little guy, that takes nothing. Demand that the superstar does the same; don't kiss his ass. Players notice, and it's an easy way to lose your team and your respect.

My senior year was a big one. I hit .500, led the city in home runs with 8 and drove in 23 runs, RBIs, in 19 games. I was All-State catcher and was invited to the state All-Star Game at the Astrodome in Houston. (I didn't go, as I went off to pro ball, but that comes later.) University of Texas came calling, and I knew I would be faced with a big decision because I knew I'd be drafted high. Cliff Gustafson was the head coach at Texas, and he was legendary. I never met him in person. College coaches got most of their info from scouts about who can play and who their high school draft picks will be, so the only call I ever got from Gustafson, he offered me a full ride. I also received recruitment letters from Stanford, University of Oklahoma, Oral Roberts and some other good baseball schools. They sent questionnaires.

With the questionnaire from Stanford, you had to fill it out and take it around to teachers for them to answer a couple of questions. Then they wanted me to write an essay on something. An essay? I couldn't remember ever writing one, and I was a senior. I knew I was going to Texas, so I half-assed it. I wrote in pen, crossed out words everywhere, used whiteout, wrote it freeform, off the cuff. A couple of weeks later, I got a letter noting that I wasn't Stanford material.

Texas didn't need any of that. Gustafson just called and said I was in. I don't think I ever told my parents about that Stanford essay . . . Hook 'em Horns.

My dad was a big education guy and talked up the great offer I had to the University of Texas: full scholarship, not too far from home. Bill had gone the scholarship route, and I knew my parents liked that idea too, but it was my choice. Either way, they wouldn't have to pay.

The annual major league Draft was getting closer. It was always the first week in June, with the Mets having the first pick and the Blue Jays choosing second. Some Toronto scouts came to town to put me through a private tryout. Al LaMacchia was one of them (so maybe me dropping six pitches in that bullpen session didn't bother him too much, or maybe it did since they passed on me). The Blue Jays, I heard, were looking closely at me, at Kelly Gruber up in Austin and at Gary Harris, an infielder out of San Diego.

The day before that tryout, my dad bought a brand-new car, a big Mercury, so he came to watch my tryout and his car was the only one around. Normally during batting practice, a cage surrounds the hitter to save foul balls. For this tryout, they didn't want one so the scouts could watch my swing without anything blocking their view. The balls they use are softer (unlike the hard, brand-new ones Coach Perez let me hit) so they can gauge your raw power better. The first dang swing I took, I knocked a pop-up into the parking lot and it hits right off the trunk of my dad's brand-new car. You kidding me? What are the odds, only one car in the whole parking lot. It dented it good. But I guess every time he saw the dent, he would think of me.

The rest of the tryout went fine. Then the Jays went up to Austin to give Gruber a look. They ended up taking Harris number two, and Gruber went to Cleveland in the number 10 spot.

Deep down I was hoping the Dodgers would pick me. Their AA Texas League team was in San Antonio for the longest time. We used to go watch them play and dream. I saw so many future great Dodgers players come through — Mike Scioscia, Steve Sax, Orel Hershiser and Fernando Valenzuela to name a few. The last game I saw before the Draft and before I headed out to begin my own career, Valenzuela threw a gem. He got called up soon after, and Fernandomania was on.

Finally Draft day, June 3, 1980. I was at my field, hitting some base-balls. School was out. My coach came running over.

"Hey, you've got a phone call."

I ran to the fieldhouse, and Jay Horwitz was on the phone. He was the PR guy for the Mets for years, a wonderful guy. But it was his first year on the job. He said, "You've been selected by the New York Mets in the first round."

"Really?" (I couldn't tell you if a Mets scout ever came out to see me — if he did, I never met him.)

I'd been told I was probably going to go in the first round, but you never know for sure. Now I knew — I was taken 24th. Hearing it, I felt a mixture of being excited and having partly expected it a little bit. Jay told me a scout would be in touch.

Then I called my parents.

The scout that called me was Jim Hughes, this old country boy who scouted in Texas for the Mets. Great guy, but didn't say much. He was the quietest dude. We arranged for him to come by the house.

High school kids couldn't have agents or you'd lose your college eligibility, so it was just me and my dad. We didn't know what to expect, and most people hadn't ever been through it either. Now, Dad never talked much, and I was quiet back then, and here's Jim Hughes, quiet as can be, so needless to say, it was a quiet room. I could have used my mom giving us a song and dance — she's actually the most talented out of us all.

Jim says, "This is what we can do for you: forty-five thousand dollars, and we'll give you some money for college when someday you decide to go." But there was a time limit on that. Dad asked if that was as high as they could go. Jim said it was.

Though quiet, he was a real personable guy. He hung around and talked a little bit about pro ball, how it worked. I would be likely sent to Kingsport, Tennessee, or Little Falls, New York, to one of the two rookie teams.

Jim packed up and headed back to the little hotel he was staying at down the road. After he left, I said, "Dad, I don't think they want me if that's all they will give me." I knew first-round money had to be better than that.

We didn't know anything about negotiating. My dad was in the military — it's not like you can negotiate your contract there! You do what you're told, where you are told to do it, and any raises are structured by rank. I was only 17 at the time, so he'd have to cosign regardless. Dad and I had a real heart-to-heart. I knew what he wanted, but I wanted to play pro ball. His advice was to take the deal then. I suggested we call Jim and ask for a little more.

"Mr. Hughes, we've been thinking about it, and if you can offer fifty-five thousand dollars, I'll sign right now." He said, "I'll be right there."

My father and I signed the deal a short while later. It only took three days from the day I was drafted to when I signed my contract. The *San Antonio Express-News* had a big headline: "MacArthur's Gibbons 1st Round Pick."

The Mets GM, Frank Cashen, told the media he expected big things out of me: "We consider John the top catching prospect in the country. He has a fine arm and the potential to be a bona fide power hitter. He should have an outstanding career."

A few days later, I shipped out to Kingsport, Tennessee.

Looking at that first round of the 1980 Draft is pretty interesting. Darryl Strawberry was everything he was supposed to be and was deservedly taken number one overall by the Mets; he should have been a Hall of Famer. Player-wise, there were a lot of misses that year, with Gruber and Glenn Wilson as the only All-Stars. But if you consider the people who ended up in baseball as coaches, managers and in management, it's a better-looking draft list.

Terry Francona was an outfielder from the University of Arizona and an Expos draft pick at number 22. Injuries killed him, 'cause he could really hit. But as a manager? The Phillies, Red Sox and Guardians all benefited from his guidance, and he's got two World Series rings.

Billy Beane, an outfielder, was taken from Mt. Carmel High School in San Diego, 23rd pick — right before me at 24 — by the Mets; he is, of course, the famed Billy Beane of *Moneyball*, trying to make the most of a meagre budget in Oakland. Beaner really made a name for himself in the game, parlaying an untested philosophy into a fortune. Billy was always going to be successful in whatever he chose.

Rick Renteria was a high school shortstop from South Gate, California, who had a decent run in the majors; he later became only the second person to manage both the Cubs and the White Sox.

When I got to know Strawberry and Beane, I asked them about their negotiations. They both said the initial offer was the same as mine, $45,000. Neither of them signed as quickly as I did. Straw held out as the number one pick in the country and got somewhere around $220,000. Beaner got in the $130,000 range. Heck, Jay Tibbs, who the Mets took with their first pick in the second round, got $90,000. What a difference compared to today's money. Dad and I talked about what we missed out on, and his advice was, "If you're good enough anyway, the money will be there in the end. If you're not, you've got a little money and promised money for college."

Now it was time to move on from Syl Perez's tutelage. After coming out of a rough part of San Antonio, Coach Perez mentored many, many students through the years and went on to become superintendent of a couple of different big school districts. He had two players make the big leagues: me and Norm Charlton. Norm played at one of our rival high schools, but he was a year younger and went the college route, playing for Rice University. Coach Perez ended up coaching at James Madison High School, and Norm fell under his wing. Norm carved out a great career as a reliever, and, nicknamed "The Sheriff," he was a part of the Nasty Boys with the Cincinnati Reds that won the 1990 World Series.

Later, Norm was the bullpen coach out in Seattle, and so Coach Perez came up to Toronto for a series between the Mariners and Jays, and we all got a photo together. It was a great reunion for all of us.

Frank Arnold and Syl Perez were elected to the San Antonio Sports Hall of Fame, a real honor. Both were honored for their accomplishments as coaches and mentors on the athletic field. Some of my buddies and old teammates still get together occasionally, and Frank and Syl are always included. It shows you the impact they had on many young men's lives.

There have been a few major league players from San Antonio, including Cito Gaston, the two-time World Series champion manager who replaced me in Toronto in 2008. There's also Cliff Johnson, Danny Heep, my future manager Davey Johnson, Randy Choate, Pat Rockett and the Mahler brothers, Rick and Mickey.

But there was one who went to the same high school as I did and was also a catcher for the Mets: Jerry Grote. Talk about following a legend — I used to see his photo on the alumni wall at school before I even knew who the Mets were.

At MacArthur High, Jerry was a baseball star (catching, pitching and playing third), but he also competed in track and field and cross-country. Instead of going pro in 1961, Jerry went to Trinity University and got better at baseball, learning from an old catcher named Del Baker, who'd played for the Tigers from 1914 to 1916, and then was a manager and coach in the majors. Jerry only stayed a year at Trinity and then signed as a free agent with the Houston Colt .45s (later renamed the Astros). After some time in the minors, including with the hometown Missions of the Texas League, Jerry made it to the majors in late 1963.

In 1965, he was traded to the Mets, and, after years of crappy teams, they became the "Amazin' Mets," and Grote was the guy catching Tom Seaver, Nolan Ryan and Jerry Koosman. Not bad for a local kid. He was so great with pitchers and defensively that the Mets basically considered any offense they got from him a bonus. He played out his time with the Mets, eventually losing the starting job, and then backed up with the Dodgers, going to the World Series both years but losing to the Yankees.

This is where the baseball gods worked in my favor. He sat out the 1979 and 1980 seasons, living in San Antonio, where he owned a meat market. Jerry decided to return to the bigs and had an offer on the table from the Royals, so he needed to get in shape again, and, in the offseason after my first year of rookie ball, I was his training partner.

We'd go out on our high school football field and run, and he was 39, but he'd run me into the ground. "Don't worry about it, kid, I used to be on the cross-country team," he cracked. I loved listening to his stories about Seaver, Koosman and Ryan, and he'd bitch about the game, the good and the bad that he'd experienced. As much as it was educational, it was entertaining.

I was a sponge for any catching tips he had. We'd talk about a catcher's footwork, and he'd give me tips on how to speed things up.

He told me story after story — it was beautiful. He said he was always trying to think of a way to distract the hitter in the box. There was a great left-handed hitter, and he said, "Man, I couldn't distract him at all. Finally, I started to throw the ball back to the pitcher right in front of his face. I did that a couple times. Finally, the guy said, 'You do that again, I'm going to whip your ass.' But I broke his concentration, and that's all we wanted."

Now Jerry could throw some bullshit around too. He told me there were certain guys that you knew were going to get one hit a game. He explained, "So the first time up, nobody's on base, we give him a fat fastball and give him his one hit. He's happy. You don't have to worry about him anymore."

Jerry was one of the true characters in the game. I love that guy.

3.

RIDING THE BUS

What did I do before heading to rookie ball in the Appalachian League in Kingsport, Tennessee? I looked at a map! I really had no idea where I was heading, and it was my first time leaving home. But I was excited to get on the plane that got me to the Tri-Cities Airport, which is located between Johnson City, Kingsport and Bristol. I was told someone would be there to pick me up, and I was thinking of a limousine. But I get there, and it's this tiny airport, and this really big guy, wearing a gray T-shirt and sweating bullets, approaches me.

In his heavy Southern accent, he asked, "Are you John Gibbons? I'm Doc Lowe, I'm the trainer. I'm here to pick you up." We got into his beat-up car, and he took me to the team hotel in downtown Kingsport, just a little rundown place. He told me that the team was meeting in the lobby at 6 p.m. Back to reality.

The rest of the guys in the lobby were a lot like me but were mostly college guys, yet still unsure of things. We were told we'd have to find a place to live, and it was suggested we find a roommate. Chuck Hiller was the manager — we ended up becoming really good friends. If you were breaking into pro ball, you couldn't have a better guy.

They all thought I was a bonus baby — though they had no idea how little I'd gotten — and almost immediately guys started asking me about rooming with them, figuring I'd handle the rent. (Strawberry hadn't signed yet, and Beane would sign but was assigned to High-A ball in Little Falls, New York.) I ended up renting with Dave Stone and Rich Greenfield. Just by opening the newspaper, we found a woman named Betsy who had this house with five bedrooms, like a rooming house. I told my mom about her, and she thought it was wonderful that there would be a motherly influence for me; I just found Betsy a bit weird. I think we paid $600 a month, and none of us knew how to cook on our own, so we muddled through or hit the fast-food places. The most popular place was Shoney's, and we practically lived there because they had a buffet. Our per diem on road trips was seven bucks, if I remember right.

A few days after we moved in, the guys were heading to a party, but I passed, thinking in my mind that I was there for baseball. They came back later with a gallon of moonshine — remember, we're in the Tennessee hills. They asked me to take a swig. I said no but took a whiff of it, and damn . . . we don't need electric cars in the future, we can use moonshine.

As soon as I got to the field, I began to think I'd made a mistake. The University of Texas had a beautiful diamond, and here I was on this rinky-dink high school field in Kingsport. It was at the bottom of a hill, so the fans could only sit on top of the hill looking down on us, not close to the action.

Back then, we had one coach who was the manager. There were two roving pitching instructors, Greg Pavlick and Bill Monbouquette, along with a roving hitting coach, and that was it. They'd drop in every now and then because they had to cover eight teams. I got to the field and Pav told me to get my catching gear and catch a pitcher named Alfie Faust. Alfie was from New York City, and they told me he was a legendary street-basketball player. He had a great arm but was just learning how to pitch. I got back there, but I knew I was in trouble when none of the hitters wanted to hit off him. The first ball he threw before the hitter stepped in nearly missed the cage. I was diving everywhere while he was getting loose, and I thought to myself, *This is pro ball?* Come to find out that Alfie had that mental block that everyone called "The Thing." He didn't last long.

Now, my first professional baseball road trip. We hop on this beat-up old Greyhound bus bound for Paintsville, Kentucky. It was an old coal mining town and home to the New York Yankees rookie ball team. The battle for the Big Apple was just beginning. As we were going down these back country roads through Tennessee and Kentucky, the guy next to me opens a window and pukes — so now there's vomit on the window and along the side of the bus. After our series in Paintsville, no one had cleaned the puke off the side of the bus, so you can imagine the smell. Pro ball at its finest.

I didn't start the first game, and instead Hiller put me in late in the second game for defense. It was a misty wet night in Paintsville. There was a runner on second base and a base hit to right field, and the guy was coming around to score. I never left my mask on as a catcher. Our right fielder threw it home but it skipped off the wet grass in front of the plate and hit me dead center in my nose. It buckled me and down I went. Great start to a promising career. I had to have surgery. I could have sworn I heard "The Eyes of Texas" playing in my head when the anesthesia was wearing off.

I think I missed about 10 days, but my first game back was in Bluefield, West Virginia. Everything's healed, and I'm at bat for the first time, and the pitcher lets one fly that goes for my head. I turned, and it caught half my earflap and half my face . . . I got lucky, as it deflected a little. Son of a bitch, it was going right for my nose!

The good thing is I started playing every day after that, one of the perks of being a so-called bonus baby.

Finally, July rolls around and Strawberry signs, and they have a big press conference at the field in Kingsport. I'm thinking, *I didn't get this!* His scout, Roger Youngward, brought him into town. There was a ton of media, and Darryl's up there talking away, and we were all watching him, but we hadn't met him yet.

The first game Straw played, the newspaper guys and TV cameras were all over, coming to watch this kid because they called him the Black Ted Williams. He was thin and strong, but you could tell he was a natural.

We went back to Paintsville again, not long after that, and they had a Strawberry Festival for Darryl — remember, this was a Yankees town! They marked right field as the "Strawberry patch," and before the game started, they had a helicopter fly over and drop a bunch of strawberries there. Once Strawberry joined us, we started getting better crowds in Kingsport too. (The biggest crowd was the night the Padres' mascot, the San Diego Chicken, visited.)

Straw had a tendency to half-ass it to first on a routine ground ball when he got there.

Chuck Hiller — this is beautiful, man — after a night game, he told Darryl, "Meet me at the ballpark tomorrow at ten o'clock. We're gonna have a little fun." Darryl asked, "We going to do a little hitting?" Chuck replied, "Just be there."

As we were walking in for our normal arrival time, we could see what was going on. Chuck had this big ol' bucket of balls, and he was throwing BP to Darryl. He had told Darryl, "After every ball you hit, I want you to run as hard as you can to first base." He did that with the whole bag just to prove a point: No more loafing. You're gonna bust your ass like everybody else. We were all happy this was going on because what's good for one is good for all, right? Plus, it would make Darryl better.

Chuck had a big influence on Straw, and on me. Hiller kept his thumb on Straw, but over the next few years, the managers Darryl played for let him do his own thing, and I think that hurt him. He was the team's boy wonder, as he should have been, but he shouldn't have been treated any differently than anybody else.

Frank Cashen came to Kingsport (probably because Straw was there), and he spoke to the club — which the Mets owned. In general, Frank never said much. It was good to know the boss knew who you were at least, plus he wanted to see who he'd drafted.

At that point in time, the Mets were a laughingstock franchise. The team had just been sold to Nelson Doubleday Jr., who had 51 percent, and Fred Wilpon, who owned the rest. I met each of them during my years with the team, and I can say they were totally different people. The

Mets were a toy to Doubleday because he came from all that money from the publishing world. He'd come around every now and then, looking like he just got off his yacht, out of place at the ballpark in his colorful plaid. Wilpon was a self-made guy, so he watched things and was involved in organizational meetings. Fred also played, so he knew the game, and he wanted to learn about the players, coaches and everyone involved.

One of the main moves that they made was to convince Cashen, who'd had years of success in Baltimore, to return to the GM role after he'd been hired as MLB's administrator of baseball operations. Cashen helped rebuild the Mets through the draft, and I was supposed to be a big part of that.

Looking back, rookie ball really was something. It's a short season, but it felt like it was going on forever, since none of us had ever played that many games in high school or college. Now we were playing every stinking day. We had to learn the professional baseball grind, which is a big, big part of the game. We finished 35-35-1, but I have zero recollection of how we managed to get a tie.

It was also the start of my many connections in baseball. Lloyd McClendon was on that team and later made it to the majors as an outfielder and then as a manager for the Pirates, Mariners and Tigers. He was sent up to High-A partway through the season though. "Hondo" was tough, out of Gary, Indiana, but what stands out is he had a big ol' ass, I don't know how he squatted, because he started out as a catcher. That didn't last long. Great guy and one tough competitor who could really hit.

Dave, Rich and I chipped in and bought a car. After I told my dad, he advised, "Don't put your name on that title or insurance. Give them your share of the money, but you let someone else sign for the car. If something happens, then they aren't coming after you." Which I did. It was a real beat-up old junker. But now we're big-time, styling around town. We used to give guys a ride to the ballpark, and they'd pile in, hanging out the window. That's what you did in the minor leagues back then. It's part of growing up and survival. Nowadays, they do everything for these kids. I think it's both good and bad. Some never learn how to survive or appreciate the little things, and we create a lot of prima donnas by doing everything for them. Not their fault.

In rookie ball if you're a catcher, you have a lot of work to do since the pitching staff is so big. There are only so many innings to go around, so the pitchers threw in the bullpen all the time to try to stay sharp. Catchers kept their gear nearby. We had two Latinx pitchers on our team, Fernando Alba and Elvin Pina. They couldn't speak a lick of English. Chuck would have to go to the mound, which he knew was kind of useless. It would be the three of us at the mound, and he'd try something simple, "Sky is blue" and point to the sky. The pitcher would repeat, "Sky is blue," and then walk off. I used to laugh.

I told you earlier that our coaching staff was Chuck Hiller and an occasional roving instructor. At least we had a full-time trainer, Doc Lowe. At some point in the season, my shoulder started bothering me. It came from playing almost every day for the first time. I told Doc that my shoulder was acting up. He was a big, heavyset dude, always sweating, and wore these jeans that hung off his ass. But this guy could touch his palms on the ground. It was amazing. My gut gets in my way. He must have been a yogi not a doctor. But anyway, he brought out this tackle box that was his medical kit, and he started looking through these pill bottles. He pulled one up and told me to take this pill. They were prescription bottles, and the name on the label was not his. "Who's Mary Lowe?" "That's my mom. These are leftovers." It was Butazolidine. Later, I was talking to my own mom on the phone and told her what I was taking. She went, "What?! That's what I give to my horses for inflammation. Is that guy nuts?" I just said neigh . . .

There were other things that were not exactly on the up and up. Some guys had DMSO for sore body parts, which was an ointment that I'm pretty sure they could only get in Mexico at the time. You'd rub it on your skin, and it made your breath smell like garlic. But again, it worked. Survival.

Rookie ball is really about players learning about pro ball, the life-style, being away from home. Just let them play, and don't get carried away with evaluating them too much. Just make sure the pitchers get X number of innings, and the batters get a certain number of at-bats.

And, just when you thought the year was over, the chosen few were off to the Florida Instructional League. Actually, I did get to go home for a couple of weeks, and then went to the Sunshine State, which was my first introduction to St. Petersburg, our spring training home till 1988. St. Pete is on the west coast, on the Gulf of Mexico. It wasn't a great facility. Things improved greatly after the Mets moved to Port St. Lucie, a beach town on the Atlantic side. I saw the changes in philosophy as well as the improved facilities. In 1980, they used to frown on weights because they thought it tightened you up and hurt your flexibility. Within a couple of years, the Mets had a strength trainer, and if you wanted to go lift weights, he'd take you over to a local gym in St. Petersburg, and he'd pay the guy and you could work out there. Later, a real weight room was added to the new facility.

Straw was my roommate that first go-round in the instructional league. We lived on Madeira Beach, right in St. Pete. We got along pretty well. Then a family member passed away back home in California, and he left and never came back. While I learned some stuff — they jokingly called it the Instruggle League because it was definitely a struggle for young players — I just kept dreaming of heading back home.

Since my father wasn't going to let me sit around, every offseason I had some sort of job. It's a blur: what job, which year? But I worked at the post office during Christmas, stocked shelves at an electronics store and stocked and bagged at a grocery store. I had the bonus, but I didn't want to burn through it.

I splurged before my first spring training and bought a 280ZX, a sweet ride, the nicest car that I ever owned. Driving from San Antonio to spring training became a tradition starting that year.

It was really something to be around big-league players all the time. They didn't necessarily have a lot of time for the young kids, but you had someone to look up to. Everybody knew how it worked: if you had a decent year in one place, you knew you were going to move up next year. The Mets had two A ball teams, one in the South Atlantic in Shelby, North Carolina, and the other in Lynchburg, Virginia, in the Carolina League — they called that High-A, and Shelby was Low-A. Well, I ended up in Hellby, as we called it, going to another crappy high school field that was somehow worse than Kingsport — but at least it was a true stadium, with fans close to the action, so you had some interactions. These two little ladies sat right next to the dugout, and they had this cowbell they'd shake, and they both chewed tobacco. I grew up in Texas, but I'd never seen a woman do that. They'd spit that big ol' load, then they'd ring their freakin' cowbell. There were big trees around the stadium, and it was in a bit of a valley, so at night, there would be a lot of moisture on the grass, and some nights fog would roll in.

The Shelby Mets were owned by Jack Farnsworth, and he owned the Cardinals team in nearby Gastonia too. It was eye-opening to realize how cheap he was. He'd have the young kids that were hanging around the ballpark chase foul balls in return for leftover hot dogs. Then they'd wash the balls so we could use them the next night. So if it was really humid, you'd be playing the game and the balls would have this soap film on them. They don't call it the bush leagues for nothing.

John Arezzi was a young go-getter who was in charge of public relations for the team, but he did all kinds of other things, too, like selling ads in programs and on the outfield fence. He invited three of us to move into the house he was renting. It was me, J.P. Ricciardi and Mike Hennessey. John had his own room, and the rest of us rotated. One got the bed, another the couch and the other got the mattress on the floor. We used to piss Arezzi off. We'd leave that place a mess, leaving for road trips with dishes stacked high and mice running around. John was very creative though; to get people to games he might try anything. We had mud wrestling one night, but the biggest hit was free grocery night. John has had an interesting career; he's been in pro wrestling, and he also managed singers in Nashville. We're still great friends. I've also stayed close to J.P. and Henny. J.P., of course, I owe my major league managing career to; Henny lives in Jersey, so we'd see each other a lot when the Blue Jays played in New York.

J.P., Henny and I would cram into my little car to get to the ballpark. On the way were a Catholic church and an X-rated drive-in theater (take your pick). All three of us were Catholic. Henny would always bless himself as we drove past the church.

"Henny, what are you doing?"

"I need some hits tonight."

Obviously, that didn't work; God was insulted. Henny was actually a better hitter than I was. Both my roomies were really good players but never received the opportunities I did. Remember, bonus babies always got the priority. I've played with so many good players that never got that shot. Some were even better than those that made it. Same holds true with my coaching and managing. I got a big break, but some better people never did. It's just like life: it's not always fair, and the game owes you nothing.

There were a lot of teams in that league back then, and we would drive two, two and a half hours to games, commuting instead of staying the night — and this was when we played a three- or four-game series in the town. You're on the road for five, six hours to play one game, and you do that three or four days in a row. But you're paying your dues, trying to make it, and we didn't know any better.

We had a red, white and blue church bus that we used on many of the trips, and the driver was a big muscular guy we called Pipes. He'd been to prison, so we gave him lots of leeway.

The Pirates farm club was in Greenwood, South Carolina, and they had a nice field, but it was right next to a dog kennel. The whole frickin' game you could hear nothing but the dogs; you couldn't hear the fans, all 20 of them.

The Braves were in Anderson, South Carolina, and that's where I met Hank Aaron for the first time. Hank was the farm director for Atlanta in 1981–82. That was the first time I really heard the racial stuff too. There was this group of old guys sitting in the stands in the little stadium. Both teams had Black players, and the comments coming out of these racists were terrible.

One time, we were coming home from Anderson, and the brakes on the bus stopped working. We were real close to home, but I can still picture Pipes pumping the brakes for all he's worth, hopping curbs as we're winding our way through Shelby late at night. The ballpark was down a little hill, and he somehow managed to coast right into the parking lot.

Boy, did I get spoiled having Hiller as my first manager in pro ball. My manager in 1981, Dan Monzon, had played a little in the big leagues with the Twins in 1972–73. He was totally different than Chuck; Monzon was a smart baseball man, but angry all the time. He was clearly in it for his own advancement and had trouble accepting a bad team. Tough guy to play for, complaining and throwing stuff all the time. We heard a few times, "Anybody want a piece of me? Stand up. Let's go!" Actually, all I wanted was a few more hits, nothing else. We did have a second coach, so I guess it was an upgrade from rookie ball. I did try to take something from all my coaches and managers when I got into managing, so maybe I got my anger from that year.

You never heard anything from management in New York: it was kind of isolating. It was nothing like it is today. They trusted the manager and coaches, and they'd get the daily reports. So much of it was learning on your own, repetition. It wasn't like there was an instructor for every little thing you do. But I got to play a lot; there were the prospects on the team, like me, that got all the game time, and then there were the guys who filled out the roster, waiting for a chance to play.

The highlight of that first season in Hellby — we finished 59-83, and I played 109 games, with an ugly .189 average — was the arrival of a high school kid named Lenny Dykstra. High schoolers usually go to rookie ball, like I'd done, but the Mets saw something in him. He was a nut, but you could tell he was a good player. We became pretty good friends and would room together the next season.

J.P. and I were different in a sense that he's a full-blown New Englander and I was a wanderer, but we hit it off from the first day we met. Both of our families are from Boston but mine saw the light and moved to Texas. We thought alike about the game, but we never sat around having deep discussions about life. We'd mainly bitch and moan about the grind of it all. His parents came to visit one homestand and, man, could his mom cook. I think she had a restaurant in Worcester. It rained one of the mornings they were there, and it didn't seem like it would stop. We figured there was no way we'd be playing, especially since we didn't have a tarp to cover the field. J.P.'s mom cooked this incredible, huge Italian feast. I've never been so full and bloated in my life. Them Italians can really eat. Even if it's raining, you still go to the ballpark where the bosses make the call on a rainout. The rain eventually stopped, and somehow we played. I can remember looking at J.P. like "are you kidding me with this?" I was useless but somehow made it through. His mom's cooking was definitely worth it.

Most places back then didn't have tarps, and if it rained, it rained. Farnsworth was so cheap he wouldn't have bought a tarp anyway, and he wanted us to play to make that $100 or whatever he got at the gate. One thing about minor league baseball: if there's a chance of rain, players beg for that rainout. Some general managers would keep you around forever before they made a decision, which made the players bitch, and they'd call the game at eight o'clock when the night was almost gone anyway; others would call it early so you could go do something.

I returned to Shelby for the 1982 season, but there was a different manager, Rich Miller, who I really liked, and I know that was a factor in me having a better year. Plus I was a year older. We finished 77–63, and I got into 99 games, for 321 at-bats, with a .265 average, with 85 hits, including 12 homers. Farnsworth had sold the team, but it was still small-time. Some days the dryer would break down, and you'd get to the park and everybody's uniform would be scattered in the outfield drying in the sun.

It was Dykstra, pitcher Roger McDowell and I sharing a decent-sized house. Any time somebody would get called up to the team or a new guy was looking for a place, they'd come live with us and help with the rent.

Lenny would never drink. Some of the college guys on the team would be drinking beer after a game. "You go to the big leagues, you can't be doing that. Blah blah blah . . ." He'd drink milk. Then he got in a slump, and Lenny didn't get in many slumps. We got rained out, so we had a party at our house one night and it was the first time he ever drank beer. I think he drank a six-pack and just got smoked. The next night he got five hits. We talk about superstitions — there's five hits in a six-pack for a guy who wanted hits — and I think that started his downfall. I don't want to take all the blame, but I was involved. Lenny wasn't a big guy back then, just a good freakin' baseball player. He just dripped confidence. Every morning we'd wake up to watch *The Young and the Restless*, then we'd grab something to eat and go to the park. That was our routine. I haven't watched *The Young and the Restless* since.

Roger used to draw to relax, and he was a great artist, but he turned out to be an even better pitcher. In AA, he got hurt and sat out a year. When they took the bone chips out of his elbow, it gave him this unbelievable sinker ball — damn, that ball dropped! Roger also spent many years as a great major league pitching coach.

I'd never been a big partier, and I didn't like staying out late. Naturally, though, you turn it loose a little more than you would at home. Shelby was smaller than Kingsport, and if we got a day off, we'd go to Charlotte to the Carowinds amusement park. One of the guys on our team was dating a girl that worked at Carowinds and helped get us tickets to see Molly Hatchet at the park. Danny Joe Brown, the lead singer, had left the band for health reasons, but the show we were going to had him back for the first time. We got backstage passes somehow. I always liked that Southern rock 'n' roll, and Molly Hatchet. We sat backstage by the speakers, close enough you could see the joint in the guitarist's instrument. Some of the guys would even talk to us briefly. That was probably the highlight of Shelby that year. And Southern rock is my go-to. Other than that, there wasn't much else to do.

Future big-league manager Bobby Valentine was a roving instructor. We got snowed out one game, and he came over to our house. We stayed there all night just talking baseball — and all he wanted to do was talk baseball: he debated it, argued about it. It didn't matter that we were young kids and that he was only in town to watch us play, he just wanted to talk ball. Bobby was ahead of the times in baseball thinking.

From that team, Randy Milligan played in the big leagues, as did a couple of pitchers, Bill Latham and Jeff Bettendorf, so we actually had a pretty good team. We had a manager who wasn't trying to fight us every night, so that helped. We had an assistant coach, Glenn Borgmann, who caught in the big leagues for a while with the Twins and the White Sox, so now I had a big-league catcher working with me every day.

Near the end of the season, I got called up to AA in Jackson, Mississippi, in the Texas League, and I met the team in Little Rock, Arkansas. They were headed to the postseason, and there was a chance they were going to play San Antonio in the playoffs, so I was excited.

I got to play in a few games but they still had their regulars, Ronn Reynolds and David Duff. I told you earlier that Chuck Hiller was great for Strawberry, but the AA manager, Gene Dusan, was just the opposite. Hiller had been strict but fair with Straw, and Dusan was trying to ride his coattails. You can't fool players; and, in the end, you can't fool the front office either.

One game, Strawberry was in right field and the second baseman was Jim Woodward. (He didn't make it to the big leagues but ended up being a scout for the Mets.) The hit was a little pop-up to short right field, so Woody's going back from second to get the ball, and Strawberry's coming in from right. They collide, hard. Woodward hit the ground, and Straw staggers and starts to stumble back to the outfield, and then he drops to the ground too. The manager, this heavyset dude, makes his way out there, barely glancing at Woodward, right to Straw. I can remember a few of us on the bench looking at each other and laughing. *Are you kidding me?* You can't hide your motives from players, and it bites you in the end.

I'd met Billy Beane in instructional league, but our time in Jackson cemented our long friendship. We hit it off and had a bond because his dad was a career naval guy, so he'd grown up in a military family too. Then, from there on out, we'd try to live together, whether in instructional league or spring training.

One time, we lived on Madeira Beach, right on the water, and Billy would always have a football with him — I think that his true passion was to be a quarterback. He could whistle that football, and we'd flip it around. Billy was going to Stanford, and John Elway tried to recruit him for football. His baseball career turned out pretty damn good, but I think he regretted not going to play football. He was a big six-foot-four stud, and he attracted lots of attention on the beach. I was pretty good looking back then too.

What hurt Billy in baseball was that he was very aggressive, a football mentality. He had trouble slowing things down. I was a lot like that too. He'd get very frustrated. He had trouble controlling his emotions sometimes. A great player blows things off — Billy let things eat at him. That's just who he was. I saw him destroy many toilets in the dugouts and plenty of other things.

In the winter of 1982, I went out to live with Beaner in San Diego — well, Rancho Bernardo — for about a month, and he had us playing pick-up games two or three times a week at San Diego State with other local pro players. One of them was Steve Ray, who I'd played with in Shelby. Stevie's dad was a Navy SEAL, the biggest stud I've ever seen. His dad would get us wetsuits and we'd go snorkeling in La Jolla Cove.

Of course, Beaner ended up in management, running the A's, and had the *Moneyball* book and movie. I do remember him saying a few times that Cashen had the right job, running a team.

The thing about playing in AA is that everybody can play, the fill-ins are gone, and The Show is within reach. It certainly inspired me, and 1983 was my best year. My average was .298, with 18 homers — best on the team — and I was named an All-Star and received the Doubleday Award as team MVP. I had to go to New York for that honor. I was in shock and awe of the size of New York City — I couldn't believe the hustle and bustle. I'm a low-key guy, I like some peace and quiet, and you ain't getting a lot of that in New York.

Things were starting to come together.

But first, spring training. All the minor league players stayed at a hotel right on Tampa Bay, around the corner from where all the other major league teams stay now when they go play the Rays. It was a one-level motel, with your car parked just outside your door. I can remember standing with a group of guys, and this sports car drove up and a guy got out. His license plate said DR. K and everybody's going, "Who's this asshole? Come on, dude." A few months later, everyone knew Dr. K. Dwight "Doc" Gooden was just one of many gems the Mets had in the minor leagues, and he would play a huge part in the resurgent major league team.

Another was Kevin Mitchell. In Jackson, the bus was nicer, but it didn't have a toilet. Going to Tulsa, Oklahoma, or Little Rock, Arkansas, were some long-ass bus trips. Every couple of hours, the bus would pull over on the side of the highway so we could get out to take a leak. A group of guys always sat in the back to play cards and drink beer. To solve the bathroom problem, they would pee in a big KFC bucket. Somewhat brilliant. Mitch had just bought a brand-new leather bag, and he was big-time proud of it. Well, someone moved the bucket, and the soggy end ripped. The pee rolled down the bus, and the only thing in its way was Kevin's brand-new bag. All hell broke loose.

Kev and I became really good friends, and he was one of the true characters in the game. He hadn't been drafted but signed as a free agent. Everyone thinks they can play basketball, but the true hoopsters would secretly get together and play after practice during spring training. Straw was a big player in California, and Gooden and Mitchell both played. At his first spring training, the story I heard was Mitch obviously didn't know about Straw, and when they got into it during their pick-up game, Kev body-slammed Darryl. Now, these are two big dudes. So Straw landed on his shoulder.

I love telling Mitch stories. He took no crap and grew up fighting. We had an off day in Shreveport, Louisiana, in 1983 — Sleazeport is what we called it. Mike Bishop, who played a little with the Angels in the big leagues, had just arrived in town after being sent down from AAA, and he'd rented a car and wanted some of us to go eat with him. Me and Mitch hop in Bishop's rental car and go to Taco Bell, on the tough side of town. It was empty, except us, until this redneck couple came in and sat next to us. Mitch had been showing off pictures of his daughter, but his language was foul. The lady says, "You need to tell your friend to shut his mouth. We don't talk that way around here." Mitch hears, and his ears go up. The husband says, "Yeah, if he doesn't, we're gonna have to go at it." Everyone stands up, and the wife is in the middle between Mitch and her husband. The husband reaches around his wife and pushes Kev (big, big mistake). Kev knocks him down. The wife grabs the tray with the food on it and is trying to hit Kevin. We're trying to hold him back. There's food flying everywhere. We dragged him out of there, got in the car and drove off. The employees got the license plate, and they sided with the couple. We got back to the hotel, and our manager, Bob Schaefer, called a team meeting by the pool. A cop was there with the couple, who wanted Kevin arrested. Schaefer did a great job, he talked to the cop and he talked to the couple and told them how Kevin had a bright future; asks if he apologizes, would that be enough? (Even though they started the whole thing.) They agreed, and Kev ate some crow and apologized. Who knows what could have happened otherwise. Kev had a heart of gold and would do anything for you, but don't challenge him unfairly.

We lost in the finals that year to the Beaumont Golden Gators (Padres), so I went home. I wasn't home long when the Mets called and wanted me to join our AAA team, the Tidewater Tides, in Louisville, Kentucky, for the AAA World Series. It was a three-team tournament between us and Denver from the American Association and Portland from the Pacific Coast League. Mike Fitzgerald — Fitzy — got called up to the big club, so I was there to replace him. Dwight Gooden also got called up from A ball, and I got to catch him in the clinching game on ESPN. We won, of course.

But my biggest thrill, I have to admit, was Mickey Mantle threw out the first pitch, so I got to stand right next to the Mick. How am I looking? He's a baseball god.

We won the AAA World Series under manager Davey Johnson, and while I hadn't been there long, I knew most of the guys on the team. The fact that I got to play in a game was pretty cool. Gary Rajsich was the MVP and won a beautiful motorcycle; we were later scouts together with the Atlanta Braves.

Gibby's Greats: Chuck Hiller

If you caught Chuck Hiller in the right mood, he'd sit in the corner of the dugout, smoking away, spinning story after story of his days in the big leagues. I was fortunate to sit under his learning tree. Tales could include his days growing up in Johnsburg, Illinois, or playing ball at the University of St. Thomas in Minneapolis. A second baseman, Chuck started out in Cleveland's farm system, until he was pulled over to the San Francisco Giants in the 1958 minor league baseball draft. He made the Giants roster in 1961, platooning with Joey Amalfitano. Hiller couldn't get his bat going and ended up being sent down. In the 1961 Expansion Draft, Amalfitano went to Houston, so Hiller stepped up for good. He benefited from the power behind him in the lineup — Willie Mays, Willie McCovey, Felipe Alou and Orlando Cepeda. The Giants faced the Yankees in the 1962 World Series, and Hiller became the first NLer to ever hit a grand slam in the World Series, in Game 4 — though New York won the series. He later played for the Mets and the Phillies.

In 1969, Chuck retired from play and started managing in the minors, where he truly befriended the Mets director of player development, Whitey Herzog. Whitey, of course, went on to manage the Rangers, Royals and Cardinals, and he usually brought Hiller along with him. Chuck could be a hardass, smartass, pain in the ass . . . and one time, someone asked Whitey why he always took Chuck with him. His response was something like, "Every team needs an asshole. He does all my dirty work."

Chuck took a liking to me in rookie ball, but he rode my ass pretty good, *because* he liked me. That one season with him really set the template for how I wanted to manage, minus the smoking (I gave up my chew after 20 years, when Major League Baseball started their campaign to end the use of smokeless tobacco in the league).

When I was first-base coach with the Blue Jays, we'd play the Rays down in St. Pete and I'd arrange to see Chuck, who lived there. He'd come get me, and we'd have lunch. Chuck ended up with leukemia, and he died October 20, 2004, so I honestly don't know whether he ever learned that I'd become a major league manager myself. I miss him, and the game misses him.

4.

UP AND DOWN AND CARTER

Even though I was brimming with confidence after the great season in AA and the AAA World Series win, I still had to spend my time in the instructional league. I was a better player now so no need to call it the Instruggle. Davey Johnson had been hired as the new manager so he came out and watched us play, looking for future help. I always played well in front of Davey, except I guess when it really started to count. I loved his confidence, and the way he treated and managed his players.

I arrived at the 1984 spring training ready to go. This was my year. I worked my butt off that offseason preparing for my chance. I can remember there was this big hill near my home, and I watched this show one time in which football star Walter Payton ran up steep hills to prepare for a season, so I started running hills. I would always add a few extra, one for each of my spring training competitors. I was in great shape. But it just goes to show you that being in tip-top shape doesn't help you hit a breaking ball. Maybe I should have joined the military like my dad.

There were five catchers vying for the big-league spot: me, Ron Hodges, Junior Ortiz, Mike Fitzgerald and Ronn Reynolds. I was a Mets first-round pick, coming off a good year in AA. Hodges was a lock, a veteran player and under contract. As for the other spot, they would let us battle it out. I had the inside track — but you have to produce.

I had a good spring, offensively and defensively, and they told me I won the job. My career is rolling now, get out of the way! We had a couple more games left to play in spring training before we headed to Cincinnati for the traditional opening game. The Reds, I believe, were the first officially recognized franchise, so they always got the first official opener. That lasted until 1989.

I was catching one of our final games, against the Phillies. There was a fly ball hit to left field, not deep, so there should be a play at the plate. Joe Lefebvre's running at third. The left fielder's throw starts fading up the line into the runner, so I go up the line to cut it off since we have no play. Lefebvre throws an elbow out and hits me on the side of my face. Stupid me never left my mask on for plays at the plate: that would have made Joe think twice about throwing an elbow. It wouldn't matter now in modern baseball since you can't have contact anyway.

It seemed like a cheap shot, and just to be sure, his next two at-bats, pitchers Ed Lynch and Tim Leary smoked him good. That's how the game was played. Teammates protected each other like they should. The Mets were coming together. Thanks, boys.

The inning ended and when I'm sitting on the bench, my face hurts but I don't do anything. One of the other guys said something like, "God, look at your face!" and called the trainer over. My cheekbone was collapsed. They took me to the hospital to get it fixed. It was a quick plastic surgery where the doctor just pulled my cheekbone back in place.

So now I'm starting the season on the Disabled List (which they call the Injured List now) and bummed out since our second series was in Houston and I expected a lot of friends in the stands. We played in Cincinnati, then off to Houston. I still had a pretty good friendly crowd come see me, which was nice. Back in those days, they didn't do minor league rehab assignments, so I just took my batting practice and did some catching drills, waiting to be put back on the roster — which would be at our next stop in Atlanta.

My major league debut was in Atlanta on April 11. It's go get 'em, cold turkey. I was not real confident at that moment since I hadn't seen live pitching in a couple of weeks, plus it was my major league debut, so I was nervous to begin with. Dad flew in for the game, so that helped. One of the pitchers we faced was Rick Mahler. Rick was from San Antonio. One of his old high school teammates at John Jay High School, Paul Lindy, was an assistant coach on my high school team. So Rick used to come over during the offseason and work out with our team to get in shape for his season. I'd catch him in the bullpen. And now my debut is against him . . . I went 0-5 but did get an RBI on a ground ball to second base. I caught Walt Terrell for the win, which is all that mattered.

So now it's off to the Big Apple and the home opener. I was feeling a little better (at least for the moment) since I had a winning game under my belt. We checked into the team hotel, which was a Sheraton, directly across the street from LaGuardia Airport. You wake up every morning to frickin' planes. I got a decent night's sleep but was a little nervous since it was the home opener. I went downstairs and had breakfast, and when I came back, the door to the room right next to mine was open and there were maids cleaning blood off the wall. *Damn, where am I?* It was time to head to the ballpark for a day game and when we got outside, I saw a few cars up on blocks, no tires and broken windows. Now it's *Where the hell am I?* all over again. I'd seen the movie *Escape from New York*, but I didn't expect to live it.

Opening Day at Shea was April 17, and I'd be catching against the Expos. I got to present the ceremonial ball to Mayor Ed Koch. I should have said, "Hey, Big Ed, can you clean this place up for crying out loud?" Pete Rose was the lead-off hitter and stepped to the plate . . . and someone threw a grapefruit or something between us. Welcome to the jungle.

I was 0-13 before I got my first big league knock. It came off Bryn Smith in the opener. Rose was playing first, so when I got there, he said, "Nice going, kid." Wow. I really should have said, "Thanks, Pete, now I only need four thousand more." (I thought I kept the ball, but damned if I can find it.) We got blown out 10–zip, and our future teammate Gary Carter hit a grand slam. Tomorrow's a new day.

The next day, Pete Rose tried to score from second on a base hit. Mookie Wilson threw a strike to the plate, and Pete and I had a good collision and I knocked him on his ass. He was out. I loved it. That was for my good buddy Ray Fosse. We both would have been ejected in today's game. Let's go, Commish, get out of the way of the game — it's too good and pure.

I don't know how many times I heard, "You get that first knock, they'll come in bunches after that. You'll be fine." Bullshit. They were all lying. Mom came to her first game on April 22 in Philly. I remember it being a cold, dreary day. Ron Darling was pitching, and we were down 6–0 before we knew what hit us. Ronnie wasn't necessarily quick to the plate; well, no one was, as a matter of fact, since coaches didn't control the running game by calling for throws over to first — the catchers did. I loved it. They even gave you the freedom to call a pitchout if you had a strong feeling that they were stealing. The Phillies had some good speed, and a runner took off from first. I tried to compensate for the great jump he got by trying to get rid of the ball quicker, and I ended up throwing sidearm. I felt a burn in my elbow, and I knew something was wrong. Now I was having a tough time throwing the ball back to the pitcher. But I managed — I wasn't coming out. I must have had some flashbacks to my old high school football days. Our coaches would tell us, "If we have to come out on the field for an injury, we had better have to carry you off. Otherwise, get up. You're delaying a great game."

I got through it and after the game went to see the trainers. (This was before the league used MRIs.) They had to put me on the DL again. What was happening to my promising career?

The team was going out to the West Coast, and they sent me to see Dr. Frank Jobe while we were out there, who's the surgeon who did the first Tommy John surgery, where they replace the elbow ligament. His patient, you guessed it, was Tommy John. I got an x-ray, and he bent my arm every which way. He thought I had some ligament damage, but instead of surgery he gave me exercises to do for the next two months. If it didn't heal through that, I'd go under the knife. (Incidentally. got to know Tommy when I was managing in Norfolk AAA. He did the radio broadcasts for the team in Charlotte. He came down after some games, and I would pick his brain. I asked him one time if he got royalties for every Tommy John surgery. He said heck no, that he needed a better agent.)

I make the big leagues, I've never been injured and now I'm worrying about a bad elbow. Relax, you're only 21. Yeah, right.

So I hung around New York with the team, doing my exercises with the trainers, driving myself and them nuts. I just wanted to play. I had gotten to where I could swing a bat, but I was far from throwing. One day I decided to go see our general manager, Frank Cashen, and see if they'll let me go down to AAA and be designated hitter (DH). He was shocked, I think, but also admired it. He agreed, but said I would have to sign a consent form, as they couldn't send down an injured player. I even asked him if they could pay me my major league salary, but he just smiled and said no, they had to pay the minor league rate. It didn't matter, I just wanted to play, but it was worth a try. Back then in the majors, minimum salary was around $25,000. Nowadays, you would be crazy to go down like I did. Players soak up major league service time towards their pensions, even on the injured list, plus they make great salaries.

Down in Tidewater, I kept doing my exercises, and I got to DH. Eventually, I got to the point where I could catch again, but my arm never was the same.

The Mets called me back up in September, and I got into two late-season games, but I was thinking, *Thank God the season's over*, because it was a rough year. How bad? In total, I played 10 games, with two hits in 31 at-bats.

As I look back now, I wasn't ready, or I should have been sent down after the initial cheekbone injury. I didn't have enough experience or a track record to fall back on. What I learned and am very conscious of now that I'm managing is to not rush players, especially if they lack experience. Make sure they're good and ready. It wasn't just the physical injuries that hurt me; mentally I needed it, too, especially after the delays.

Being in New York didn't help either. It's a tough town to play in if you're established, and it gets even worse when you're a struggling young greenhorn. They ride your ass pretty good. So next thing you know, you're making a bunch of changes to your swing when all you need is a mental adjustment. I have never understood why, when players finally get to the big leagues after success in the minor leagues and have a slow start, all of a sudden everyone wants to change something. And if you're very coachable, you're done. Just because our title is coach doesn't mean we have to coach all the time. The good ones know when to back off and just let a player clear their mind.

This is where I could have been much wiser. At the end of the year, an organizational party for the team and front office was held in one of the rooms in Shea Stadium. I'm standing there, like a wallflower, when the team photographer, Dennis, comes up to me and goes, "Hey, this girl would like to meet you." I was a single guy, so, sure. He brings over this pretty gal, nothing extravagant. Dennis says, "This is Nelson Doubleday's daughter." So the takeaway of my story is if I had played my cards right, I might have owned the Mets now and it would have been easy getting a publisher for my book.

The day that dictated my baseball life more than any other was December 10, the day the Mets traded for Gary Carter. The Mets farm director, Steve Schreiber, called me. He beat around the bush with some small talk, but I knew right away something was up.

So, what does it feel like going from being the "catcher of the future" for the Mets to being stuck behind the best catcher in baseball? It was a kick in the nuts. And he took the shirt off my back, too, as I had been wearing No. 8 and that was his number.

If anything, Carter's greatness was underappreciated, since he had been playing in Montreal and the Expos didn't get a lot of exposure in the U.S. He was drafted in 1972 and was playing full-time in the majors three years later. He was an 11-time All-Star and was inducted in Cooperstown in 2003. By the end of his time in New York, everybody knew who Carter was. Gary put the Mets over the top. It was just one of those circumstances where the Mets would have been crazy not to get him. I'm sure they had doubts about me at that point too. Now, if I'd had a really good year in 1984, who knows? But it was Gary Carter; they still probably would have gone after him — he's a Hall of Famer for a reason.

"Camera Carter" never turned down an interview; hell, he was even learning French to become more of a star in Montreal. "The Kid" was a PR dream for a ballclub, and one of the most personable guys I ever met.

Gary treated me like gold. He was who he was, a clean-cut all-American kid out of California. A good, strong family man. He always had a smile on his face. He loved what he was doing. On the field, he gave me some good advice. I'd watch him just to see how he did things. I'd seen Gary play enough that I knew there was an opportunity to learn something from him. There was no animosity there. I've got nothing but good things to say about him.

I knew I had no shot when Carter was there. I was thinking, *I'll back him up*. Fitzgerald had gone to Montreal in the Carter deal. But I was at that age when they tell you that you need to be playing every day. You're too young and can't be a backup, you need to get your game going.

My game was going to be, once again, in Tidewater. At least I got my first official baseball card, from Donruss. Now I have proof that I'd been there, regardless of what the future holds. It's not a very flattering shot — I'm just standing there with a bat, and I look like a goober. I don't remember the specific photo shoot for the card, but there are photographers everywhere at spring training, and even more of them when you're playing in New York.

So now with the trade for Carter, I'm getting a taste of the business side of baseball. It's a big business that owes you nothing. You come to realize that it's time to look after yourself. I stopped worrying about everything and started focusing on my strengths. I could catch, I knew that — catch, throw, work with the pitchers. I understood what a catcher is supposed to be. I always disagreed with teams that only wanted a catcher that could hit. Working with the pitchers was the most important part, and focusing just on hitting hurt your team. It goes back to Jerry

Grote, who was known for being great with the pitchers, and they took any offense they could get from him.

Every pitcher is different, and I had to learn how they differed, how to approach them, when to challenge, when to back off. Part of it is instinct: You get a feel for what the hell's going on. You've got to be able to recognize what that pitcher's got, and not just what he's got all the time, but on that particular night, what's working and what isn't.

You hear the evaluation often: This guy isn't a good game caller. Well, okay, most guys are better game callers when they've got a better pitcher out there because you can do more things. Some guys have a little better instinct, a better feel for what's the right pitch at the right time, or what are the right things to say to that particular pitcher that get him going or what have you. I don't necessarily think it's something you learn, I think it's just something where you've got it or you don't. It's a sixth sense, an instinct. And I think that's why so many catchers end up as managers.

The idea of catchers becoming managers is perhaps a little overblown, but there is no doubt that a catcher has a different perspective on the game. It's the way they view it: looking out at everything. The nuts and bolts of baseball games are the pitching and catching, since there is so much of it. You can't be a rockhead and go back out there. What hurts the game now is that in high schools and colleges there are coaches that call every pitch, so some catchers have never called their own pitches once they get to pro ball.

That season in Tidewater was when I realized I was not the hitter that I wanted to be, or thought I was, or was when I was younger. It gets tougher the higher you go. The pitching is better and brings more guys to their knees than in A ball. In my eyes, it was a down year — .259 average, nine homers — but maybe that was my reality. I'm pretty good at looking in the mirror and not fooling myself.

Today, they'll sit with the player and watch a thousand at-bats to see what changed with his approach. With me it wasn't physical, my confidence was just eroding, I was scrambling to find help, and then I couldn't remember how I used to hit. Once you find yourself changing everything, well, that's not a good road to be on.

To vent, I'd talk to my dad. His advice was, "Wait a minute, you don't know what can happen. Some other team may want you. Don't slack off." I wished I had been Mike Fitzgerald, who got a new chance in Montreal. I heard they'd wanted me in the Carter deal, but the Mets chose to keep me.

Now, I was both happy and jealous of Ed Hearn and Barry Lyons, who were Carter's backups in New York. They both were good friends. In this game, you have to be a little bit selfish, you have to look out for number one. But I also knew the Mets had options on me, they wanted me playing; I was the youngest in the group — so there was no way in hell I was going to be a backup. Plus they both outplayed me.

We haven't talked much about the money I was making. That was the least of my worries. Plus my dad had told me, "If you're good enough, it will be there for you in the end." The amount of money in the game today is staggering and much different. We need to thank all the old-timers who went on strike and sacrificed so much to get today's players where they are. But me, I was always on a split contract, my salary was determined by whether I was in the major leagues or the minors. Standard for everyone. By this point, I was up to $65,000 a year if I was in New York, probably around $20,000 if in Tidewater, if I remember right. Each year, you got sent your new deal in November and December, and your contract got bumped up a bit; you either signed it and returned it, or you didn't and they renewed it.

I didn't even hire an agent until 1984, when I hooked up with Alan Meersand, and that was on the recommendation of Dykstra, who used him. But there was really nothing he could do, because until you start making some decent money, what is there to negotiate? I had no service time. He might call back and ask for $5,000 more, and we'd settle for another grand. I liked the guy. He never had to do anything for me. I never had to pay him a dime either. He took a percentage over a certain minimum, and I never made that.

I came to spring training with a great attitude, but I knew my only shot would be if someone got hurt, and even then there was no guarantee. Maybe a trade? No chance.

Virginia Beach had become home away from home. It's a great city. I spent many years there as a player and then managed there for three more. But having tasted The Show, it was back to the early morning flights, then right to the ballpark. Repeat.

The only difference in 1986 was that Sam Perlozzo had taken over as manager of the Tides. He was a real gung-ho guy, upbeat. He'd make us laugh and shake our heads by saying, "Boys, keep it close. I'll figure out a way to win this." I did play regularly, 96 games, a .246 average, but only three homers. My batting had slipped.

It was an exciting time in the Mets organization, as the big-league team was kicking ass and running roughshod over the National League. I'd get my chance, too, thanks to an injury.

Gibby's Greats: Rusty Staub

A veteran on that Mets team in 1984 was Rusty Staub, and he looked out for a young guy like me — and took me to my first hockey game . . .

Naturally, there's not a lot of hockey history in San Antonio, but there was in Montreal, where Rusty was an Expos original, from 1969 to 1971, and then brought back in 1979. The Quebec fans loved him and dubbed him Le Grand Orange. Yeah, the nickname was about his hair color, but it described his outgoing personality too. He was always good to me. He was good to everybody.

When we were playing in Montreal in the spring of 1984, we had a day off between games, and Rusty got some playoff tickets, the Canadiens against the Islanders on April 24. A bunch of us went to the Forum that night.

That was my first indoctrination to NHL hockey. And then a week later, we were back out in New York, and, again, Rusty pulled some strings, and we saw the Isles play out at Nassau Coliseum on Long Island. (The Isles beat the Canadiens and eventually lost to the Edmonton Oilers in the Stanley Cup Final.)

He owned a rib restaurant down in Manhattan, Rusty's, at 73rd and 3rd. We used to go down there and eat sometimes — great ribs.

As far as baseball goes, Rusty had The Job there at the end, great hitter, great career. But he was paid good money for one at-bat a night, to come in there and pinch hit: that's all he did. Most of the time he didn't even have to run, they'd pinch run for him. Now that's the job, but you earn those.

I can remember being in the clubhouse in the middle innings, and he'd be lying on the training table getting a rubdown while the game was going on, to prepare for his big at-bat. But that sucker, man, he could come through with the best of them. "Rusty, that's the life!" He'd snicker — he had a unique laugh. Le Grand Orange.

5.

THE '86 METS

B y my count, this has to be the 1,403rd book about the 1986 World Series–winning Mets. Not that I've read 'em all . . . or any of them. Lenny Dykstra sent me his autobiography, but I never cracked it open. Now, I *have* watched a couple of documentaries on that wild bunch, including the ESPN special and the *30 for 30* episode focusing on Darryl Strawberry and Doc Gooden.

I was a minuscule piece in the championship season — I was the bullpen catcher, and not on the active roster during the playoffs — but reveled in the moment just like everyone else. If you must, I'm briefly in the infamous Mets music video, "Let's Go Mets!" too.

But I'm struck at just how that team continues to mean something to Mets fandom, and baseball lore. Even before I managed in the bigs, I was included in some of the baseball card shows or autograph signings celebrating the team.

Gary Carter went down on August 16, he was playing first base, and he dove for a ball and fell on his left hand and broke his thumb. I was called up from Tidewater to backup Ed Hearn. I got into eight games — and we won them all; that's the important thing, team wins. If you just looked at my stats, you'd mistakenly think I was one of the stars — I batted .474, with nine hits and a homer — my one and only major league dinger. It was special to me, in my fourth at-bat in the game on September 20, 1986, against the Phillies at Shea. Michael Jackson is the trivia answer if you are wondering who I hit it off (and not the King of Pop!).

When Carter came back, it was back to the bullpen, so in reality I was a player but not a player. Most of the guys on the team I had known for years now, so that made everything worthwhile. It was very frustrating just sitting there, watching from the bullpen, and then occasionally getting to warm-up a pitcher. But I contributed somehow whenever I was called upon. It's hard to become a regular on a major league team, but it's extremely hard on a great team, so I felt lucky too.

Nowadays, most of the bullpens are behind the outfield walls, but there used to be a few that were on the field, like you see in Tampa with the Rays. Now it's no big deal during the regular season, but come play-off time, you'd better concentrate. We don't need any game delays. You might be wondering why I'm talking about bullpens, but don't forget, that's my home away from home. We were playing in the Astrodome during the first round of the '86 playoffs against the Astros. I'd warmed up pitchers there before, but this was different — a lot of people were watching. I can remember air-mailing the pitcher a couple of times and the ball rolling towards home plate. Now they have to stop the game. Great. Not the way you want to get noticed. Plus, it wasn't just me, the pitchers threw a couple of wild ones rushing to get loose, and those caused a delay too. It's one of those small things that get in your head and are tough to shake. A similar thing happened my first year with the Blue Jays as the bullpen catcher. We were playing in Fenway Park, and their bullpen is behind the right field wall, but it's level with the seats, and you're surrounded by fans that are ragging on you hard. Hurrying to get the reliever loose, I air-mailed one over our pitcher and hit some guy square in the back. Now they're all over me, thinking I must have done it on purpose. Nope, just the yips. I would like to have hit a couple of them right between the eyes, trust me. I tell people that I have New England blood running through my veins: that's the asshole in me. So you think being a bullpen catcher is easy? It can be hazardous duty, at least for the fans ... I laugh to this day, but it's not a good way to get noticed.

A lot has been written about Game 6 of the NLCS on October 16, when it went 16 innings, and the Mets won, 7–6, heading to the World Series. Yet we only used four pitchers — try getting away with that today in a game that long! Heck, today they use four guys in four innings.

Now, the documented famous plane ride home. It was a wild group that lived hard and enjoyed life, but I've never seen a more focused, competitive group in my career. These guys fought each other and didn't always get along, but, boy, once game time came, they turned it on and fought for each other. There was a group that sat in the back of the plane called the Scum Bunch, four or five of them who could throw back the beer.

I was like a fly on the wall. I'd enjoy a cocktail now and then, which just made everything I was observing more entertaining. Straw would occasionally get up and walk to the back to check things out, and sometimes the excitement turned up. But on this ride home from Houston, it was crazy. We beat that plane up pretty good, seats were wrecked, a couple of wives were puking — the plane needed a good cleaning. The airline sent the Mets a bill, which Frank Cashen handed to Davey Johnson. Davey told the team that they were going to make so much money as World Champs that the fine didn't matter.

Next up was Boston in the World Series. So much ink has been spilled about that series, but what sticks with me, and was something I took with me managing, was that when the manager has confidence, the team does too. When we were down two games to the Red Sox, no one panicked. Davey was the ultimate players' manager, and he just wanted you to show up and do your part; he didn't pay attention to any of the extracurricular stuff. Players today are micromanaged, to the point their sleep is monitored and they're even given scheduled days off. I know for sure some of those '86 Mets played games without sleeping a wink the night before and did just fine. And a scheduled day off? It was a badge of honor to try to play 162. That's what you did, plus the fans pay a lot of money to see certain guys play. It's not like football, basketball or hockey from that standpoint.

I look at the ball Mookie Wilson hit that got by Bill Buckner at first that led to an improbable Game 7 differently now as a manager than I did as a player.

Now, I have sympathy and understanding for every manager that has managed in major league baseball. There's all the scrutiny, and you have a lot of control but you also have no control. Everybody makes mistakes, sometimes your best moves backfire on you and your worst moves have you come out smelling like a rose. It's easy after the fact to say you should have done this, you should have done that, but not everybody understands what led to that decision at that time. Now it's different in the postseason, winner-take-all games.

Boston manager John McNamara chose to leave Buckner in the game, instead of his usual late-game replacement, Dave Stapleton. Billy Buckner couldn't move very well anymore; he still had a great glove, but he had no range. Was McNamara managing with his heart, wanting to reward Buckner by allowing him to be out there when Boston won? Well, it backfired. If your emotion, your heart, gets in the way of your head, you're in trouble. That's the baseball gods punishing you.

After the comeback Game 7 win, mayhem broke out, but you won't find me in the pile on the field. The mounted police had taken over the bullpen and were going out onto the field, so the bullpen guys went to the club-house celebration through the under-stadium walkway where all the rats that lived in dumpy Shea Stadium hung out. I got to see some big, beautiful police horses before they hit the field, but remember, I keep my distance from horses. I told my horse-fanatic mom, and boy was she jealous.

The ticker-tape victory parade was incredible. People hanging from windows. I was in awe. There was confetti and toilet paper and all that stuff being thrown from every direction, including the high-rises. There was a little panic before it started; word was going around, "Nobody can find Dwight." I'm thinking, *Well, I'm here. I'm going to enjoy myself.* It turns out Gooden was strung out and missed it. I've got a great photo where I'm shaking the hand of Mayor Ed Koch during the parade, and it complements the one I have of him and me on Opening Day at Shea in 1984.

With the talent on that team, everyone expected more championships. I just wasn't sure where I fit in, especially with Carter entrenching himself in Mets lore.

After that season, they started breaking it down, moving and trading guys. My two old A ball roommates, Dykstra and McDowell, were traded to the Phillies for Juan Samuel. Ray Knight, the World Series MVP, was gone because they didn't want to pay him. They unloaded some pretty good players. And management likely knew some of the behind-the-scenes stuff, how could you not?

Going up and down like I did, I really was oblivious to some of the wilder stuff. I had no idea Gooden and Strawberry were into what they were, especially the drugs. I knew they lived it up pretty good. I was shocked with Dwight; I didn't expect it at all. I kept to myself, and I had my head in the sand with a lot of it. Dwight was the best pitcher I ever saw — he just dominated. Then the lifestyle caught up with him. I may be a little biased since I saw him up-close and I caught him, but it would be tough to argue against me. I'll debate that any day.

Straw had the talent to be one of the greatest ever, but he became his own worst enemy. Still, I love the guy. Years later, he was speaking at churches, giving his testimonial, and I went out to see him in San Antonio. It was great to see how he'd turned his life around, and I'd rate it the best sermon I've ever heard.

Gooden and Strawberry both should have made it into the Hall of Fame — they had the talent, that's for damn sure — but their lives took wrong turns. Very few guys ever take the baseball world by storm the way they did. I love both those guys, they're good human beings. They just made some terrible decisions, and it cost them. But either one of them would do anything for you.

On November 13, 1986, the Mets were invited to the White House. It was pretty awesome, though the Iran-contra scandal was just breaking, so I'm not sure we got President Reagan's full attention. Somehow, I ended up in a prime spot for the team picture, just to the side of Reagan and George Bush Sr., the vice president. (We could use Reagan again.)

It's been great going to reunions for the team, though Carter died in February 2012, of brain cancer. And he was probably the one guy from that team that took impeccable care of himself.

We know baseball ain't fair — but life sure isn't either.

Gibby's Greats: Sid Fernandez

Sid Fernandez pitched some big innings in the '86 World Series. He was a starting pitcher during the regular season but came out of the bullpen in the playoffs.

I lived with Sid for the two months I was with the Mets in '86, out in Port Washington on Long Island.

Sid was a simple guy from Hawaii who didn't have a care in the world. At one point, he was struggling and missed Hawaii. He said to me, "I'm going home to work on the docks and smoke weed." I told him, "Sid, you pitch a couple more years and you'll own those docks." He was that good, but he didn't realize it.

We first squared off as opponents in 1983 in the Texas League. Sid was a top prospect in the Dodgers organization, which was based in San Antonio, my hometown, and I was in Jackson, Mississippi.

The game I faced Sid was my first time playing at home since I'd been drafted, so there were a lot of my friends and family there.

Sid only gave up two hits, a home run and a double, both to me!

What a homecoming.

After Sid was traded to the Mets in 1984, we always joked about that, and I could always say that I owned him . . .

6.

THE TIDE SWINGS

A quote I gave to a newspaper after spring training with the Mets summed up my situation very well. Going back to Tidewater was not something I wanted.

"The last two years I've been voted most popular Tide. You know you've been around too long when that happens," I said. "There's got to be teams out there that need a catcher, maybe a new atmosphere would be best. I just want a chance to play. A lot of guys come and go, maybe it's my turn to go." Being popular was associated with familiarity, not being the best player, especially in the minor leagues.

I'd been taught to not vent in the media, to not create animosity. Usually, I was a team-first guy, but for the first time, I was committed to another team. Before the 1987 season started, I married Julie MacFarlane. We were married 32 years, and raised three great kids, but that's jumping ahead a bit, both in my story and in the book.

My dad was someone I could vent to, though. I can remember telling him, "Dad, I've had enough of this." He replied, "Are you a quitter? Plus you just got married. You need a job." Great point again, Dad.

The competition for the Mets catching job had changed a little. Ed Hearn had been dealt along with some others to the Royals for pitcher David Cone — Julie and I were actually having dinner with Ed and his wife, Trish, when he got the call. When that happened I thought, *Okay,*

I'm gonna be the backup catcher. Nope. The Mets went with Barry Lyons and deservedly so. They also converted Clint Hurdle from infielder to catcher. That was even more writing on the wall that I wasn't going to get a real good shot, and my days were numbered. Clint, Greg Olson and I split catching duties with the Tides. (I'd heard my name batted around in trade rumors, to the Blue Jays, Royals and others.)

I had a decent enough year stats-wise in 1987 with Tidewater. I think I played a little better in some areas because I was accepting my fate instead of fighting it. It's the old, don't fight the system, you can't do anything about it. And don't cry; there's no crying in baseball. The team was good, finishing first, but it wasn't what I wanted. Let's say it was a ho-hum year.

When the rosters expanded in September, the Mets did call me up. And then I sat there and did nothing except accumulate big-league time. Well, that's not quite true. I ate sunflower seeds, chewed some tobacco, chatted with fans, warmed up our pitchers in the bullpen, so I guess that counts as doing *something*.

On the last road trip of the year, in St. Louis, when GM Frank Cashen came out during warm-ups, I asked if I could talk to him. This time I did let myself vent, expressing my frustrations about not playing. I told him, "I get it when you're in contention, but we've been eliminated, and I can't sniff an inning." To his credit, he listened, but he also made no promises.

That winter, I got the standard one-year contract sent to me, still the same old split deal between the minors and the majors. I did some soul-searching, now consulting with my wife, and decided to go back for spring training with the Mets, with the intention of getting a fresh start somewhere else.

Throughout the winter, my agent kept on Joe McIlvaine, Cashen's right-hand man and future successor, requesting a trade. When nothing happened, I stopped him at spring training: "You've got to get me out of here, man," I begged. He told me to be patient. So finally, they did it, and on April 1 — no joke — I was traded to the Los Angeles Dodgers in exchange for infielder Craig Shipley.

Ship was kind of in the same spot I was in with the Dodgers. He was out of options too. I only spent a couple of days in spring training with the Dodgers. The Mets sent him to AA, and I went to AAA, to the Albuquerque Dukes.

Even in my short couple of days with Dodgers AAA in spring training, I realized the Dodgers were different. The Dodger Blue thing was real — they had a tight clique. If you were an outsider with the Dodgers, you knew it. And I was an outsider. But I really respected the way they took care of their own. If you'd been drafted by the team, they invested in you, they wanted you to make it. Manager Tommy Lasorda came as advertised, a larger-than-life presence, and there was a lot of great talent. It's not a surprise the Dodgers won the World Series that year, thanks in large part to the historic pitching of Orel Hershiser and Kirk Gibson's Game 1 heroics. To get to the World Series, they beat my old Mets team — notice the correlation. Some guys are winners, some are not.

I didn't get called up that September, though. Instead, Gil Reyes got to go up when rosters expanded. We had shared the catching duties with the Dukes, and I only played 76 games, on a team that won its division. It's a good example of having thought the grass was greener on the other side, but it wasn't. At least when I was with the Mets, I played more.

Terry Collins was the Dukes manager, and I was around some really good baseball people and some great players. Sandy Koufax used to go around and visit all the different Dodgers teams (I'd met him before — he was old friends with Mets owner Fred Wilpon, high school teammates I believe). I can remember getting into the shower one time, and he was in there, and he looks at me and he goes, "You know, I'm getting a little tired of this shit." "Sandy, you think *you* are? At least you've done something." What an awesome man, and what a career — a legend.

In November, I was released outright. I kind of expected it. I knew I wasn't going anywhere with the Dodgers. Honestly, I was fed up with the whole game — not because I was getting screwed or anything, just that my career was slowly coming to an end, and it hadn't happened the way I dreamt about it.

I'd been through so much that nothing fazed me at that point. I figured being a free agent would allow me to zero in on a team that really needed catching, and I could pick and choose from a list.

The Texas Rangers manager Bobby Valentine called me from the winter meetings. He'd been in the Mets organization for years and was third-base coach in 1984, my rookie season, before taking the manager's job in Texas midway through. So we knew each other. Bobby told me to come to spring training and promised me some playing time. That's all I needed to hear.

It meant a lot that the manager called, even though I knew they had a young kid, Chad Kreuter, in AA that they liked. In the end, I couldn't sniff an at-bat or any time catching, and it was disappointing. Bobby is known for his BS, but I get it; plans and circumstances change in a hurry in baseball. When somebody gives me their word, I take it seriously. And I made sure to honor that in my years managing.

I got to know Jim Sundberg, who was always one of the top defensive catchers in baseball. He and I used to have this little competition, because he was at the end of his career, and I was never going to get in a game anyway. During the game, we'd go onto the backfield and set up a big metal garbage can, and we'd measure the distance from home plate to second base away from that drum. We'd see who could put the ball in the drum the most often — an accuracy contest. It was a way for Sunny and me to stimulate ourselves. Man, was he good. I see why he was always regarded as one of the best. I won't tell you who won the contest, though, because I hate to brag.

Nolan Ryan was on that team. I only got to catch him in the bullpen. But I was always a huge fan, and to get to watch him up-close was special.

Charlie Hough, the knuckleballer, was there, and that was my first time trying to catch that pitch. Charlie could make the ball do some amazing things; he could make the knuckle move left or right intentionally — trust me. I don't think even R.A. Dickey could do that. I only caught him in the bullpen, and thought, *Shit, I don't want any part of that in a game!* I didn't have the big mitt either. Geno Petralli was the guy that caught him all the time and did a good job. I think they should ban that pitch in baseball, though. It will drive you nuts watching it, let alone trying to catch it or hit it.

I got to hook onto one of Charlie's foursomes in a round of golf; what a golfer, and a great man. I saw him riding an exercise bike in spring training with a cigarette in his mouth — now that's baseball. See, all that training they do nowadays is overrated. Charlie was one of the great characters of the game; we need more of that in today's game. Players don't seem to have as much fun. What a beauty he was.

Then you'd see Nolan running to stay in shape even if his body was hurting so bad. Old warhorse.

Charley Pride would come to spring training every year as a celebrity guest, and he had actually played pro ball. One day, I walked into the shower and there's the great Charley Pride and he's singing a little bit. I told him I had seen him at the San Antonio Stock Show & Rodeo a few years before and loved his music. I can't remember what he was singing, as I was too much in awe. Hope it was "Burgers and Fries" — my favorite. For a crappy playing career, I met some really legendary people.

Off to Oklahoma City. Funny thing is, I never was officially sent down. During the cut-down day, they told me to sit tight and someone would get to me. Nobody ever did, so I said screw it, and I just showed up the next day to minor league camp. So, I sent myself down. I guess that was me preparing for my future role as a manager.

The Oklahoma City 89ers weren't very good — we finished 59-86 — but it was one of my most enjoyable seasons because of the guys on the team. We had a lot of older guys that were in a similar situation and had been around, we were just hanging on for that last cup of coffee.

Jim Skaalen was the manager, and he was one of the best guys you'll ever meet. Stan Hough, the third-base coach, was an old friend. Ron Roenicke, Mike Berger and Danny Rohn were guys I'd known from other teams, and Ruppert Jones I didn't know, but he'd been around a long time, so we had a lot in common. Then I'd meet someone, like pitcher Brad Arnsberg, who was there maybe half the season and ends up as my pitching coach in Toronto my first go-round. And there were the youngsters to keep an eye on, like Sammy Sosa. He'd been in AA in Tulsa and was promoted towards the end of the year. He was a bean-pole. I'd seen him at spring training, thin, lean, strong. Then he gets to the Cubs three years later, and, pfft, he ballooned. If they knew what he would have become, I'm sure the Rangers never would have traded him.

There were some serious hitters in the system. Rubén Sierra, Rafael Palmeiro, Juan González, Pete Incaviglia — some monsters. I'd never seen such big guys on a baseball team. It could have been an NFL team — but what great hitters. I know some of them have been mentioned in steroid conversations . . . regardless, these guys could mash. But they couldn't all fit in the weight room at once.

During spring training, position players hit off our pitchers throwing live batting practice to work on their timing, but mainly to let the pitchers face actual hitters. I was catching on the field while Palmeiro was hitting live BP. I have never seen a better, smoother, easier swing than his. He used to hit that live pitching — and most guys struggle with it because they've been off all winter and don't have their timing yet. But it didn't matter. Palmeiro had the sweetest swing I've ever seen. And for a guy that supposedly took steroids, he never got really big and bulky.

The pitching coach was Tom House, who was a forerunner in using bio-kinetics in baseball. He had all the Rangers pitchers throwing footballs, which was fun to watch. I've never seen a quarterback that couldn't whip a baseball. So I started doing it too; I had the best throwing year of my life, and my shoulder felt the best it had ever felt. House and Valentine were forward thinkers.

AAA was still a loose atmosphere with so many veterans, and I loved that the football continued. You know how if you go to a professional game at any level, you see the players playing catch in front of the dugout up until game time? We did it, too, but we were throwing bombs with a football not a baseball. A bunch of wannabe NFLers.

While House was the major league pitching coach, locally it was the legendary Fergie Jenkins, who lived nearby. I'd seen Fergie pitch at the old Arlington Stadium when I was a kid, so I was looking forward to getting to know him.

Fergie was an easygoing gentleman and a class act. He had this big house that he was fixing up, and the property had two nice fishing ponds. He told us that if we ever wanted to fish, just come on out. So we did. We never helped him work on the house, and he worked long hours on it. He would occasionally show up to a game in his overalls with paint on him. Another tough Canadian; when he would throw us batting practice, he could still pinpoint it, but if you hit a couple hard off him, he would turn it up just to remind you who he was. One of baseball's all-time greats.

Towards the end of that season, I took a foul ball wrong, broke the knuckle on my right index finger and that was it for me. I was at that point anyway, thinking, *Screw it, I'll go home early, what the hell.*

The offers weren't exactly flowing in for the 1990 season.

Have you seen *Bull Durham*? I was Crash Davis (Kevin Costner's character), without going all the way back to A ball.

Bill Dancy was the manager of the Scranton/Wilkes-Barre Red Barons and we knew each other a bit, so I thought this would be a good place to end it unless a miracle happened.

Essentially, I was there as insurance if something happened up in the big leagues with the Philadelphia Phillies. Tom Nieto and I split time. But I was kind of fried. As excited as I was at spring training, getting a new look by a new team, deep down I knew this was going to be it for me. Julie and I had been talking about starting a family, so I started thinking about supporting more than just myself. We went off to Pennsylvania, and it was a miserable-ass year.

Scranton and Wilkes-Barre are two towns, and Scranton is older and Wilkes-Barre seemed newer. Julie and I lived in Scranton, and it was a depressing place. I butted heads with Dancy a couple times over stupid stuff. There were lots of youngsters on the team, and Dance was a disciplinarian, which is what that team needed. I was sour and resistant, a combo of the older guy that was hanging on plus thinking I was getting screwed and should have taken the scholarship to the University of Texas instead of going pro.

I guess the only thing I did good that year was pee in a cup for a buddy of mine for a drug test. It wasn't for steroids but for recreational drugs, which you can test for in the minor leagues. Now that's loyalty . . .

At the end, my confidence was gone. It was too hard. I wasn't having any success. And baseball's a bad business when you ain't having any success. I found myself wondering, *What the hell happened? Where did it all go wrong? What could I have done differently?*

I took the money and gave them my best effort, but my playing career was over.

A lot of players hang on too long, and it delays their next career. Some guys just can't admit that it's over. Nowadays, they're paid decent money to make it worthwhile to stick around for six months, but it doesn't help you in the long run.

Catchers with a little bit of experience can always get a job in AAA; I could have played another five years. My body held up pretty good. My knees and everything are bad now, but I've never had a knee surgery or anything like that. Physically, I felt okay. There were a few more aches and pains, but that wasn't the issue.

Through it all, when things were starting to trend the wrong way, I started thinking, *Okay, it's too late to join the military.* Maybe I could be a coach — but I also knew that in high school and college you had to have a degree, which I did not have. I was thinking, *What am I gonna do now? Get a minimum-wage job? Doing what? Digging ditches?* That reality hits you between the eyes.

Gibby's Greats: Steve Springer

Steve Springer knew me better than most during all my years with the Tides, and, like me, he made the big leagues but only for short stints.

But there have to be reasons beyond that for us to have remained pals all these years later, even surviving living together. Partly, it's that common bond, knowing the dream of being a (full-time) major leaguer is so close and yet so far.

He still teases me to this day about my patented swing. I got to the point where I couldn't pick up a slider thrown from the pitcher — ever. So I became the king of the check-swing, you know where a hitter takes a half-swing when he's fooled by the pitch. It used to really frustrate me. Now, when he's out scouting and he sees a kid check-swing, he can't help but think of me. I guess I'll be in his mind forever. We have a good laugh.

Neither of our playing careers worked out. Springer became a scout for Arizona, but then he found his true calling as a mental coach, especially with regards to hitting.

When I had some clout in Toronto, Springer wanted to get back into pro ball, and I talked to the right people, who then hired him. It was great having him alongside again — and he even lived with me during spring training.

Spring loved playing online poker, and my outlet was fishing. One day after practice, he lost some dough, then switched gears, grabbed one of my fishing poles and came and found me at one of the ponds. (During spring training in Dunedin, most of the players stayed at Innisbrook Golf Resort. They play the PGA Tour Valspar Championship there every spring, so it's cool. But the best part about it is there are ponds everywhere, with four or five 18-hole courses on the property. We always had a lot of fishermen on the team, so you could go out on a golf course any afternoon and see half the team fishing. The funny part was, the golfers would get out of our way. Big fish in there, and gators, so watch yourself.)

It was his first time fishing, ever, so I hooked on a plastic worm for him and showed him what to do. Sure enough, he catches a 10-pound bass. Catching a 10-pounder puts you in an elite club — very few people ever catch one that big, and he did it on his first day. I've never done it, my biggest is nine pounds. Spring was hooked.

Spring now speaks across the country about the mental side of hitting, while working and training with major league all-stars. He has a very successful website, Qualityatbats.com — check it out. While on the road, he always manages to find a fishing hole or golf course (he can really play). Full credit to him for creating a market for his knowledge. There's been a book about his life, and now, apparently, a movie is in the works. I wonder who'll play me in it? Brad Pitt was already used in *Moneyball*. Maybe Jack Nicholson; the older Jack. People say we look alike, and some even call me Jack. My mother's not too flattered. But Jack's line from *A Few Good Men* — "You *want* me on that wall. You *need* me on that wall" — fits me perfectly.

7.

MANAGING JUST FINE

In my first couple of years in the minor leagues as a player, I would see these roving instructors come around. They were all older guys. I thought, *That can't be any life. There's no way in hell I'll be doing that at that age.*

I wasn't as old as them, but I ended up in the same place. (I see now why guys stay in baseball so long. Baseball is addicting: you fall in love with the competition and the camaraderie, and you never have to grow up. Maybe that's part of my problem — I've been told to grow up a few times, mainly by my wife.)

That place was back in the Mets organization.

Vern Hoscheit — who'd been my catching instructor — announced he was retiring. He was a beauty. An old country boy from Nebraska who loved to talk about his dogs and hunting. But he was a hell of an instructor. Funny how times change. Nowadays, one of the big categories for a catcher in analytics is pitch framing, which is making a pitch look like a strike even if it isn't. Ol' Vern used to scream when someone would say "framing the pitch." "You frame pictures, not pitches! Just catch the damn ball and let the umpire decide!"

Vern was a longtime major league coach and was on the staff of those great Oakland A's teams of the 1970s. He told us his main job was to drive manager Dick Williams around when Dick had been drinking. Chauffeur. Now that's job security.

In 1991, Steve Phillips and Gerry Hunsicker hired me to replace Vern. They knew I was done playing, and simply asked, "Do you want the job?"

After spring training, I'd go on the road 20 days out of the month, and I'd be home in San Antonio for the rest — our daughter, Jordan, had just been born when I started, so it was the perfect job.

At the games, I'd lock my focus on the catcher, make notes and then address my observations with him the next day just like my instructors did. My catchers and I all developed a great bond, our fraternity, but it's different when you're a rover and not with them every day, so you make the most out of the few times you visit their town. At the end of the year, I filled out evaluation reports. The sad part was knowing most wouldn't make it.

The next career move coincided with the birth of Troy, in 1994. I was an assistant coach for the Capital City Bombers, A ball, in Columbia, South Carolina. Julie was pregnant with Troy during the season. We rented a house from Marlin McPhail, who was a Mets coach in Norfolk, Virginia, so we helped pay the mortgage while he was out of state. The house was probably about 45 minutes from the ballpark, which is a lot, but in a nice area.

Ron Washington was the manager, and he'd later go on to manage the Texas Rangers. Wash is a workaholic; nobody can outwork him. He'd been an infielder himself and would especially work on hand drills.

The organization instituted a new policy, where they wanted low-level players — in rookie ball and A ball — to start talking about more game situations that happened that night or recently while it's fresh on your mind to help speed up your development. So after the game, we'd all get together and talk about that night, which would lead the discussion. Example: — "We have a runner on second, no outs; we've got to get him over to third base. What options would we have?" The important things from that game. Talkin' baseball. It was also an attempt to make things more like they used to be. When I was coming up, we'd play a game, and then the players would hang around the clubhouse, drink some beer and talk baseball. But things got to where everybody just showered and left after a game. Before my time as a player, they say it was non-stop baseball on and off the field. Players must have had more fun back then, it was still just a game. Wash could *talk*, and he's a funny dude. It was probably the funniest and most entertaining year I ever had. The problem was, we were doing it damn near every night. We'd get to the park around lunchtime, then do early work with the players, then the game at 7 p.m. Then we'd have our postgame meeting, as it didn't have to be every night. It was overkill, but I look back and smile. Wash went on and did a great job managing the Texas Rangers and is known as one of the best infield instructors in baseball (bet he didn't have those postgame discussions with his Rangers players).

So here's my wife, Julie, with our daughter, Jordan, who's not quite two, and she's pregnant with Troy and we have one beat-up old car. How we looking? She would drive me to the ballpark around noon every day, head home, then come right back and get me after the game, while waiting for Wash's lessons to end. Not only that, but it was about a 30- to 45-minute drive. She's spending all damn day in a car in one of the hottest places on earth, Columbia, South Carolina, all for $25,000, chasing the bright lights on Broadway. People think professional baseball is all fun and games and everyone makes a fortune. Nope. But I wouldn't trade it for the world. Julie got her breaks, if you want to call them that, when I was on a road trip. She went home early to San Antonio, and I can't blame her. She had Troy in September.

I do wonder how we managed that without quitting or hitting a breaking point. We weren't making much money. The fact is that I loved the game and I wanted to advance. More importantly, I didn't know anything else.

That opportunity came the next year, 1995, when the Mets gave me my first managing job, in Kingsport of all places. The Gulf Coast, New York–Penn and Appalachian rookie leagues, where Kingsport was, were all short seasons — so, three months long.

First there was what we call extended spring, where some lower-level players who didn't make a full season team and the three rookie-level coaches and managers stayed behind in Port St. Lucie until their season started in June. I had rented a place for my family to come out, and then we were going up to Tennessee together. Something happened where they said they were going to pay X amount of extra money to anyone who stayed down for the extended spring, and it fell through. Now we couldn't afford to rent this house we had reserved. At the time, there was one hotel in Port St. Lucie, because it was a new, budding town that only came to life when the Mets moved there. But it was a nice Holiday Inn and our only option. Another coach, Ron Gideon, was in the same boat with his family, so at least we had company, and we became friendly enough that years later I'd go fishing with Ron up in East Texas. It wasn't necessarily a crowded hotel, but there were people coming and going, and we really had no peace and quiet. I think it must have been the only hotel in Florida, because once high school prom season started, it was chaos every weekend. Unusual for a one-horse town. As for me and Julie, we had two youngsters. We had a suite, which wasn't much, but at least there was a pull-out couch. Somehow, we managed to stay there for two months, at which point my wife called bullshit and went home with the kids. I can't blame her. I'll say it again, it ain't all fun and games, especially for your family.

As excited as I was going to Kingsport to manage, I was on my own and missing my family, and I would try to call home every day. The guy who owned the Kingsport Mets at the time was a prominent defense lawyer in town named Rick Spivey — I loved that guy. I asked him to find me a place to live. He found a place all right, but it was in the worst spot, run down, just me and the bugs. I thought he must not like me or he just stuck me near all his clients so he could visit us all at once. Every night I was there, I thought I might get jumped. But I survived.

Thank God my family went home. It was probably for the best, all things considered: I was damn busy and had little time for anything other than being a rookie manager.

I would drive the team van all over town to pick up the guys who didn't have cars, which was almost the whole team, then have to take them all home after the game, which was not in the job description I received. Now the fun started, as it turns out the groundskeeper that Spivey hired — a client of his — got thrown back in jail for violating parole. So now I've got an extra job. I'd finally get to the park, then I'd hop on the tractor and drag the infield. Then I'd have to bring all the screens out and set them on the field. Then we'd have early work or early BP. Back then, we only had me and the pitching coach to throw all the batting practice, with an occasional roving instructor coming in to help. But a few days before we broke camp, my pitching coach Dave Jorn broke his throwing hand hitting a refrigerator or something — guess he was pissed the milk was sour. So now I'm the only BP pitcher for three groups of regular batting practice and occasional early hitters. I was begging for the roving coaches to show up. But that was minor pro baseball back then.

Roving instructors would come through every now and then, but not often enough. One time, Chuck Hiller came to town. After the game he asked why I was leaving the ballpark so quickly. I told him I had to drive the players home. He said, "What? You're the manager. Bullshit, you ain't doing that." So he grabbed our trainer and told him, "You're the new official van driver. Managers don't do that." Now the trainer had an extra job. Thanks, Chuck!

It was an enjoyable year, with all the hungry rookie-level ball players, but I put up with a lot of crap. Winning helps though — we finished first in our division. In the Appalachian League championship game, I got ejected in the first inning for arguing a call at first base. There was no need to get ejected. I didn't say anything inappropriate. It was some young umpire, and just like the players, they want to move up, and he chucked me. The clubhouse was attached to the dugout, so I was able to watch — and manage a bit — through a window. The team made a huge comeback. It was awesome. The boys earned me a manager of the year award too.

In 1996, I was bumped up to High-A ball, in St. Lucie. I was being rewarded: they liked the job I did in Kingsport. Though it was a higher level, we had lesser talent relative to what we had on the rookie team. In Kingsport, we had some flyers who could run you out of the ballpark; here we didn't have one great strength other than being a close team.

One kid that stood out was my shortstop, Guillermo Mota. He had the best hands, the most accurate arm you will ever see. He was just too big — six-foot-six — to hit: he had those long arms and a long swing. But he could really defend. Every ball he threw to the first baseman hit him in the chest. He had a cannon. Half the coaches told the front office to put him on the mound, try him out as a pitcher because he's not going to hit in the big leagues; the other half said to give him time. The Mets didn't protect him, and the Expos took him in the Rule 5 Draft and made him a pitcher — and he was in the majors a dozen years! We screwed up there.

It was a split season in St. Lucie, where the winners of the first half — the Vero Beach Dodgers — would face the winners of the second half. Come August, the last month of the minor league season, we were a few games out. Somebody put a rubber duck in our dugout one night, floating in a little container. I don't know who did it or why. We won that night, so the next night, someone put it back out there. We kept winning. We made up five or six games and jumped into first place.

I don't know if you call this good managing or just reading your players, or maybe we were all just a bunch of ugly ducklings. It's the end of the year, and these young guys are all worn out, and it's hotter than hell down there in Florida. So we bucked organizational policy and decided to give the guys a break: One day we took batting practice and played the game, but didn't take infield practice, and the next day, we'd skip BP but take infield practice. At those levels, they wanted you to do it all, so scouts could see and to keep the players active and help their arms, but it can get to be too much. Some days we would just show up and play — players called that cold-jocked. We kept doing it, and we were rolling. The front office (and the Mets scouting department, stationed in St. Lucie) was miffed, but I told them too bad, it's working.

We get down to the final game of the year, and we've got to win to make the playoffs and we're playing up in Brevard, against the Marlins farm team Fredi González was managing. Our farm director and the field coordinator in charge of all the teams wanted to come up to the game, and he wanted to know what time we'd be hitting. Well, it was a non-hitting day by my schedule, and I knew the players would revolt if I switched — plus I'm the manager, and I know what's best for my team. Not only that, the baseball gods punish you when you get in the way.

"We ain't hitting," I told him.

"What?"

"No, this is the way it is. We're gonna roll the dice."

It goes to extra innings, and we get out of a bases loaded, no outs jam, and we go on to win. The other team we were fighting with blew a lead, and we got into the playoffs. It's all thanks to the ducky and the rotation of BP and infield practice — don't ever mess with the baseball gods.

In all seriousness, baseball players are very routine-oriented and superstitious; if you change something that's working, shame on you. Plus, if they know you're a front-office puppet that can't or won't think for himself, you're done in their eyes.

We beat the Vero Beach Dodgers and then the Clearwater Phillies to win it all. What a fun year. You get them young kids, they all think they're going to make it, you get a great effort every night. All they want is a chance. You've got no sour attitudes, or very few if any. The boys stepped up.

The Hawaiian winter league ran from October to December, but it was only in existence from 1993 to 1997. The Honolulu Sharks and West Oahu CaneFires both played in Oahu, and then there were the teams in Maui and in Hilo on the Big Island.

In 1996, I got to be a coach on the team stationed in Hilo, and DeMarlo Hale was the manager. We lived together in a condo overlooking the Pacific Ocean and became such good friends that we made a pact that if one of us got to the big leagues, we'd bring the other one along. Sure enough, I made him the bench coach when I became the Blue Jays manager my second go-round. You had every Monday off. So, let's say you play six games in Hilo; you're the home team, you play two three-game series. Then you take a day off. Say that last game is in Maui on Sunday — you'd stay there with a day off and nothing to do, then you might fly to Oahu and stay on Waikiki Beach. It was just like a vacation. The guy that owned the Hawaii League, Duane Kurisu, was a major automobile dealer. He had this big condo right there in Hilo, right on the water, and he let us live there for free. There was a beautiful lagoon in the backyard — swim, snorkel, and all that — and then you had the big breakers just beyond the lagoon, in the Pacific Ocean.

The teams were a fascinating mix, mainly of players from A ball, but a few from AA. Each team was made up of players from five different major league organizations plus six Japanese players and six from South Korea. The Koreans and Japanese would not acknowledge each other or even sit near each other, let alone try to communicate — but they played the game well together. We eventually asked the translators, and they explained the history, how Japan had invaded Korea during World War II and all the atrocities committed. Neither side could let it go; I can understand some of that.

Our team was in Hilo on the Big Island, and it rained every frickin' day in the afternoon, just about the time we took batting practice. We finally said screw it and told the players to just show up for the game, but early enough to get loose. Cold-jock it.

After every game, the locals did up a barbecue, which was always incredible. All we did was show up and play games. You go to the beach or golf or whatever during the day, play the game at night and then they'd feed you afterwards. Tough assignment for two months.

We did a little fishing while I was in Hawaii, too, but I really associate my time fishing with spring training in Florida. Right from my first days as a young player, I'd go out fishing with some of the other guys, Ed Hearn, Billy Beane and, really, whoever else wanted to go. That continued when I became a coach and then a manager, especially in Dunedin when I was with the Jays. I'd see Justin Smoak and Aaron Loup out there every day. They both could be on the Bassmaster fishing circuit; two Southern boys, not surprising . . .

Mel Stottlemyre had been a pitching coach for the Mets when I was playing, and later, I got to know his sons Mel Jr. and Todd — both became great pitchers too. One year during extended spring training, Mel Jr. was down rehabbing his arm, and he loved to fish. He had a bass boat that we took out a couple of times on to Lake Okeechobee, which is a great bass fishing lake. It's also known for alligators. His boat was a 16-footer, and we saw gators longer than the boat. In 1997, I returned for a second year to High-A ball in Port St. Lucie. Three of the Mets top prospects were Preston Wilson, Terrence Long and Fletcher Bates, and they were all heading there with me. Preston had a connection to an old teammate of mine, as he's Mookie Wilson's son. What a first-class kid, just like Pops. I was given a bump in pay, and my main job was to see that these three improved. I learned a lot that year. The two prior years managing, I didn't have any big-time prospects on the team. This year I had three, plus pitcher Jason Isringhausen, who ended up being a great closer, pitched some rehab games for us. Preston and Terrence both made the bigs. Management expected a lot out of those guys, and being able to shape them into something was a big responsibility of mine. Two out of three ain't bad; maybe Meatloaf wrote the song about us?

The game and the competition are the fun stuff, but there's a crap job for all minor league managers: endless paperwork. After each game, the pitching coach would write up the pitching report with all the actual statistics, how many pitches were thrown, the breakdown, that sort of thing, on that night's game. The starting pitchers help out by taking turns charting our pitcher, then giving it to the pitching coach to file. As the manager, I would give an overview on how each pitcher did. They gave the factual stuff, and I gave my opinion.

I would do the same thing with the position players, how the night went, any key plays, that kind of thing. By then, we had started to use computers, so you'd type it in and send it off. But you'd still have to call in a game report. The real pain at that level is you've got to file end-of-season reports on not only your players, but every player you saw on the teams you faced. One year, I had to do one on every position player and every pitcher. It was ridiculous because you can't lock in. You can't be objective or be fair because you've got too much going on in the game. We complained enough and it was eventually changed, so now the manager only did the position players, and the pitching coach did the pitchers. Common sense. The poor guy that still got screwed was the coach, since he had to do both.

The postgame reports took about a half hour. The other stuff you just had to stay on top of and chip away at. Say you play the Vero Beach Dodgers; you play them enough times, you know the players, so preparing the reports goes a bit more smoothly. But there are teams in that league you might play only twice a year, so you need to do those reports in the moment you play them. A lot of it's overkill, because you can't be fair to these guys when you don't see them enough.

After that season, the Mets told me I'd be going to Binghamton, New York, to manage the AA team, in the Eastern League. It would be my first extended time coaching in the Northeastern U.S. My family's all from Boston, and one cousin married a girl from Bainbridge, which is right up the road from Binghamton, so I got to see a lot of family during this assignment.

At AA, the baseball is getting better, guys know they can go from AA to the big leagues — not as often as they do in today's day and age, but it was not unheard of back then. It's a more polished game. We had a nice bus for those trips, up to Portland, Maine, or down to New Haven, Connecticut. The travel was pretty easy. We didn't have to go very far; it is one of the easier AA leagues for travel.

Of course, the difference between these bus rides as a coach and the ones when I was playing in the minors is that now I'm "El Jefe," and bosses sit up front. I wasn't big on rules on the bus, though I liked a clear path to the bathroom since I'd get up and go pee a lot and didn't want to have to jump over players lying across the aisle. Some guys would crawl into the luggage racks to sleep.

Nelson Figueroa, who had come up from my rookie ball team, was on that Binghamton team, and he made it to the big leagues. Octavio Dotel pitched in the majors for 15 years on 13 teams. Scott Hunter was my best player and top prospect. He never got the opportunity he truly deserved. He's now the scouting director for the Seattle Mariners.

Derek Aucoin came to us later, a Canadian kid from Montreal. He was a big dude. He'd become pretty popular in broadcasting but died from a brain tumor in December 2020. His wife got in touch with me a couple of years later and asked me if I could do a little video for their son, Dawson, talking about his dad. What an honor and compliment. Those are important things in life. I got a nice note back from her. Derek was a gentle giant and a great man.

We had a good team in Binghamton, finishing 82-60, but lost in the first round of the playoffs to the Twins farm team, which was loaded with A.J. Pierzynski, Torii Hunter, Jacque Jones and Doug Mientkiewicz. I can still picture our outfielder camping out under a flyball, but the ground was wet and he slipped. The ball dropped in, and they scored the go-ahead run. That's all it takes.

Teams were starting to sign more players from Latin America, more than when I was a young player. I learned to say a few words in Spanish, but I can't string phrases together. When I started coaching, there would be English classes for the Latin American players. I used to think, *Hell, we're in the U.S., you learn English. If I'm going to Venezuela, I'll learn Spanish.* The big-league teams were investing in these kids, and helped them adjust much quicker. Dealing with the culture shock can't be easy. Baseball truly is an international game.

For a lot of the players out of Latin America, major league baseball is a ticket to a better life. If they can get that opportunity, make big money, now they can really help their families. I greatly admired those guys. They wouldn't be making much money yet, but they'd still send funds home to help. It's easy to take things for granted in North America, but I tip my hat to them. What they're having to do is admirable but also kind of sad.

I was the manager of the year for the league, and the Mets gave me their Casey Stengel Award as the organizational manager of the year. Any time you get an award like that, it means something; you're being recognized for your accomplishments. Did I save it? I don't know where it might be. My mom might have it. Let's not kid anyone, though — good players win those awards for you.

Before diving into Norfolk, and AAA, where I'd spend three seasons, how about a round of applause for the Clown Prince of Baseball? In the minors, I saw Max Patkin so many times I knew his act down pat. He could twist his face in all kinds of funny ways, and he excelled at pratfalls and skits. He played every little rundown town. What a rude, crude dude he was! When the crowds were small, you'd hear him mutter under his breath, "Screw this stupid act." I've been in parks where he's coaching first base. The fans aren't very far away, and he's doing his gimmick, whispering to the first baseman, "You're screwing up my program!" I'm keeping it PG.

After his performances, he'd be in our clubhouse after the game, sitting there naked, drinking beer, telling stories. His star power increased after being in *Bull Durham*.

Back to Norfolk, where I'd spend eight years total, between playing and managing. I loved where I lived, down by Virginia Beach; it's a beautiful area. Norfolk is a big military town, home to the largest naval base in the world. And we weren't far from Naval Air Station Oceana, where they park all the carrier jets. You didn't need an alarm clock since you'd wake up every morning to roaring jets, practicing dog fighting: *Top Gun* on the East Coast.

There is an area where you could park and watch the jets practice touch-and-go landings, just like on an aircraft carrier where they hit the deck and take off again. There's naval personnel everywhere. I befriended this guy who ran a navy equipment depot. He was a big autograph collector, so I helped him get some signatures from players. In return, he got me some navy hats from the various ships and even two Navy SEAL survival knives.

The team relied on the military as its biggest supporter and was always holding a special night for whatever ship had come into dock, USS *so-and-so*, you name it. The sailors wouldn't pay, but friends and family would come out to see them honored. Brings out the pride in everyone.

When I was managing there, I got to tour the massive carrier USS *Theodore Roosevelt* with my two oldest kids. It wasn't a public tour, just a favor, so we got all kinds of unique access. I got to sit up in the catbird seat, where the admiral sits, looking down on the flight deck. It's unbelievable how big those carriers are. The *Roosevelt* was being repaired, then was heading out for sea trials, then off to the Persian Gulf.

I was in Norfolk on 9/11. That place mobilized rapidly when it was time to flex some muscle. As much as we all love baseball, there are times when we realize how unimportant it is in the greater scheme of things, and this was one of them.

Once again, just like when I was a player, I was knocking on the big-league door. I thought I was going to have a great playing career, and when that never materialized, now, maybe, as a coach . . . I was one step away. AAA is the one level where you truly experience the difficulties of managing people, grown men living a dream and so close to success or failure. These guys are older, some have families, so you have to treat them a little differently.

I had learned from Davey Johnson to limit the rules to: be on time, play hard, be a man. For a lot of players, time is not on their side. You see if you can make a difference to help them make it. It can be a difficult level to manage because there're three types of players: You've got the up-and-coming guy, who is climbing through the system. Hasn't been to the big leagues, but he's going that way. He's locked in, on fire and enthusiastic. Next, you've got the guy that's pissed off because he got sent down from the big leagues, so he thinks he's getting screwed. Last, you usually have the guy that's just hanging on. He's been in baseball his whole life and sees it as a job where he gets paid decent money, but he's got nothing else he can do.

It can be a tough balance. If you have too many of the guys that are pissed off and think they're getting screwed, that can present a problem. I could relate to all of them, since I had been all of them, and that helped me manage.

I had a ready-made speech for the guy that thinks he's getting screwed, that thinks he was dealt a bad hand: "You can't let that get to you, because that's not actually reality. If you let it get to you, it will affect your game. You are proving those guys up there right; prove them wrong, that you should have stayed. Play better. Even if you have a great playing career, you're still a young man when it's over. The real world comes fast."

The players found a little inspiration and a good meal when someone was sent down for a rehab assignment. The big club would call and say, "Hey, give so-and-so three at-bats," or if it's a pitcher, "He's got fifty pitches, just yank him after." They'd lay that out pretty good for you. As the manager, I just made sure they got their work in. Which brings me to Bobby Bonilla coming down for a few games. I didn't know Bobby when he first showed up. He had a bit of a surly reputation, but I didn't see it, he was a great dude. Bobby's got a heart of gold. And he got a heck of a contract with the Mets. Bobby went on to work for the Players Association so I'd see him every spring when he'd come to town with that group — Steve Rogers, Donald Fehr, whoever it was. It was always good to see him.

It energizes the young kids to meet these guys. If they haven't been to a major league spring training, then they haven't been around the big-league players. Then they can see for themselves: what's different about this guy? Naturally, Bobby Bo was a beast.

The protocol is that any time a big leaguer comes down for rehab or anything, they buy the team a meal after the game. So you always looked forward to one of these guys coming down. It might be steak and shrimp, or lobster. They'd always find one of the best restaurants in town and get it catered. You'd come in after the game, and there it was.

I've had the privilege to manage some great players. One of them is Octavio Dotel. He had an 18-year career and played for 13 different teams. Talk about a hired gun. Octavio, who we called Pato because he walked like a duck, came along when the organization was becoming real protective of their young pitchers. They had all three of their top pitching prospects get hurt: Jason Isringhausen, Bill Pulsipher and Paul Wilson. They were going to take over New York, even appeared on the cover of *Sports Illustrated*, so, suddenly, the brass became really conscious of injuries, almost to the point of babying the guys.

There's always been a big argument in baseball where some say that injuries result from throwing too much in the minor leagues — you've got to structure it. The old-timers will tell you the problem is players don't throw enough, because back in the day guys used to throw all the time and they didn't have the same problems. Some will say it's the weights because you get too tight . . . That's been the ongoing debate. Regardless, human arms were never designed to throw 100 miles an hour, so pushing them to that limit means you're going to break down sooner or later.

Dotel was one of our top prospects, and one of the nicest kids in the world. He had the damnedest arm, so bendable and flexible, loose, and he could pop it out of its socket. He was double-jointed.

He was pitching a game in Norfolk and had a no-hitter going. He always threw a lot of pitches because he was a high strikeout guy and he got a lot of foul balls. I think it was the 6th inning. I know he's got a lot of pitches because he got a lot of foul balls and he's striking guys out. I asked the pitching coach, Rick Waits: "Waiter, how many pitches has Dotel thrown?" It was between 70 and 80.

One thing you should watch for, with pitching, is if they're laboring at all — that's a sign — but if it's effortless, there's less concern. Dotel was definitely at the easy point still. "Okay," I said. "I'm not going to ask you again. And don't you tell me." The crowd was into it.

Pato goes into the 9th and gets two outs. Bob Hamelin comes up with two outs and boom! Home run. Breaks up the no-hitter. I think Dotel punched out the next guy. Barely broke a sweat.

Later, when I asked Rick about Dotel's pitch count, it was in the high 130s. Oh, shit. "I guarantee in the next five minutes, there will be a call." Sure enough, the assistant GM Jim Duquette called. I explained everything, how he was pitching easy, how he was caught up in it all. No way was I taking him out. Duquette told me about others bitching about it and noted that if Dotel was going to throw a no-hitter, they wanted it to be in the big leagues. Fair enough. We agreed that in his next outing, it would only be five innings.

So we go to Pawtucket, and he's got a no-hitter going after four. He showed no signs of labor after that long outing. But he did give up a hit and was out after five. He turned out to have one of the most durable arms in baseball, ever.

I do think teams baby pitchers today. They restrict what these pitchers can throw in the minor leagues, and when they get to the big leagues, it's all about winning. A guy hits the point where he's never thrown more pitches, but he's pitching a hell of a game and you don't want to go to the bullpen or the guys in the 'pen may need a break — but he's never been beyond this . . . now you're kind of screwed. You want to push him past his norm because the team needs him, but he's never thrown more in his whole frickin' career in the minors.

Melvin Mora's story with the Tides is another great one. He was signed out of Venezuela by the Astros in 1991, but never made it to the bigs. Instead, he went to the Chinese Professional Baseball League where he played for the Mercuries Tigers in Taipei. Then the Mets signed him as a free agent, and he landed with me. Nobody expected anything out of him. All of a sudden, he turned into a great player. The kind of utility player every team needs, he could play anywhere. A lot like Jose Bautista, he didn't figure it out early on, but stuck with it and learned how to play, how to hit. In 2001, Mora's wife, Gisel, had quintuplets, so all of a sudden they had six kids, including their eldest daughter. He played from 1999 to 2011. Good thing — he needed the money!

As the manager, you know it's a tough racket, it ain't easy to make it. You've got to get a break, somebody's got to like you and all that. And then when you get that opportunity, you've got to do something with it. Some guys get a lot of opportunities, some might get only that one shot, so you'd better do something, you'd better be ready. I root for them all. Of course, there are some guys that are a pain in the ass, maybe you don't root for them quite as hard.

And the sad truth is some guys have zero shot. That was the case with country music icon Garth Brooks, who came out to the Mets spring training. It was for charity, sure, but he was really into baseball. He worked out with the team, did everything the players did. The fans knew he was there but there are always big crowds at Mets camp anyway.

When the team was done with their day's workout, he stayed late and would do extra fielding work and BP with Tim Foley, who'd played in the big leagues with the Pirates. Garth would stay at least an extra hour or so, to try to improve. These fans would all wait, and when he was done with his workout, they would get in a long line and he would sign every autograph, take pictures. People would get on their phones and say, "Hey, can you say hi to my friend?" It was incredible to watch, he was so patient, and this was after a normal day plus his extra work. Garth gave out signed guitars to players too. That's why he is so beloved.

Garth had bought this new blue truck, a dually, and he told Tim that if he got in a game and got a hit, he'd give him the truck. Garth hit a long line drive once, but the outfielder caught it. Foley was hoping he'd get a truck, but never did.

One day, we were on a backfield, going over bunt plays or something, when Make-A-Wish Foundation brought a young boy who had cancer out to meet Garth. Garth borrowed a cell phone and called home, as his wife and his kids were staying nearby. I heard him talking to Sandy: "What are you making for dinner night? Can you prepare four extra spots?" So, Garth took that boy and his family, the mom and dad and two kids, home with him that day to spend time with his family. Incredible.

At the end of camp, he threw a party for the players. Really, a cool dude.

A decade later, when I was bench coach in Kansas City, the clubhouse manager, Jeff Davenport, had befriended Garth at some point. When Jeff was getting married, Garth let them have the ceremony on his property in Oklahoma, where he had a little chapel.

It's not true that there's never pressure to win in the minor leagues. You're a competitor, so you want to win. But it's a fine balance. They want you to develop these guys, but winning is a big part of development. In analytics, they say pitcher wins don't matter. I get that there are so many factors that go into a starting pitcher getting the win. And players coming and going absolutely affects the team and its performance. The 2000 Tides finished 65-79; we had 45 different players go to bat and used 23 pitchers.

Now, up in New York, the Mets went to the World Series, losing the Subway Series to the Yankees in five games. So, there was success as an organization, and the AAA team contributed big-time.

In my 40 years in baseball, I can confirm that some guys figure out a way to win, some guys figure out a way to lose — that's just the way it is. It's a mentality, what they've got inside. You may leave with the lead in the game and the bullpen blows it or something — but I'm just telling you, in close ballgames, at certain times, there are certain guys that figure out a way to get tougher, and the other guys collapse. It's psyche, confidence, so that's why I argue wins do still matter.

AAA can be a logjam, a holding ground. Back to my career as a player, I kept going back down, because they wanted me to play every day. That's what you did. Generally, if a guy can't break the big-league lineup, but they like him, he's going to be playing every day in AAA. That poor guy in AA, unless he's a better prospect, he's going to have to stay in AA. It can be two, three, four years, until you get a break.

The front office would call, "Hey, we traded so-and-so." I would call the player into the office and tell him, and then the front office would phone him up and give him further details. It was important to be human about it, you're uprooting him from a comfort zone.

The best part about that level, though, is that a lot of times you get to tell the player that he's going to the big leagues for the first time. That's the thrill of it all. It's tough when you've got to release a guy or you're sending him down. But it's the best to be the guy delivering the news to a kid going to The Show.

There's always a nice hug. The wide eyes. It's pretty cool. Sometimes I would screw with a player. I'd call him in. "What happened? What did you do?" And as he's starting to freak out, I'd say, "I got this call from the general manager. You're going to the big leagues." I got to have a bit of fun with some of these guys.

With a few of them, the long shot or the one nobody thought would make it, I brought them out into the clubhouse to tell all their teammates, so that everyone could share in the moment and celebrate with them. Every locker room has that guy who is beloved, the Rudy of the team. It helps the other players believe they can make it too. Then you might see them two days or two weeks later back in your clubhouse.

Now, management can mess up too. One afternoon before a night game, I received a call from New York to be told, "Don't play so-and-so. We're calling him up tomorrow, but you can't say anything yet because the player up here left the ballpark before we could tell him he was going down." They must have said, "Don't say a word to anyone yet," about five times, and I swore I wouldn't because the move to send the player down was controversial.

About a half hour later, I go into the training room, and the guy who runs our clubhouse has a little office in there. There are two players in his office with him, and he asks me in front of them, "So-and-so's going up?" I asked him where he heard that. Valentine had just called him. So now everyone knows because the two players let it out.

Management was insistent that I not say a word and the team's own manager is doing the opposite. In my 10 years managing in Toronto, I very rarely spoke to our AAA coaches but definitely not the clubhouse boss.

If you think everything is always done the right way and professionally, the way it should be, think again. But that's what happens when the general manager and manager distrust each other.

In season, you hear from the major league front office, the GM and the assistant GM, a lot about what's going on with the ball club. They don't tell you everything, but they kind of give you an idea if there's something they are planning, just so you can plan accordingly yourself. They might say, "We're going to bring this pitcher up in two days." He might be scheduled to pitch today or tomorrow, so if you pitch him that night, he can only do two innings. They help you plan so that you don't overuse somebody, so you're not sending someone up after a night with 130 pitches. But when you take him out of the game that early, he knows something's up. Organizational meetings were held at the end of the year during the instructional league, where the scouts and the coaches and the front office people would get together and talk about all the different players.

A manager or coach needs to be able to rate players. If you're a terrible evaluator, you really have no value to the team because you can't help them make decisions. And this is all before they did everything just based on numbers; I don't think every team has organizational meetings anymore. So much of that has disappeared. Numbers are really good because they help improve evaluations — you can tell when a guy had a good year, and when he didn't — but the eyes and ears and just being around somebody and getting to know the guy is a big part of it too. That's something numbers can't do.

In this one meeting, Frank Cashen was there, helping out, as he had retired as GM. He still meant a lot to the team. He was sitting in the front row where all the power players were. Someone mentioned that a player reminded him of Axl Rose, the lead singer of Guns N' Roses. I guess Frank had been half asleep, but he heard the name and started flipping through his organizational book. He finally says, "I can't find Axl Rose in our book." That gave everyone in the room a good laugh.

Daryl Johnson, who managed the Red Sox in the 1975 World Series and managed the Seattle Mariners, was a big influence on me on the coaching side of baseball. DJ was Cashen's right-hand man. He was a great baseball mind, great judge of talent, just a good dude. When I was playing in AAA, DJ had an apartment in Norfolk, so he'd often watch our team. Cashen respected DJ's opinion. DJ would sit out in the crowd, with the scouts, everyone smoking their cigarettes.

At the organizational meetings, there might be some debate — some people like a guy, some don't. In the end, Cashen would always go to DJ: "Hey, DJ, what do you think?" DJ wouldn't say a lot, "Can't play" or "I like him." And that was it, there was no more debate and we'd move on to the next player. Frank trusted him more than he trusted anybody.

One time in the 2001 Tides season, Cashen came down to watch us play, and he was sitting in my small office after the game, when outfielder Tony Tarasco — one of the vets on the team — walked by on his way out. Tony was a fun-loving, carefree dude, and he was real casual that day in a tank-top and camo pants, his hair in the small 'fro he kept at the time and his music blaring. I called him in to meet Frank. He comes in, all happy, and puts his arm around old-school Frank, who was all brush cuts and collared shirts. Frank didn't know what to make of Tony.

I went into that season seriously questioning things. My family was young — Kyle, the lovely surprise, came along in 1999 — and I wanted to do right by them.

The team itself performed better on the field, finishing 85-57, and it was a squad with lots of fresh faces, some up-and-coming youngsters.

We got knocked out of the playoffs in the first round, but the championship series was cancelled anyway because of 9/11. Norfolk was on high alert as I was packing up to head home.

I came to the conclusion that I needed to get a job closer to home for my family's sake. They had already sacrificed a lot. After three years in AAA, I hadn't broken into the big leagues yet as a coach, and they were changing coaches left and right. They were looking for a new third-base coach after that year. Duquette told me that they wanted me to stay at Norfolk, even if I didn't get the job. I told him, "Duke, I can't do it." He offered more money. I told him I still couldn't. If I didn't get that job, I needed to find work closer to San Antonio.

My family and I were driving from Norfolk to San Antonio, and Jeff Wilpon — Fred's son — called me. You knew when Fred got complete control, Jeff was going to be pretty much running the team. Jeff and I had always gotten along. We talked about Norfolk, and he reiterated that the Mets wanted me back, and I told him my side. We left it with him telling me to call him before I took any other job. He even offered to create a job for me.

Later, I went to New York for the third-base coach interview, and I met with Valentine in his office. Then I was supposed to go meet with Steve Phillips in his office, and it took a while. You could tell there was a disconnect between the two. Both Phillips and Valentine had known me a long time, but I ended up not getting the job.

Marty Noble was one of those very knowledgeable New York beat writers, and he was always a thorn in Valentine's ass. He called me for a little piece, and I laid some things out.

Phillips called me and said, "I read that article and didn't appreciate it. I think we're going to have to part ways."

"Steve, it's too late. I already told Duke I'm not coming back, so you've got nothing to worry about." Turns out I had lots to worry about.

Gibby's Greats: Scott Stewart

Scott Stewart was one of my favorites. He was an old country boy — a real goofball, but a very friendly guy. I had him in AA and then in AAA. He was born in Stoughton, Massachusetts, but I believe he lived in the Carolinas. He ain't no Yankee, I can tell you that. He's a proud redneck and a volunteer firefighter. He just loved the paramedics and firemen. "Hey, Gibby, if you need me tonight, if I get called up or something, I'm staying at the firehouse." He'd go down there and befriend those guys and stay the night. I'd tell him, "Don't worry about it. You're not getting called up." The Mets never gave him his shot, but he turned into a darn good left-handed reliever for the Expos. I loved that kid.

Throwing left-handed, he'd always fall off to the third-base side of the mound. When a ground ball is hit to the right side, the pitcher has to cover first base, and he had a hard time getting there because he was always finishing his pitch on the opposite side of the mound. He was also a heavyset guy and couldn't run real well — and he used to have trouble remembering stuff. I used to ride his ass. "You've got to get over to first!"

One game, and the ball's hit, and it ricochets to first base, but Scott doesn't cover first. I was pissed off anyway, the game was going bad, and it didn't even register with me that the ball had hit him. We had a reliever getting loose, and I told the pitching coach, "I've seen enough of his BS. He never covers first base." I went out there and yanked his ass and lectured him again. Then when he was back in the dugout, I ripped into him again. The pitching coach, Rick Waits, comes over and says, "Gib, you know that ball hit him." I'd completely missed it and never saw him hobbling around. It damn near broke his leg, but I had seen him not cover first so many times that I just figured he was loafing again. I apologized, as he was sitting there with ice on his leg.

Sorry, Stew.

8.

J.P. THROWS ME A LIFELINE

"**H**ey, if you ever want to come and work out here, let me know."
I'd heard that line dozens of times from my old pal Billy
Beane, who was in charge in Oakland. This preceded his stint as general
manager too; even when he was a scout for the A's, he told me that.

So, when I walked away from the Mets organization, my contract ending on December 31, 2001, I thought Billy was my ace in the
hole. The problem was I didn't check with him first, before notifying
the Mets.

The A's were good and cheap — but a playoff team. There was no
need to make any changes to the coaching staff, those guys were doing
something right, plus they didn't have the money to carelessly add. I
wasn't looking for a big-league job, just something in the organization so
I could be home or closer to home.

Fortunately, another old friend was able to look out for me.

Over the years, J.P. Ricciardi worked in the minor leagues in various jobs with the A's and rose to become Billy's right-hand man. And,
since he was both an old teammate and roommate, we were still tight.
J.P. knew my plight and called around. I interviewed for a couple of
spots, like the AAA job for the Astros, but nothing was happening
for me.

But something was happening with J.P.

On November 14, 2001, I called Beane, and he couldn't talk: "J.P.'s got a press conference." Press conference? J.P. was supposed to be helping me find a job . . .

It turned out that J.P. was being named GM for the Blue Jays. Well, shit, he never said a word about that. I think it developed fast.

My next thought was obvious: *He'll have something for me.* When things settled down for him after the whirlwind of the announcement, he called me and said, "Listen, we're going to need a third-base coach and a bullpen catcher. Those are the only jobs we've got open." He promised to bring me up to interview for the third-base coach job.

Buck Martinez, another old catcher, was manager of the Jays, and I flew up to do an interview with him and J.P. I thought it went okay, but they ended up giving the job to Carlos Tosca, who'd been the manager in AAA Richmond. J.P. hired a lot of people he knew, as a GM should do, including director of player development Dick Scott; special assistant Bill Livesey; national scouting cross-checker Jack Gillis; and Tosca, who he knew from the minors.

Later, J.P. called me and said that the bullpen catching job still hadn't been filled. I laughed at him, "I ain't squatted in ten years!" He said he'd pay me what the Mets were paying me to manage in AAA: $65,000. "Physically, J.P., I can't do it." We left it at that.

Family-wise, we'd been living in Ruidoso, New Mexico, for three years to be close to my wife's family. It was a small town and too isolated (felt like Shelby all over again), so we moved back to San Antonio. Now I've got a new house, three kids and two weeks left on my job.

Julie and I talked about it, and it's tough to pay a mortgage with no paycheck. I called J.P. back to take the bullpen catching job — not bullpen coach, there's a big difference . . . but it was work. I sat back and had to laugh, thinking, *Heck, I spent my whole career catching in the bullpen, this is perfect for me.*

I'd be lying if I said that I spent the rest of the offseason getting in shape to catch again. Instead, I just enjoyed time with my young family, settling back into San Antonio.

Toronto had its spring training facilities in Dunedin, which is close to Tampa on Florida's Gulf Coast. Catchers and pitchers always report first to spring training, so there I was, putting the gear on for the first time in a decade, squatting down to catch some pitchers. Next thing you know, *Pop!* My knee just blows up. So now I'm the only bullpen catcher in baseball that can't catch. *Son of a bitch, I knew this was gonna happen!* Now I can't help take the load off any of our catchers because I can't catch in spring training.

The swelling went down in time.

We went into the season, and the Jays pitching just wasn't very good. Every night, it seemed like 20 guys were up in the pen throwing and we only had seven or eight relief pitchers. The only person hurting more than me was poor Buck — his job depended on the pitchers performing well. So I'd just get down on one knee and try to catch.

Dan Plesac, one of the best relievers in baseball, was on the team. He used to sit there and laugh at me, as he was an old-timer too. Danny and I'd laugh and joke: I honestly thought that by June I'd have to find another job, scouting or something, because physically I couldn't do it — nor did I want to.

About a month into the season, I sidled up to longtime Jays radio voice Jerry Howarth, who was watching BP. "I'm a Blue Jays coach too," I told him. Jerry laughed. I stuck out my hand. "John Gibbons." It was the start of a beautiful friendship, but it's also a good example of how little an impression I was making.

Buck had played for the Brewers and Jays and was a tough son of a bitch, once making a tag at home plate with a broken leg. After playing, he became a Jays broadcaster and got some time in the U.S. on ESPN too. So Buck was hired as the Jays manager by GM Gord Ash after Jim Fregosi was let go. But then Ash was gone and J.P. came in, and you just knew the leash would be short. Sure enough, Buck was fired 53 games into the season, when we were 20-33.

The timing was a bit odd, though. We went to Detroit and swept the Tigers, and J.P. fired him when we got back. Maybe J.P. was thinking if things started rolling too good he wouldn't be able to do it. Baseball's a rough business, and every GM deserves their own hand-picked manager. But I have to thank Buck for giving me an opportunity — another great man.

Garth Iorg, who was Buck's guy at first base, was fired too. J.P. promoted Tosca to manager, and I got the first-base coaching gig. We called the first-base coach the Celebrity Coach, since usually it's a great ex-player who stayed in the game. I was one of the few first-base coaches that wasn't a great everyday player, so people would ask, "Who's that guy?" We also called that position the Get Back Coach, because all they said was "Get back!" when the pitcher threw to first.

Brian Butterfield, who had been managing the Yankees AAA team at the time, but got fired midseason there, was hired to be the third-base coach — Brian (who we called Butter) went way back with J.P. too.

Now I didn't have to go find a scouting job.

In the first-base and third-base coaching boxes, you really have to pay attention, but it is hard to do since you're also trying to watch what's going on in the field. So many close calls on foul balls that go flying by. Mike Coolbaugh, from San Antonio, was a minor league coach for the Rockies who got hit in the neck, and it killed him. I played with his brother, Scott Coolbaugh, and I knew Mike. Great family man. A line drive caught him in the wrong spot. That tragedy finally pushed the requirement for base coaches to wear helmets. Another thing I noticed when at first was how fast the balls travel into the stands, so thank God they finally started getting netting up. It was unbelieveable how many balls went into the stands and that more people didn't get seriously injured. Nets don't interfere with your view, and they add a lot of safety.

Butter used to do a thing at third base where he'd give the outs and I had to give them back to him to make sure we were on the same page, that we had it right. People forget the outs; we've all seen the guy at first base who just takes off, thinking there are two outs but there's only one, and the ball's hit and he just keeps running, and then they double him on first. It shouldn't happen, but it does.

Let's talk about giving players signals. Now, in the minors, we drummed the signs into the players, but in the majors, they almost forget it all, or they don't pay as much attention. Say you're going to hit and run: you put the hit and run sign on, and if one guy doesn't get it, you're in trouble. So you might have a verbal sign, you might say a certain word that means hit and run. You always see the first-base coach right behind the runner because they are both watching the third-base coach's signs. You might have a hand lightly on his back and pinch him or something — that might be the signal, the "Okay, you're going on this pitch." Of course, the good runners have the green light to go whenever they want, but they still need to know the "hold" sign to know when we don't want him to try.

As the coach at first base, you remind the runner of how many outs there are, where the outfielders are positioned — stuff the runner should know automatically, but they don't. You can say, "Hey, the right fielder is playing more in the gap, a ball down the line should get you to third base." That's the toughest one for a runner on first since every other hit is in front of him. You often have to remind them when to tag up depending on how deep the fly ball is and the situation. A lot of times, they get to first and just bullshit the first baseman. You see it all the time.

There's not a lot to being first-base coach, but you can screw up a lot of base running by not getting the signs right. So it's more of a reminder position. I learned so much from Butter, the most knowledgeable coach I've been around. He had great attention to detail and was very demanding.

I liked Carlos, and he respected the opinions of his staff. Every coach has a specialty. When I was a coach, catching was my specialty, so I'd spend time with the catchers working on their mechanics, footwork or whatever it was; they know their bodies, so you work together to figure it out. Someone else was in charge of the outfielders. Of course, you had your hitting and pitching coaches too. The coaching staff is its own little team within the bigger team, sharing scouting reports, talking about where to position people. Today's players often carry a card in their pocket so they don't have to memorize everything and they know what's going on.

Coaches can be more buddy-buddy with the players than the managers. Often, a coach will put out a fire before the manager's even got to deal with it. Usually it relates to playing time, so you take a moment to listen, but you also reinforce that the manager knows what he's doing. Coaches have a say in decisions on somebody's career, but they don't have to make the call, don't have to be the bad guy. And you're spending so much time with these guys, around them every day, throwing batting practice, hitting fungoes, ground balls. You've got a 20- to 25-man roster, and there are five or six coaches. You can't help but get to know somebody because you see them so damn much.

Now, not every player is curious about the coaches. They kind of know who you are, they'll know if you played at all and if you got to the big leagues, that carries a little bit of weight. Often, I was asked about those '86 Mets — everybody wants to know about how wild that team was.

The Jays finished the season 78-84. Highlights included seeing Roy Halladay finally put it all together and become who he was meant to be — he had 19 of our wins, against seven losses. Vernon Wells was another who came into his own, as our centerfielder, and since he was only 23, you could see big things ahead for him. A surprise was the play of third baseman Eric Hinske, J.P.'s first trade acquisition, who ended up being named Rookie of the Year.

And there was nothing like watching the confidence of Carlos "CD" Delgado. He was a wonderful guy, the ultimate professional, great face of the team, well-spoken, highly intelligent . . . you name it. Carlos had it all. He was a hell of a hitter, one of the best I ever saw. I was coaching first base when he hit four home runs in a game. What's too bad for Carlos is he never got to play on any really good teams until he went to the Mets. Vernon Wells was in the same boat, and never got to be celebrated in the postseason at all.

Carlos was the first player I ever saw who religiously sat down after each at-bat and made notes in his big, thick book of all the pitchers he'd ever faced in the big leagues. He kept track of how they would pitch him, their tendencies or little things he might pick up on a pitch or something — he always wrote it down.

My contract as first-base coach was extended on September 3, 2002.

In 2003, the team seemed to turn a corner, finishing 86-76. That was only good enough for third in the American League East, though, as the Yankees and Red Sox were again dominant. Delgado and Wells were monsters at the plate, and we were overall a good-hitting team, could pound it pretty good. We just didn't have enough pitching — though we did have that one guy.

This was Doc Halladay's first Cy Young season as the best pitcher in the AL. Every time he went out there to start a game, we believed we were in it. Halladay's going to give you a shot to win nine out of 10 times. It could be a low score, so score a couple of runs for him, you might win. The bullpen loved it because they knew they were pretty much getting the night off because Halladay would go deep into the game. If Roy were playing today, he'd be yanked after the second time through the lineup. No, nobody is that stupid.

Halladay's work ethic was legendary, from spring training right through the dog days of September. Coaches would get to the ballpark early, but he always beat them there.

When A.J. Burnett came over from the Marlins, at spring training in 2006, he started going in early to work out with Roy. That lasted a few days until Burnett said, "Screw this!" A.J. could not keep up with Roy. Doc lived near the spring training facility too, which helped. He was impeccable in so many ways, but you might not get two words from him all day long. Just a real gentleman, a manager's dream — and not only because he was good. He never complained. If you took him out of the game, and he didn't think you should, he didn't bitch and moan — he might look at you funny when you came to get him, but he'd never show you up. It's tragic what happened to him.

I don't remember where I was when I heard about his personal plane going down on November 7, 2017, in the Gulf of Mexico, near New Port

Richey, Florida, but I was shocked like everybody else. I first thought he must have been doing aerobatic stuff; he'd always had a passion for flying, and his dad was a pilot. At spring training, we flew out of the smaller airport in St. Petersburg, not Tampa, and one time, we were all getting off our buses to get on a plane to fly somewhere to start the season and Doc was taxiing in after a day of flying.

The beauty of Doc is he never took anything for granted. He was a humble guy. Everybody appreciated him more because it didn't come easy to him. He had tremendous skill and natural talent, but he got to the top and got knocked down and went all the way back to A ball. He made it back and turned into a great one. That showed his character there.

But Doc was a tough guy to get to know: he kept to himself, very quiet, intense, introverted. There were a couple of times he walked by my office and I invited him in. I'd ask him about how things were going — life, not just baseball. He loved to talk about his family, and that would always bring out a smile in him. Then he'd thank *me* for asking about his family.

The Jays stuck with Doc, but they gave up on Chris Carpenter after the 2002 season. The word on the street was Carp was soft and got hurt a lot, but that wasn't the case at all. The Cardinals took a leap of faith with him, since he needed surgery, but their patience paid off. After Doc and Carp left the Jays, you had two of the best pitchers teeing it up, one for Philadelphia, one for St. Louis. It just shows that sometimes it takes guys a little bit longer to figure things out. Some teams can't wait that long. But that's why you never want to write somebody off too soon.

Carp and Doc were very tight, and they both had guitars, and they'd take them on the road and learned how to play the guitar together.

In May, I got my first shot at managing in the big leagues. Carlos told me about a week before, "I'm going home for my daughter's graduation — you're going to manage these games." I don't know if it was his call or J.P.'s, or both of theirs, but on that particular staff, I had the most minor league managing experience, I guess. Butter had done it, but he hadn't done as much as I had. Plus, he was too good at third.

My thinking was to go out there and have some fun with it. It wasn't like I was taking over and the players have to learn about me. We won those two games. "Good pitching always makes for good managing," I told the press after the second win, 7–1, over the Angels. On August 26, Tosca got into it with umpire Tim Timmons in Boston, and he was later suspended for a game for spraying Tim with spit while arguing a call. I managed, and we won while Carlos served his suspension on September 5.

In January 2004, I was blindsided by the news that Joe Breeden had been hired as the Jays bench coach and was in charge of the catchers. Breeden was an old pal of Tosca's. About a week before spring training started, I was told I'd be coaching the outfielders — and I didn't even hear that from Carlos first! Instead, it was Gil Patterson, the pitching coach and my roommate, who told me. Gil then told Tosca, "You might want to tell Gibbons what his job is!"

It's important to have a competent guy with you to be your bench coach, I get all that, and that's what Breeden was to Tosca. But the fact that they waited so long to tell me about my reassignment meant I really couldn't prepare. That's what bothered me and made me think, *Maybe I'm not thought of very highly around here.*

I knew the basics about outfield play, but I didn't know all the techniques. My job in spring training was using the ATEC machine to fire fly balls. I tried to study up and ask questions, but these were pros who had played outfield for years. If they can't catch a fly ball by now, we're in trouble. What was I supposed to do? I was definitely out of my element.

Since I hadn't been in Toronto that long, I didn't realize the significance of June 3, 2004, when Tom Cheek didn't call the Jays game, as he had to attend his father's funeral. He'd been the Jays radio play-by-play announcer since day one, on April 7, 1977, and his streak stopped at 4,306 consecutive regular season games and 41 postseason games — that's the 4,306 beside his name on the Jays' Level of Excellence. The media guys were a part of the team, too, especially those employed by the club, and I spent a little time with all of them — Buck Martinez and Pat Tabler from TV, Tom and Jerry from radio.

Injuries were a huge problem in 2004, with Delgado, Wells and Doc all on the injured list.

On August 8, we were in New York and lost an 8–2 stinker. The old Yankee Stadium had a real small clubhouse. I crossed paths with J.P. He said, "Hang around, don't leave without me talking to you."

Gibby's Greats: Pete Walker

I can remember J.P. asking me about Pete Walker, whether the Jays should acquire him via waivers. I'd coached him in Norfolk. Two words: "Get him." If I'd said, "He's an asshole, we don't want him," the Blue Jays wouldn't have bothered. So it never hurts to be a good guy.

And Pete was just a first-class dude, did everything right, the Ultimate Pro. He'd been drafted by the Mets out of UConn in 1990 and eventually debuted with them in 1995. He bounced around after that, until ending up back with the Mets when I was managing in Tidewater. Pete had two go-rounds with the Jays as a pitcher, bookending a year playing in Japan. He did a great job when he came over to Toronto, too, kind of that valuable swing guy in the bullpen.

You knew that if he got into coaching, he'd be a very good one. That's how it all played out for him, starting in 2012 as the Jays pitching coach. He's one of those guys, he never did anything wrong, you never got pissed off at him because he always gave his best effort. He was pretty damn good, and now one of the best in the game — if not *the* best.

9.

TORONTO, ROUND 1

There were rumors that Tosca might get fired. It's part of managing. I'll say one thing: in Toronto they can run out of patience fast. That's a good thing, I guess, since it shows the fanbase wants results. That's the way it is in New York and Boston, and that's why those are such great sports cities. But it doesn't make it easy for the manager or coach. Heck, there are some guys out managing who never feel the heat and never win anything. Guess the media loves them or something. Could be worse though — try coaching the Leafs! Now, that's pressure and scrutiny. Someone said J.P. and Carlos were doing a press conference and Carlos was done. It's very rare for a GM and manager to do a press conference together after a firing — I'd have said, "No way, I've got nothing to say" — but they got through it.

I'm smart enough to put two and two together, but it was still a surprise when J.P. found me after and said, "You're taking over, so when we get back to the hotel, come up to my room."

Now my head was racing. You've got to be kidding me!

Back then, the Jays always stayed at the Plaza at Central Park.

The beauty of being the general manager and manager of the team is they give you a suite in whatever town you are in. The Plaza is extra special, and I went up to J.P.'s room and could not believe it — it was like a palace in Rome, perfect for an Italian dude.

He asked me to take a seat. I sat down and he explained his thinking. The main takeaway was: "Have fun with it. At the end of the year, we'll look at you and see what's going on." There was a small bump in pay, as I was making less than $100,000 as a coach, and the raise was pro-rated because it was just for two months.

The next day was my first game, and Josh Towers was on the hill, and we beat the Yankees in my debut. There aren't many baseball cards of me, but one of them is me shaking hands with catcher Gregg Zaun after the game, a wad of chew bulging in my cheek. That's when reality set in. When you win your first game in Yankee Stadium, with all its ghosts and history, you're sure things are going to be easy, right? Wrong. We limped to the finish line, with the Jays at 20-30 under me, and 67-94 overall, last in the AL East.

I don't even remember when J.P. told me, "All right, we're going to bring you back next year." It was before the season was over. J.P. was always cool about it: "Do your thing," he'd say.

That was a learning experience, dealing with the media, dealing with the players in a different role. As the manager, even in the minor leagues, you're watching everything that's going on, your head's got to be on a swivel, facing every direction through the whole game. Now I'm back doing that in the big leagues, and things happen much faster up here. You have to be on your toes.

Take pitching changes. If you leave the pitcher in there one hitter too long: Boom, home run. The game swings the other way, or it may even be over. You'd better plan ahead, be prepared, ready and decisive. I've been burned along the way, but every manager can remember in-game decisions that backfired and bad moves where you came out smelling like a rose.

There are so many demands on your time, distractions, that I never worried about as a coach. Eventually, I settled in and enjoyed it.

But dealing with the media every day? Shit. I saw other guys do that, and thought, *What a pain in the ass*. But you get used to it. Some guys love it, they're politicians and love to talk. I actually made so many friends in the media, and I miss them all — some really good, genuine people. You just need to understand that they also have a job to do. And if we stink, we stink, they'll tell it like it is.

The Jays radio co-host, Jerry Howarth, always tried to help me. I used to have to do his radio show, and we'd catch lunch occasionally. I asked him one time for some pointers. He offered me some really constructive thoughts. He pointed out my constant use of the phrase "you know." He noted, "If they knew, they wouldn't be asking you that question, so stop saying, 'You know.'" There were no crash courses from the front office; J.P. had enough battles with the media himself. Bostonians speak their mind whether you like it or not.

This is as good a place as any to talk about the Toronto media, and there's a lot of it . . . I wasn't prepared for the amount I had to do. It was every stinkin' day. It used to drive me nuts. There were commitments to the team radio and TV every day. Usually, there was an on-air interview hours before the game, which the station could use to promote the game that night, or more than one, so you'd have to give the same answer a couple of times. The beat writers were always around, and the Jays had more of them than just about any other place other than New York and Boston, if only because it was a four-newspaper town at the time. Postgame, there would usually be either a full-blown press conference if it was a game in Toronto, or some sort of scrum if we were on the road.

In my career, I attended one media training seminar, and that was in spring training when I was still a Mets player. The team had hired a woman from New York to instruct us young players on how to talk, how to listen. On the final day, they brought Bob Costas in and a couple of others, and they fired off questions at you for practice. It was a cool and valuable experience. But it did not prepare me for Toronto.

I understand the good and the bad of the media. They've got to report what's happening. That doesn't bother me at all. I look past it. Just because we disagree on something or you've got to write the truth and that truth affects me, it doesn't mean we can't be friends. That's just the way it is. Some guys have problems with it. If those things bother you, you're not fit for the job.

If you ask any of the regulars, like Richard Griffin, Jeff Blair, Ken Fidlin or Bob Elliott, the only Canadian writer honored in Cooperstown, hopefully, they'll say I got better at communication. Throughout my managing career, major and minor league players teased me that I was like the mumbling Farmer Fran character from the Adam Sandler movie *The Waterboy*. So true. Now that may not be ideal when you're dealing with a large, competitive media, but if the players can't figure out what you're saying, it keeps them on their toes guessing. I made them work for their quotes, or their misquotes! Plus Bobby Cox once told me to talk a lot and say nothing. That's perfect. I've actually done that naturally my whole life.

What I enjoyed most towards the end there, was that members of the media would come into my office and we'd shoot the shit — and I knew them all well enough that I could push the buttons of real left-wingers like Larry Millson or Mike Rutsey, or I'd ask Rosie DiManno about being shot at in Afghanistan or some other hot spot. But I could always lean on Shi Davidi for some balance. I actually looked forward to that every day. Toronto has some really good people in the media, some a little more colorful than others, but quality. The city of Toronto is lucky. (I became a fan of tennis when my son played in high school, but really became a fan from taking in Arash Madani's expert coverage and tips on the game.)

When I first started out, we used to all talk in the dugout. And then my second go around there, I told Jay Stenhouse, our PR guy, "Let's just do it in my office." I'd get to sit in a comfortable chair, and they'd get chairs, couches.

I could go on and on with media stories, because if you think about it, they control a lot. That's why baseball is so lucrative. The game couldn't exist without the coverage.

The team would head out to stretch around 4 p.m. The media would usually come into my office about 3:30. We might talk five minutes,

10 minutes about baseball, what's going on. I'd often start off with, "Nothing's changed since we talked after last night's game." That was usually the truth, but sometimes things came up. So, we'd talk about baseball for a little, and then about politics, life, whatever. Of course, I was outnumbered politically, but man did I have fun getting them going. (Still do.) I'd often be late for BP and would mosey on out after throwing our BS around, and then I'd have to do my hits for the broadcast people.

Most of them became great friends. Shi Davidi and John Lott were writing a book on what was supposed to be a 2013 championship season. We were crowned before we ever played a game. We'd made the big trade with the Marlins and with the Mets for Cy Young winner R.A. Dickey, but it's never that easy, so hold your horses. Plus we weren't that good, but the manager can't say that before the season even starts. They still tease me about screwing up the team enough that we didn't have a great season, costing them sales on the original book. Sorry boys, but they regrouped with *Great Expectations: The Lost Toronto Blue Jays Season*. They spent a ton of time around the team that year. Both Griffin and Stephen Brunt came down to San Antonio for articles, and I showed them around and took them out to meet my mom, the true celebrity in our family.

I wasn't exactly sure how life would be different in the offseason before the 2005 season began. J.P. and his front-office guys were always talking about moves, but now he consulted with me more frequently. It was more than just a courtesy to ask my opinion; I know J.P. listened to it.

Every year MLB hosts its winter meeting to make trades and sign free agents, but it's really to promote the game. Managers would meet to discuss possible rule changes and other issues.

The highlight of most meetings is the possibility a big-name free agent may sign with your team. The agents parade their guys around like show ponies. Now, not every free agent is a bank-breaker. There are many that are just good fits on each team and won't put you into bankruptcy. In these cases, the agent will bring them to each team's suite just to feel you out, or the agents might come alone. It's a great time to ask questions.

"So-and-so loves the way you treat him," or something along those lines. They all try to feel out the manager, which is smart, but in the end it's always about the money. Heck, a team will change the manager if he's not getting along with the prized free agent. I guess that's fair. But usually it's general questions. They might ask, "How are you going to use my guy?" That's pretty obvious, but I'd rather not venture into that and affect the deal. "Ask the GM — he's paying you the money! And he can lie to you. I can't lie to you. I don't want to answer that one."

In Anaheim we'd sit around the Marriott, eating snacks and talking about players, waiting for calls on trades or decisions from free agents. That year, J.P. landed third baseman Corey Koskie, a good Canadian kid from Manitoba, at those winter meetings.

Then we'd go out and eat a good meal somewhere.

Another day would be a meeting with all the other managers. That's when the Commissioner's Office and umpires would tell us about any rule changes, or any possible changes. They weren't asking our opinion, but telling us, so there wasn't a lot of discussion. Finally, they'd open it up for questions.

The last day, we'd have a little luncheon, the managers would sit at a table with all the media from their respective city. At the end, you'd take a picture as a group and boom, you go home, all of us under the gun, knowing we had to make our teams winners.

Spring training was a little different, being the boss. Instead of being a valuable part of the staff, I was the leader, and people reported to me. And the coaching staff had changed too. Pitching coach Gil Patterson and first-base coach Joe Breeden were gone, and so my coaching starting lineup was Ernie Whitt, another former catcher, as my bench coach; Mickey Brantley as both the hitting and first-base coach; Brad Arnsberg, looking after pitching; Bruce Walton, running the bullpen; and Brian Butterfield on third base.

It's a massive job organizing everything, and that usually falls to the bench coach, at least on the major league–team level. The pitching coach has a ton of work, too, because pitchers and catchers report early, and they have so many players to look at, from the minors on up, to get them ready for the season. There are trainers and the strength and fitness people arranging for their time with players, too, and conditioning is so important with the grind of a long season ahead. Fortunately, the days of guys getting in shape *at* spring training were gone. The money is so big that they keep in shape year-round.

When the position players arrived, it got even busier. It was divide and conquer, with my staff working on what they knew best — so I spent a little extra time with our catchers, watching them work on block balls, pop-ups, throwing to the bases, all the basic stuff. We went from individual fundamentals to team fundamentals, so the whole team would get together and maybe go over bunt plays, or cutoffs, relays. At batting practice, everyone wants to get their cuts in. The Grapefruit League games, when we got to them, were a sign that we'd made progress. Dickie Scott and Charlie Wilson were in charge of our minor league teams, and they would send some extra players over for the games. The minor leaguers always played the last couple of innings when your big leaguers were finished after getting their two or three at-bats or having got their work on the mound. Having toiled in the minors so much myself, it was very important to me to get these guys in the game and let them hang around major leaguers. It goes a long way to building their confidence, plus it's just the right thing to do.

Finally, after six or seven weeks, we packed up and headed north to the SkyDome, er, Rogers Centre. That took some getting used to. With Rogers Communications finalizing the deal for the stadium, owner Ted Rogers promised to increase payroll over the next three seasons. It was J.P.'s job to spend the money, and my job to get the most out of the players. Fans noticed the bigger, better jumbotron videoboard in the outfield, and players appreciated the FieldTurf, which replaced AstroTurf. I mean, it still wasn't real grass, but it looked better and was easier on the players.

Baseball has so much dead time. It's funny, my wife, Julie, would say, "Why are you going to the ballpark so early?" I told her that's just the way it was. "What do you guys do, just sit around, eat and bullshit?" I had to think about it. "Yeah, there's a lot of that." Nowadays, with all the video stuff and analytics, the time fills up a little more, at least for the coaches.

The manager and the coaches have got to be there — especially the manager — before the players start getting there, otherwise it looks bad. What if the GM wants to come down and talk about something? The front office has been there all morning. As manager, I used to get there later than the other coaches. I never obsessed about getting there too early. Plus, my wife made me feel guilty. To me, it made no sense because I can lay around in my hotel room and watch TV or whatever . . . I learned that I went nuts if I had too much time before the game. Coaches will often fill that time working out in the state-of-the-art weight rooms that every stadium has now. I'd do that too. We're smarter and healthier now in baseball. You get a top-notch physical every year. They check you out pretty good. They don't want the stress getting to anybody. They want us *all* healthy, not just the million-dollar players. But we're definitely easier to replace.

Which brings me to food. In my rookie year in Kingsport, before the game, you might have had to bring something, a snack, if you wanted to eat before the game — PB&J was a favorite. At my first spring training with the Mets, we'd come in for a pre-game lunch, and it was like the army, where we'd line up for salad and then for soup. They'd fill our Styrofoam cup with salad, then we'd go back for soup and crackers, if there were any left. Tom Miller was the crusty old clubhouse guy with the Mets, so that was his job, and he had a rotation, like every Tuesday might be bean soup, and minestrone soup was another — we'd always rag him, "Hey, Tommy, menstrual soup again?"

Nowadays, it's unbelievable what you can eat. It's obviously helped the game, but it's hurt it too. Some players have become prima donnas. Whereas players used to have to rough it, and didn't know any better and appreciated it, now, if anyone tried to pull that, players would go on strike. You can remind them about that poor bastard busting his ass in the real world, who gets a 10-minute lunch because he's got to get a job done, but these kids have never lived in the real world. I guess I never have either, so what am I complaining about?

Another comparison is how players were released from the team. When I played, the spring training clubhouse had these little lockers where we put our valuables and kept the key, just like a safe-deposit box at a bank. At the end of spring training, when it was time to release players, if there was no key in your locker when you got to the ballpark, you had to go see the person in charge — and that's how you knew they were releasing you. They'd try and get you before you put on your uniform and went outside. But then there were times when you'd already be out on one of the four or five big fields. The full season clubs all had a field — two A ball teams, an AA team, and AAA; the rookies stayed on the half-field. Guys would be dressed and going through the team stretch, and here comes somebody from the front office, and they walk onto your field and everybody's looking at them. They'd go up to somebody and tell them to go see the farm director or whoever. It was their mistake in the first place that they didn't get you beforehand so now you have to make the walk of shame in front of all your boys. I don't think that happens much anymore. I guess front offices are more humane.

The game has changed so much and mostly for the better. Another big difference between now and then are the facilities. We had no batting cages; get your swings in on the field and hope it doesn't rain . . . but it always rains in Florida. When it did rain, what about position players? It was, "See ya, go home." Pitchers and catchers hung around for a long day. There were only two pitching mounds that were covered, so the pitchers and catchers would be there all damn day, until everyone threw — and there were a lot of guys. I often wonder how could there be so many good players back then, with all the bad facilities and lack of extra work. I guess it comes down to the same as today — when you're good, you're good.

We started off the 2005 season great, even leading the AL East at one point. But shit that you can't control always happens. Koskie broke his finger. That can be both good and bad depending on whose perspective you're viewing it from. Up comes Aaron Hill, and the rest is history. If Gary Carter hadn't broken his thumb in 1986, I may have never enjoyed the playoffs in '86.

Doc was our ace. At 12-4, he was off to another Cy Young–type start.

Miguel Batista was our closer — he's kind of out there, but he had a great arm and did a good job for us. But I can remember there was a stretch he didn't pitch, with no save situations. He came by my office one day. He spoke English but didn't talk a lot. Straight to the point, he asked why he wasn't pitching. Halladay threw a gem that day, and that's what spurred him on. I said, "What do you mean? There have been no save situations. Halladay just threw a complete game." He said, "So when Halladay pitches, it's all about Halladay?" I said, "Yeah, pretty much."

Miguel left the office pretty pissed off. He thought he was going to be traded, so he stacked all his clothes in his locker, waiting for the deal. Or maybe that was a protest thing.

On July 3, we were playing a game in Fenway, Doc goes eight, he could have easily gone nine, but we had a 5–1 lead. Batista hadn't pitched in a while, and I told Doc that Miggy needed a little work. I put Miggy in there, and he gets the first guy to pop out but then all hell breaks loose. They scored a run and loaded the bases. Line drive rocket to centerfield, and we got it. I couldn't take it, so Scott Schoeneweis got the last Red Sox. It almost proved my point. As I'm walking the field, shaking hands, I'm wondering, *How do I explain this one?*

I found Halladay on the way back, and I said, "Listen, that will never happen again. I don't care who needs an inning of work, they can get it tomorrow night." He smiled and said, "Don't worry about it."

Don't mess with fate. It's Halladay. It's almost a guaranteed win. Take it.

On July 8, in Texas against the Rangers, Kevin Mench smoked one right off Doc's shin bone in the 3rd inning. Broken leg. Uh-oh. Obviously terrible news for the team and him. But — this is so Halladay — he went out and bought a portable hyperbaric chamber, and he'd take it on the road with him. I'd get to the ballpark and walk into the training room, and Roy would already be there in his machine, you could only just see his face. He was so focused. I'm pretty sure he thought he'd be back and able to play, defy the odds. It didn't happen. Same went for any Wild Card hopes.

Those Yankees and Red Sox teams back then, they were fighting each other to the death. The Yankees had Jeter, Martinez and Rivera, and the Sox had Ortiz, Ramirez and Schilling — like two All-Star teams, as both teams were loaded. Usually they both pulled away in May and left everybody else behind. When your top dog goes down, it's like, "Okay, thank you very much." We finished 80-82.

Shaun Marcum was a September call-up. He could really pitch. He was a shortstop in college. Great changeup, great competitor. I loved seeing the young guys get their opportunities.

Throughout the season, J.P. would be consulting me, and soon enough, he was bringing along his new assistant GM, Alex Anthopoulos. Originally from Montreal, Alex had started with an unpaid gig with the Expos, sorting fan mail, and worked his way up. J.P. hired him in Toronto in 2003, as the Jays scouting coordinator. Alex could have been successful even back in the 1970s and '80s, as he is extremely talented and would do whatever it took.

Over the course of the season, it could be either J.P. or Alex, or both, sitting with me, as we talked about different players and the needs of the team — and that ramped up as we got towards the last couple of months. Who's available, who might not be available. The informal chit-chat suited all of us.

I always gave them my two cents. It wasn't my job to put the team together, but I wanted them to know what I thought we needed. I understood, *That's the GM's job, I don't want to meddle with that.* Once they had my opinion, and usually it was pretty obvious, it came down to whether they could get that player or not.

Gibby's Greats: Justin Speier

Managing a bullpen is one of the toughest jobs for both the manager and the pitching coach, but I think it's a strength of mine. You want everyone to succeed, but you also know who you want in what situation, and you need to be clear and fair with the decision. They all needed to know their job, their role.

I'd secretly ask players on my team about the bonuses in their contracts, especially the backup type players or relievers (though bonuses weren't a part of most contracts like they were in the '80s). If I liked the guy — and I liked most of them — I'd work with him to make sure he got his games-played or innings-pitched bonus. "If it's possible, I'll try to help you get it." I work for the organization, but I'm with these players every damn day, and if I can make their life a little easier, I'm going to do it. (Bonuses didn't matter as much my second go-round as contracts were skyrocketing.)

In 2005, we had a pretty special bullpen, with Miguel Batista, Scott Schoeneweis, Pete Walker, Vinnie Chulk, Jason Frasor and Justin Speier. Those primary guys all had ERAs of 4.10 or under, which was rare.

At the end of the season, as a thank-you for helping them get their bonus money, Shoney bought me a beautiful golf driver and Spy got me a gift certificate to a high-end Western store in San Antonio for some boots and a jacket. They were two of my all-time favorites, great competitors.

Speier was a second-generation player, as his dad, Chris, had been a great shortstop for those real competitive Montreal Expos teams of the late 1970s, early '80s. That meant that Justin had spent a lot of time in Montreal, so he was virtually Canadian.

He could also be a goof.

Toronto's grounds crew has always been part of the show, racing out during the 5th inning, claiming to be the "World's Fastest Grounds Crew."

One game, Speier put on an outfit, ran on the field with the rest of the grounds crew and headed to third base, which was nearest our dugout. Corey Koskie was playing third, and Speier tells him, nice and loud, "Hey, nice at-bat striking out, you jackass."

He caught my eye, and I just started laughing.

When the crew was done, I called down to the bullpen and told Speier, "That was awesome. Thanks for that. But now get out of that outfit and go pitch." He was a true character.

10.

ALWAYS IN THE FIGHT

A sk any of the players that I ever managed, and I'm certain they will say that I ran a laid-back clubhouse. They call it being a "player's manager" and, in my view, it fits. I'm easy to talk to, I get along with you, I'll fight for you, I'll have your back. You can come talk to me anytime you want. I'll have fun with you because I enjoy baseball and I enjoy the guys who play it that become jackasses and make it. A player's manager is easy to play for. The players feel like that's a manager who will protect them, not just some mouthpiece for the front office who's scared of losing their job if they speak up or express a disagreement. The other managers that become assholes or pricks and make it all about them usually don't last long. Nobody likes a micromanager, always looking over your shoulder and nitpicking, that gets old real quick. Coaches don't like it either. But remember, if I fight for you, you fight for me; it's a two-way street.

Players are different nowadays — heck, the world's different. You used to be able to rule with an iron fist. Management could get rid of a player, burying him in the minors or trading him; now, the players have all the power, they're making all the money.

That doesn't mean you let the inmates run the asylum. There's got to be that fine balance. If the wrong players — or a real powerful player — turn on you, you're in trouble, unless the team's doing well. That's just a fact. That doesn't mean you cater to them or kiss their ass or anything like that. But you can't stomp them, either, like you could in the old days. I think it was Casey Stengel who once said something like, "The secret of successful managing is to keep the five guys who hate you away from the four guys who haven't made up their minds."

You feel out the personalities in the clubhouse, you get to know each other, personally and professionally. You hopefully get to know their family a little bit and what makes them tick. Then in the heat of the moment, you see who does what.

If I had an issue, I feel I was direct, stern, and it usually passed quickly, then we'd be laughing together the next day.

But not always.

I have no idea how many times I've been asked about the Shea Hillenbrand or Ted Lilly incidents through the years, but it's a lot. So here we go again.

It was July 19, 2006, and we had just lost to the Rangers, making our record 52-42.

I liked and got along with Shea. He could be a little temperamental, like most of us, and I don't think he was really happy when he got traded to Toronto from Arizona in January 2005. Since the trade, Shea had become primarily a DH — I think he thought he'd get labeled as a DH — and he wanted to play the field; he had a few years left and wanted to maximize his earnings. But Shea played great for us and made the All-Star team in 2005.

Shea and his wife were adopting a child, and he arranged through the front office to go home. No problem. Something happened, and he ended up needing an extra day at home. Now he's missed four games, no big deal.

The guy that's pitching that next night, the night Shea's going to be back, had always given Shea troubles. So I'm thinking, *He's been out, let him take his ground balls, take some batting practice, maybe pinch hit that night and play the next day.* Shea gets there in the afternoon and sees his name is not in the lineup. You can sense when something's wrong, you can sense when somebody's cutting you up behind your back, or somebody doesn't like you, or somebody's upset about something. It's that sixth sense. Players don't think everything gets back to the manager's office, but it does. Somebody told me Hillenbrand was pissing and moaning about not playing. Somebody wrote on the chalkboard, "the ship is sinking" and "play for yourself." That got back to me, too, and then I saw it myself. I didn't know who wrote it; I assumed it was Shea, but some said Gregg Zaun. Alright, enough of the bullshit. Now we're getting carried away, somebody's *asking* to get their ass ripped because I've been more than fair. I knew I had to put a stop to it. The ship may be sinking, but it ain't going down this way. And I ain't walking the plank for a malcontent.

I got everybody in the clubhouse. I probably went a little overboard, I undressed Shea pretty good. But I can guarantee you, I don't ever do anything knee-jerk — there're things that built up to my reaction. We'd already had that deal earlier in the year where he tore his jersey off on Canada Day and threw it away. I think we played him as much as we could at first base. We accommodated him, and he was a good player for us. It wasn't like we were sticking it to him. But then the bitching and moaning and sniping . . .

In front of the team, I challenged him, undressed him worse than I should have. It shocked everybody, I think. I basically told him, "Listen, if you don't like it, take it to the front office. It's either me or you because I ain't going to put up with this shit. We bent over backwards for you."

He didn't say a word. I was hoping he would.

The meeting broke up and everybody's like, What just happened?

Shea stormed out of there, and either he or his agent demanded a trade. J.P. sent Shea and reliever Vinnie Chulk to San Francisco in exchange for Jeremy Accardo, who turned out to be a pretty good pitcher for us and closed a little bit the next year. J.P. scolded me, "You can't say it's either you or me, because with some guys it might be you." But he knew I'd meant it.

I never talked to Shea again after that. Somebody told me years later he was trying to get a hold of me. I liked Shea, he had a good major-league career, I hope he's doing well.

The way I saw it, we did everything we could for Shea, to accommodate him and his family. The incident followed me around. We both have had to live with it the rest of our careers. But I think I got some guys' attention, I'll tell you that. I was blowing some frustration off, too, there's no doubt about it.

Later, I found out Zauny wrote the comments on the board. Didn't surprise me. After that, I'd had enough of him too.

But really, I was an easygoing guy, hard to provoke. I drank a lot of water, coffee or Diet Coke sitting in the dugout, so I had to pee a lot. In Toronto, you go up a hallway, and you have to hustle — it's not far, but it's a race. Zaun nicknamed me "Flomax" in reference to my constant need to pee. Could you imagine an Earl Weaver or Gene Mauch putting up with that? Funny thing is, I take Flomax now — Zauny should have been a doctor.

The "incident" with Ted Lilly on August 21 pretty much boiled down to a couple of friends getting into it. When I was a Jays coach, I'd go jogging with Ted, depending on his pitcher's running program. We'd run stairs, too, in the different stadiums. We once ran up the upper deck stairs in Oakland, the part that's now covered. What a view from the top. Teddy could run forever and is wiry strong. The infamous game was against Oakland and at home.

First off, we built a big 8–0 lead against Dan Haren, one of the top pitchers in the game, not easy to do, so we're feeling real good. Next thing you know, in the 3rd inning, Ted has Eric Chavez 0-2 then throws him a pitch sidearm. I'm thinking, *What the heck was that? I've never seen him do that before.* So I asked Brad Arnsberg, our really good pitching coach, "What was that?" He didn't know either. I'm thinking, *Big lead, he's out there screwing around.* (I had learned by now just how tough it is to win a major league game.) Things can start rolling downhill fast.

I sent Arny out and got the bullpen cranking — 8–0 lead, you're kidding me. Lilly gives up five runs. So now's the time to go get him while we're still leading — he had every opportunity to shut them down. As I approached the mound, he said to me, "What are you doing out here?"

I'm thinking, *There lies the problem.* Now he won't give me the ball. This ain't good. We exchanged some words, and he finally gave me the ball, but he jabbed it in my stomach. The infielders were out there now, too, and probably wondering what's next. Ted left, and as I was walking back to the dugout, I saw him down the stairs at the opposite end of the dugout from where I sit. I just headed in his direction without even thinking. When I got down the stairs, I don't remember if I said something to him first or he said something, but we grabbed each other and the cage match was on. The other players came down and broke it up. I had him in a headlock, but man, Teddy's strong. Plus I was too old for this, and a little overweight, so I was trying to catch my breath. Ted headed to the clubhouse, and I headed back to the dugout since there was still a game going on. I grabbed a towel and someone said my nose was bleeding, but it was just one of those colorful Gatorade towels. Get the story straight.

The game's over — we lost 12–10 — and I went inside and J.P. came down and we talked. We tried to figure out how to explain it. The word was that Gibbons was going to snap once a month. I handled it the wrong way, obviously. Someone brought Teddy over, and we talked it out. I told him I overreacted. He said his piece like that too. It was over. We didn't have a problem after that.

It reminds me of a funny story about a Yankees pitching change back when Billy Martin was managing. They say it's true. Some Yankee pitcher was pitching in a road ballpark where they would shoot off a cannon every time the home team hit a home run. The Yankee pitcher had given up a few home runs, so Billy sent his pitching coach, Art Fowler, out to talk. Art gets out there and the pitcher said, "What are you doing out here?" He replied, "I don't know what you're doing out here, but you're really pissing Billy off. Plus, I'm giving them time to reload the cannon."

Now it's "Gibbons is a loose cannon" and has anger issues.

Those two incidents overshadowed what was a pretty good 2006. To start off the season, J.P. had brought in Lyle Overbay, Troy Glaus and Bengie Molina. A key addition was A.J. Burnett in the rotation, so we were feeling good because now we had someone to complement

Halladay. We had a good thing going and the evidence was our five All-Stars: Glaus, Wells, Halladay, B.J. Ryan and Alex Ríos (though Alex missed the game with a staph infection in his lower leg).

Ozzie Guillén, manager of the defending champion White Sox, picked me as one of the AL All-Star coaches. It was unexpected. My family all came out to PNC Park in Pittsburgh, and my boys went down on the field with me for the home run hitting contest. The visiting clubhouse isn't really big in Pittsburgh, so now you're bumping into these superstars. You've seen them, competed against them on the other side, but now you're in a room with all of them. It's a pretty impressive sight. But you can't show your awe. You're supposed to be a coach. I thanked Ozzie for the invite. One of the real characters in the game.

Thanks in part to the Red Sox slumping and our red-hot 18-10 September, we finished second in the AL East, 87-75, the best the Jays had done since 1993. There was bonus money for finishing second in your division back then. Not our goal, but we'll take it. If there had been two Wild Cards, we might have made it. See, those couple of blow-ups didn't hurt us one bit.

The other notable part of 2006 was that there was a Canadian federal election going on. Every one of the federal party leaders came to a Blue Jays game, and they all came down on the field. This would repeat in the ensuing years during other elections. Politicians love to get in front of a crowd. I can remember telling somebody, "Every time one of these politicians comes out, we lose."

Heading into 2007, we thought we had a competitive team. Wells was signed to the biggest deal in Jays history, seven years, $126 million. I loved Vernon. A real first-class guy, good human and ultra talented. He probably had as much talent as anybody. Effortless. There hasn't been a better centerfielder. In the clubhouse, he was a leader.

"The Big Hurt" Frank Thomas was signed as our DH, and he was every bit the presence you'd think he would be. But "hurt" describes the season, too, as we lost our closer, Ryan, to Tommy John surgery, and had a bunch of other injuries that kept us from ever getting going.

Me at six months old, in the loving arms of my mother.

The three Gibbons kids, Billy, me and Kris, in 1963.

Love that island life: Kris, Billy and me in Puerto Rico, 1964.

Starting my life in baseball, in Goose Bay, Newfoundland and Labrador.

I was a catcher from early on.

Mom and Dad in San Antonio.

Darryl Strawberry was, briefly, my roommate in the Instructional League in 1980.

My mom is between Billy Beane and I while we were in Jackson in 1983.

The catcher for the Tidewater Tides.

You can tell the era — early 1980s — from the type of baseball hat popularized by the Pittsburgh Pirates.

A day off at Carowinds amusement park in North Carolina in 1981; that's me and J.P. Ricciardi in the back, with Scott Merlack in the white hat and Kevin Spicer in the black hat.

Sailing along with Ed Hearn in Long Island Sound.

A day at the beach with Billy Beane.

A successful day fishing on the Indian River near Port St. Lucie around 1996.

At Texas League spring training in April 1983, in Jackson, Mississippi.

Here's a postcard the Mets made up with me on it from 1984.

I'm at bat for the Mets at Shea Stadium in April 1984, with Gary Carter catching.

The curly hair with the Jackson Mets in 1983 was just a phase.

Ed Hearn, Vern Hoscheit and me after the 1986 World Series.

Gary Carter was the greatest catcher of our era, and I was stuck behind him. It was worth it to get to know such a great man.

The 1986 World Series champion New York Mets at the White House; I'm just over President Ronald Reagan's right shoulder.

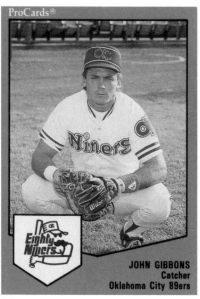

My year in Oklahoma City was fun at least.

With my #1 fan, my Nana, in Fenway Park.

A conference on the mound when I was the Jays manager, round one, with catcher Gregg Zaun and pitcher Josh Towers. COURTESY TORONTO BLUE JAYS

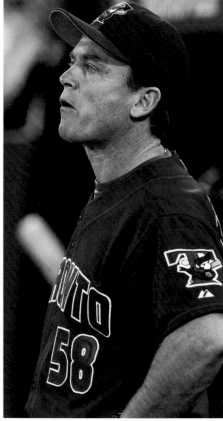

As a coach with the Toronto Blue Jays. COURTESY TORONTO BLUE JAYS

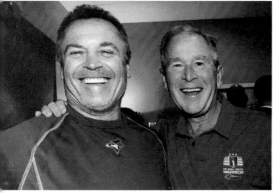

Former President George W. Bush popped in to say hi in Texas.

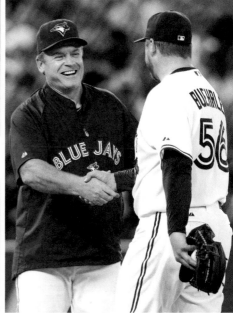

Congratulating Mark Buehrle on another fine performance. COURTESY TORONTO BLUE JAYS

Reuniting with my high school coach Syl Perez.

Mom throws out the first pitch . . . to me! COURTESY TORONTO BLUE JAYS

Jordan and her band Southtown perform at the Rogers Centre. COURTESY TORONTO BLUE JAYS

I am blessed with three great kids, Kyle, Troy and Jordan. By far my greatest accomplishment.

My wife, Christi, and brother, Bill.

Kyle and I with the 2010 Royals.

Opportunities arise from injuries, and that's how Dustin McGowan got his. Everyone envisioned him being another Halladay, or at least hoped he was. He was a big, strong kid that looked like a star. Dustin had diabetes, so he used to wear a pump on his belt to regulate things. I can't imagine how difficult that would be, but it would affect his strength and stamina on any given day. And he battled the injury bug in his career. There are some guys you root extra for — he was one of them. Great kid. He threw some gems. A highlight was Dustin taking a no-hitter into the 9th inning at the Rogers Centre against the Rockies on June 24, before giving up a hit.

Four days later, in Minnesota, Thomas hit his 500th home run. Frank would complain about the strike zone as much as anybody, and a lot of times he was right. But he walked a ton, so obviously they weren't screwing him with too many pitches. He would come back to the dugout and be hollering at the umpires about the calls. I told him, "Frank, you're going to the Hall of Fame. When you're at home plate, get on their ass out there. They'll listen to you — plus they're scared of you." But he'd wait until he got into the dugout. "Frank, do it out there." After his 500th homer, in his next at-bat, he was bitching and moaning to the umpire and got ejected. He finally listened to me ... or maybe he wanted the rest of the night off; he earned it.

Frank was physically gifted, but mentally he could really zone in and lock in. He had a tape of all his home runs that we called his "Dig Me Tape." He used to watch it to get ready, programming his mind with past successes. He knew his swing. He had a great eye. And obviously the pitchers were afraid of him — how could you not be? He knew how to train himself. He knew how to DH. A lot of guys struggle with the preparation and the time in between at-bats. Frank had all that figured out.

A good learning moment for me was when our lineup card was screwed up on September 1.

We were playing Seattle in Toronto. We pretty much had a steady lineup that we used all the time. Players know where they hit, and the GM actually signs players to hit in certain spots. In this game, we flip-flop

Lyle Overbay and Aaron Hill for some reason in the sixth and seventh spots, likely a lefty-righty deal in the lineup. Every day, I'd write the lineup out, put it on the desk of Bruce Walton (who we called "Pappy"), and he'd print it all out and post it for everyone to see. For some reason, Pappy was late that day, and I didn't tell him about the switch, and the new lineup that I put on his desk had fallen onto the floor where he didn't see it. Now the problem was we posted the changed lineup on the clubhouse wall for the players to see. When the official card is given to the umpire before the game, that's the only copy that matters, and we gave them the incorrect one.

In the 2nd inning, Hill gets a double. Mariners manager John McLaren, an ex–Blue Jay, goes to the umpires to let them know we hit out of order.

This is what is amazing. The baseball rulebook can be complicated, and there are so many things that never happen or that you hardly ever see happen. Even for an umpire, things can happen quickly. All four umpires get together, with me and McLaren behind home plate. I know I screwed up, but I don't know how they fix it. The umpires were going back and forth, and I didn't feel as bad, because they didn't know what to do either. Finally, they figured it out, and Hill was ruled out on a putout by the catcher. Batting out of order may have the most confusing rule on how to rectify it. Read it sometime and let me know what to do.

From then on, I'd make sure I'd go over the lineup card enough times that you would think I had OCD before we turned it over to the umpire. I'm actually surprised these kinds of screw-ups don't happen more often. (Well, I'd actually done something similar, on July 27 against Chicago, when I listed John McDonald as the starting shortstop on the signed lineup card but later switched to Royce Clayton because McDonald was sick at the hotel and couldn't play.)

Once again, the Jays' story was determined by the Yankees and Red Sox. They were both loaded, so we finished in third in 2007, with an 83-79 record. We always looked at the schedule — we'd love it when we played one of those two teams right after they played each other, because they played long-ass games, they beat each other up. That was back when everybody walked, and you killed the bullpens. And so if you caught them after they played each other, you almost could feel a little let down. You knew their bullpen was beat up. Then if they were coming off a Sunday night game, you knew they were going to get to Toronto late and they'd be running on fumes.

For 2008, J.P. got third baseman Scotty Rolen and shortstop David Eckstein, two proven winners. I'd seen them from afar, and I'd heard nothing but good things. I'd always been a fan of the hard-nosed way both played the game. Rolen, even if I wasn't with him long, was one of my favorite guys; there was just something about him. Eck had less natural talent than most guys but got more out himself than any other player and was a World Series MVP — the biggest overachiever I've ever seen. Two of the best guys I've ever managed.

At spring training, Rolen was on a backfield taking some extra ground balls. I was watching the pitchers throw off the mounds right by him. I saw him leaving the field, and I said, "What, you going home early?" He pointed a bloody finger at me. He'd taken a ground ball and it tore his nail up. He was out for a while, but then Marco Scutaro filled in admirably. Rolen was one of the greatest third basemen of all time, and I just wish I'd been around him longer to admire it. Plus he made everyone around him better, and winners.

Eck got off to a slow start, but he was getting older too. We signed him as a leadoff hitter. He struggled, and then later in the season we bumped him down. I called him in: "Dave, I hate doing this, but I'm going to move you down to the bottom of the lineup." He said something like, "I wouldn't blame you if you didn't play me." The ultimate dream and team guy. A lot of guys go, "You signed me to blah, blah, blah." Dave was really just a quality, thankful guy, another winner. There's something to that Cardinal way.

J.P. had always warned me that Frank Thomas — who we teased and called "The Big Skirt" when he started getting hurt — was a slow starter each season, and he was. It was complicated by the fact that Matt Stairs had to play left field, but he should have been DH at that point in his career. Frank just really never got going. And so I told J.P., "We need to juggle the bats. He's our DH, but there's some days he shouldn't play." J.P. kept telling me he's a slow starter, stick with it. He's the boss.

One day, Frank didn't have a good game, and J.P. said, "Do what you want. Play whoever you want to as DH." I got somebody to go get Frank. Butterfield was in the office with me. I always had another coach in the room for a meeting like this in case it got heated — and remember I'm an old man. Plus, you never want anything you say to get lost in translation, if you know what I mean. Always have a jury. So Frank comes in and he sits down. He goes, "What's going on?" I said, "Listen, you're still our DH, but there's other guys that we want to get some at-bats against certain pitchers and get them off the field. You aren't necessarily going to DH every day."

He got all pissed off, and he says, "This ain't about that. This is about my money next year." Well, he was on the second year of a two-year deal, $10 million per season, but it guaranteed another $10 million if he got a certain number of plate appearances during those first two years. All he needed was somewhere around 300-something. He would have gotten it easy regardless, so I don't know what he was thinking. Maybe he skipped his math class at Auburn. Hope he got his money.

I said, "Frank, I don't have a contract for next year. I sure as hell ain't worried about yours." He was pissed off and wanted to talk to J.P., and he stormed out of there. On April 20, J.P. gave him his release, and Frank went back out to Oakland.

We struggled to score runs in April, going 11-17, but had righted the ship by the end of May, as we were 31-27.

I could feel the rumblings and all that, but the thought that I might get fired never occurred to me or concerned me. Typically, you see the storm clouds developing, but I'd seen those before and nothing had happened.

I didn't suspect anything or even care. With school out, my family was in Toronto. I took my boys on the plane with me on a road trip to Milwaukee, then my wife and daughter were driving to Pittsburgh to meet us on the second leg of the trip. We got swept in Milwaukee, we didn't play well.

After the family reunion in the Pittsburgh hotel, J.P. called me on the phone, and he said, "I'll see you in the morning. I want to meet with you." I'm thinking, *Huh, that's kind of weird, he's never done that.*

J.P. drove down to Pittsburgh with his lieutenants, Alex Anthopoulos and Tony LaCava. On the morning of June 20, I met with them in their room, three of my favorite people sitting around a big table. I know what's happening. J.P. said, "Hey, we've got to let you go. We've got to change some things up." I told him, "I don't blame you, I get it. My only regret is that I feel bad. I let you down, that we didn't play better." It was a tough moment, but part of the business. I always heard if you haven't ever been fired, then you haven't done very much. They also fired coaches Ernie Whitt and Gary Denbo. Those are the guys I felt bad for since they got caught up in the purge.

Later, someone told me they'd seen Cito Gaston at the hotel, so word was spreading. Cito was there with Gene Tenace and Nick Leyva, two of his old captains.

I get back to the room, I tell my family and everybody's sad. I'd never been fired from a job before.

So I called Mike Shaw, our traveling secretary, and told him, "I'm not going back to Toronto, so see if you can find me a big SUV. We're driving home." He said he'd get one of the clubhouse kids to go over to my Toronto condo and pack it up. We hopped in the SUV, a driving adventure like the Griswolds in *National Lampoon's Vacation*, and we headed to San Antonio.

I do remember getting home and it was an adjustment because it's June and I'm used to the high pace stress of day-to-day baseball.

The stresses of baseball can really eat you up if you let them. When I started out managing up in Toronto, every now and then my heart would flutter and beat weird (I'm sure all the caffeine and tobacco had nothing to do with it). One of the first times it happened, we were in Boston, so I went over to Mass General and got checked out. They told me my heart rhythm was normal, but they wanted me to stay overnight for observation. They put me in this nice private room and hooked up all these electrodes to my chest. Before I went to sleep, I got up to brush my teeth, and my movements must have set off the alert at the nurses' station, as three of them came rushing in, panicking, to see if I was having the big one. Luckily, I was just shining my pearly whites. I told you my mom was a dental hygienist. But it wasn't until I was home after being fired that the doctors finally figured out it was atrial fibrillation. My heart wouldn't stay in an irregular beating pattern for long, so they'd had trouble detecting it. After three or four trips to the hospital over the years, I felt justified. Damn, I knew I wasn't making it up. Guess it proves I at least have a heart.

They ended up putting me on this medicine to reduce my heart rate and blood pressure; I still take it.

We had planned for that All-Star break to go to the Bahamas with the kids; since the Jays were in Tampa after the break, we would just meet them there and start the second half. After talking about it, we did the trip anyway. Arnsberg had a couple of kids that were great friends with ours. So, in Tampa, I drove to the hotel and picked up his kids and brought them back to our place. It was weird because I was supposed to be with the team, but now I didn't want to see any of them.

I caught myself watching the team. I had the MLB Network, so I flipped and watched a lot of games, different teams. It was my way of decompressing.

When I think about it, the way I got there, a lot of people took care of me along the way, which led to that opportunity. There are only 30 major league managing jobs; if somebody didn't stick their neck out for me, I'd never have gotten one. I was not bitter; I had nothing to complain about. And I was grateful. I meant it when I told J.P. that I wished I'd done more for him and the team.

Gibby's Greats: Brian Butterfield

Brian Butterfield has the best baseball mind I've ever been around — but I was only around him officially for four seasons.

We'd never met prior to him getting hired in Toronto as a third-base coach in the purge of Buck Martinez and his guys in June 2002. Butter had been a journeyman minor league second baseman, and then transitioned into coaching and managing in the minors, including the Yankees AAA team. In the majors, he served with Buck Showalter and the Yankees, and then with the expansion Arizona Diamondbacks.

We hit it off right away, and not just because he was on third and I was the first-base coach.

Butter was a lovable guy, and he had fun with the players. He was also big on discipline. Butter believed in doing things the right way — respect this, respect that, just respect the game. He had great attention to detail and was very demanding, even with things as simple as having the players learn the signs he'd be using. Even before it became popular, Butter was big on the analytical side of things — particularly when it comes to the field, shifting a position based on where the batter is likely to hit. He was almost an infielder whisperer.

When I became manager in 2004, I relied on Butter. He would keep an eye on things for me. He never ratted anybody out, but because things would bother him worse than they bothered me, I could read him. I could tell something was eating at Butter. It could be a lack of effort from a guy, or someone complaining. He was my finger on the pulse of the team.

Butter made his way to the Red Sox and was a part of the 2013 World Series win. He's been to a few other places since. It's mind-boggling that he has not gotten a shot as a major league manager. He's a reminder of what's good about the game. Play it right, and take nothing for granted.

11.

BENCHED IN KC

As happens at the end of every baseball season, teams start putting together their staffs for the following year. Often, the smaller moves barely get a mention in the mainstream media, the addition of a new pitching coach, or a trainer being replaced. But, if you're *in* the game of baseball, you are acutely aware of it all, following where your friends are going, trying to figure out who some of the new faces are, what each team needs.

Both old and new factored into my new job, announced on October 10, 2008, as the bench coach for the Kansas City Royals.

First off, the manager, Trey Hillman, was a friend of mine. How much of one? We lived together when I got to KC, along with third-base coach Dave Owen (who'd moved over from bench coach), in a small home that Hillman had. Not exactly party central, but we talked a lot of baseball. Probably too much. I liked to get away from the game, but when you're living and working together, and the team's scuffling and we need some answers, you talk a lot of baseball. The following two seasons, I lived on my own so my family could visit more.

New to me was the Royals GM, Dayton Moore, and I become a fan. He's one of the best men you'll ever meet, just first-class, a good baseball guy. He was honest and upfront about the plan. He said the Royals had some good young players on the way, but it might be a tough season; Dayton saw them being competitive in a couple of years. While that had nothing to do with my accepting the job, it did factor in to my staying later.

Trey lived in Austin, Texas, so Dayton flew down, and I drove over and met them at an airport hotel, and they offered me the bench coach job.

The Royals were owned by David Glass, who had made his fortune as one of the key people beside Sam Walton as Walmart became a massive company. David Glass and his son Dan, who was the president of the team, would often come down to the clubhouse during a homestand to sit and talk baseball with the manager. I knew them in passing, just to say hello, but I found it fascinating they'd do that — Ted Rogers was never going to do that in Toronto. But I'd rather have that than an owner who's too involved. I think in today's game, owners are more involved than ever. They must love analytics. Owners of all successful businesses understand numbers, so now that reading and using numbers is first and foremost, it allows the owners to engage more. I guess if I paid a billion dollars for a business, I'd want to know what's going on too!

Those were a great three years in KC. I liked that Midwest feel. Loved the stadium. Loved the places I lived. And it was that much closer to San Antonio.

The bottom line is that I was back on the pension plan, aiming to get my 10 years in. It was a bonus that they were paying me good money and I was working with a friend.

It was nice getting a break from the pressures of managing in Toronto. I didn't have to deal with the media, and I could head home sooner after a game, win, lose or draw. The only agonizing and sweating I did was from the intense heat you get in a KC summer. The flipside, though, was exactly that — I was used to making the decisions, and now I wasn't getting paid as much and I didn't have the final say. That's the beauty of managing: the decisions you make affect the game. But also in baseball everybody does things differently. You take 10 guys and every one of them will have a different opinion on things.

While I knew some of the players from competing against them when I was with the Jays, there was a learning curve. One rule was to give José Guillén some room because the right fielder could be a handful. All I mean by that is that he was very emotional and competitive, but also a wonderful, lovable guy. I wasn't there long before I heard stories of José's generosity, the things that he'd do for employees that worked for the Royals behind the scenes. But he was high maintenance.

One player stood heads above the rest in 2009 — Zack Greinke. What a beauty. He started the season with 38 scoreless innings and went on to win the Cy Young Award as the AL's best pitcher. And this was on a bad team that finished 65-97. Zack was credited with 16 of those wins.

When I think about that first trip back to Toronto, a few things stand out. For one, going to the visiting dressing room was odd. But other than that, it was a good chance to see some old friends, some familiar faces.

Bob McClure was the pitching coach for the Royals, and he'd been told by a friend from another team that had played the Jays that Toronto had somebody, a cameraman or something, tipping off the pitchers' signs out in the centerfield seats. Really? We kept our eyes open.

Greinke was pitching that first night in Toronto and got his ass kicked. During the game we were trying to watch for any sign stealing. We could see somebody out there in a white shirt — he'd stand up, sit down, and we thought maybe . . . or maybe we were seeing things.

The next day before BP, Hillman and McClure went out to center-field where the cameraman was and started talking. He sent them to talk to his boss, by the third-base dugout. The big red flag was that no other team had touched Greinke all year, basically a mismatch. So now he gets pounded around. It happens in baseball, but this seemed different. Probably a coincidence or just our paranoia, but it was odd. Nothing ever came of it. We couldn't prove anything. When they asked me what I knew, I cracked, "If I'd had someone relaying signs while I was managing in Toronto, I might still be there."

In August 2009, Trey had to head home for something, so I managed the Royals for three games, going 1-2, which is pretty well the way the whole season went.

In 2010, the team wasn't much better, finishing with two more wins. We would be in the game till the very end, but we just didn't have enough pitching. Still, these guys would compete right to the finish, they were never out of it. What stands out was Trey getting fired during the season, and Ned Yost coming in, who I didn't know at all.

Backing up a bit, it's notable that Dayton was a part of the Atlanta Braves organization for a long time, starting as a scout; like me with the Mets, he had many connections. Yost was one of them. Ned was let go as manager of the Milwaukee Brewers, and Dayton hired him in an unspecified role. He was at spring training, hanging around, scouting guys. So you kind of knew, if something didn't go right, maybe Ned's here for a reason. You see it a lot in baseball, teams covering themselves in case they need to make changes. Plus Ned was a good, experienced baseball man who eventually led them to the promised land in 2015. And sure enough things went south, which is how it is supposed to work when you're not quite good enough yet. Trey got fired and they hired Ned. I was, thankfully, kept around. Good, smart baseball people over there.

Ned and Trey were both very good baseball guys, but different personalities. Trey's a real outgoing guy. Ned's more like me, laid back, keeps to himself. There was a learning process getting to know Ned, but zero problems; he was experienced and, also like me, an ex-catcher. He was good with players, he let them do their thing, but was stern when he had to be. It was great working for Trey and then Ned.

In that offseason, I interviewed for two different managing jobs.

First, I went to Pittsburgh. The GM, Neal Huntington, interviewed me, along with the team president, Frank Coonelly. It was a professional chat, and they asked me about my personal ideas and about situations, how I'd handle this or that. Since I'd had dust-ups with a couple of my players, those were always questions: What happened with Lilly? What happened with Hillenbrand? I liked Neal and Frank, and I thought it went very well.

I left Pittsburgh and flew right to Seattle, where there was another opening. Jack Zduriencik was the Mariners GM, and he'd been a scout with the Mets back when I was a player, so I knew him. This was a totally different interview. Jack and I talked about some old times and had some laughs. The team president, Chuck Armstrong, sat in on the interview, too, which wasn't as in-depth as the one in Pittsburgh was. What really stands out was Howard Lincoln coming in; he was the CEO of Nintendo of America and the representative of the team, as its owner, to Major League Baseball.

Howard asked me, "I see these other teams come to town, and their players are out there signing autographs. Do you think you'll get our players to do that?" And I'm thinking, *Huh?* I thought I'd better answer diplomatically, and said, "I think that's great. Players can do that. But you also have to remember these guys have to get ready to play games. Yeah, I think it's a great concept. I would do my best, but I can't guarantee it." Then Jack, Chuck and I went out to dinner that night. The job ended up going to Eric Wedge. Maybe Wedgie guaranteed autographs?

A couple of days later, Pittsburgh called and invited me to the next round of interviews, but I pulled out. Something just didn't feel right there, or, more importantly, something felt right with the Royals. The Pirates ended up giving the job to my old buddy Clint Hurdle.

Dayton was a little surprised that I declined interviewing further for the Pirates job, but I was back in KC for a third year. Plus, if I had somehow gotten that job, there wouldn't have been a second go-round in Toronto, which I'll cherish forever. Things usually work out.

It was an exciting time in KC, and I liked what the Royals were doing. These young guys started sprinkling in from the minors — Salvador Perez, Eric Hosmer, Mike Moustakas, Danny Duffy and Greg Holland. Dayton also pulled off a major trade, sending Zack Greinke to Milwaukee for Lorenzo Cain, Alcides Escobar, Jeremy Jeffress and Jake Odorizzi. Now that was a great deal for both sides.

In 2011, the Royals were marginally better, at 71-91. But there would be no fourth year for me in KC, as over in Atlanta, the legendary Bobby Cox retired after the season. His bench coach had been Chino Cadahia, and Dayton snapped him up to do the job in Kansas City.

I was okay being cut loose, as I had gotten my 10 years in and had a lifetime Major League Baseball pension.

As for the Royals? It played out just like Dayton said it would, and they won the 2015 World Series, beating the Mets four games to one. You might remember who the Mets manager was — Terry Collins, my AAA manager for the Dodgers in 1988. And who the Royals beat in the ALCS — me. The world of baseball can be very small.

Gibby's Greats: Eric Hosmer

Baseball people love to sit around and talk about base ball. Who's the best at each position? Who was the greatest pitcher you ever faced? Which umpire missed the most calls?

A frequent one that you hear from the front office experts was, "If you were starting a team from scratch today, who would you pick?"

Well, when someone asked me that in 2013, my first pick was Eric Hosmer.

I'd seen Eric in spring training with the Royals for a couple of years and could see the potential; and then when he finally joined the big-league team for 2011, wow. He turned into a Gold Glove first baseman, he could hit, had fire and, perhaps best of all, he put the team first. Watching his heads-up, daring play in the 9th inning of the 2015 World Series, where he tied the game against the Mets, defined everything. He's young and can do it all on the baseball field.

That whole core of young Royals — Hosmer, Moustakas, Alex Gordon, Billy Butler, Perez — all came up together through the system and believed in each other. I don't think I've ever been around a better bunch of young players and good human beings. They played hard, nine innings, every night, and never quit. They got their due in 2014 and 2015, even though I felt it should have been the Jays in '15. I'm proud to have been a small part of that group.

When the Jays would play the Royals, I always found time to visit and share some laughs with all my old friends. Great memories.

12.

I LOVE UMPIRES . . .
AND THEY LOVE ME!

How about we talk about my *favorite* subject? Umpires.

For the record, I got along well with about 95 percent of them. I respect the hell out of those guys, I know what a tough job it is. But I learned that a call here or there can make a difference in the outcome, and once you're in the big leagues, it's win or lose, that's all that matters, and your record determines whether you keep your job or not.

You get to the know the umpires and to know which bunch is in town for the series. The analytics aren't there for umpires the same way, but we had basic scouting reports, the different strike zones for each guy.

I have never gone out to argue just to argue. I've always been angry about something.

One thing I learned with teams that I had in Toronto, we had some guys that weren't necessarily very well liked around the league — great players, but they were emotional: Jose Bautista, Josh Donaldson. Being respected is different than being liked. People viewed them as whiners.

Jose knew the strike zone, and I learned to look at what he was complaining about. And it's not like I'm at home on the couch, where they are zooming in and showing how the pitch missed the zone.

So when I did argue, it was legit. Probably a lot of frustration. It may have had nothing to do with that particular call, the team may have been stinking at the time, playing like crap.

But I've never faked an argument, it was never staged — I'm not that good of an actor! (I have been told that I look like an older Jack Nicholson; I don't know if that's good or bad.) People say managers go out there to fire up the team. That's bullshit. Not me.

Back when I was playing, that didn't fire me up.

But I did get fired up if my manager was defending me for all the right reasons.

I've always believed that if you want your guys to fight for you, you'd better fight for them. That is just a fact. And that's fair. I've been on teams and I've seen it where guys bitch and moan about how the other team's manager goes out and fights for them but our guy never does for us. You want to lose your team? That's how, because the players start to think that you only care for yourself.

By paying attention, I could see that someone like Jose would get hosed a lot, and partly he had himself to blame because umpires get tired of the bitching, so they'll stick it to you. Not so much now, because they're under the gun too. Now Major League Baseball can track how an umpire's strike zone is and all that. Instant replay has helped. But in the old days, umpires could really stick it to you.

In Game 5 of the 1997 NLCS, it was Greg Maddux of the Braves against Liván Hernández of the Marlins, and the umpire was calling pitches six inches off the plate strikes (check it out). Hitters had no chance. After that, I think they started cracking down. People still talk about that game. Heck, if you don't want to be out there and do your job right, call in sick or quit.

Where you are playing matters too. I'd always heard it, and then I saw it; when you are the visiting team at Fenway Park or Yankee Stadium, things are a little bit different. I'm telling you: When you're pitching, that damn strike zone shrinks up a little bit. When they're hitting, it's a little bigger.

Here's a perfect example — and I may not even be accurate, as I never went back to the video — but Gustavo Chacín was pitching for us in Yankee Stadium, when Joe Torre was their manager. He's pitching a gem, it's a close game but we're winning. It was a young umpire behind the plate, and I thought he was doing a great job. He was calling balls as balls and strikes as strikes. Torre went out there and argued, and I guarantee you, he intimidated that young umpire — Yankee Stadium, Torre on this kid's ass — and that strike zone changed all of a sudden. You could just see how it affected our guy, the pitches he was calling strikes, now he's calling balls. They love the walks over there at Yankee Stadium, and now, boom, a couple of guys are on. We lose the lead. Then Chacín made a pitch, I think it was to Derek Jeter, and it was a strike, but it wasn't called. So, I go out there and start arguing. I tell him what I saw — that he'd been doing a hell of a job until Torre came out, got on his ass — and I say I think that he got scared. I pointed at Torre. Little things like that are part of the reason it's hard to play in Boston or New York. All umpires have their deciding lines for ejection. When you call them names, if you direct a curse word at them, yeah, that's going to get you.

I've had umpires say to me, "You ain't going anywhere. If I've got to stay out here and watch this shit, you do too!"

And I'd say, "We're a horseshit team, but the only problem is you're more horseshit than we are."

Now with replay, if you question the call that comes from New York, that's an automatic ejection. But I've gone out there and said, "Listen, see that big old scoreboard out there? It's huge. And I know you looked at that damn thing too. There's no way that call is right."

They'd hem and haw. I'd say, "Who's up there protecting who down here?"

"Y'er gone. You can't argue replay."

"Are we looking at the same thing?" We've all seen that, wondering how they didn't get the call right or why it was overturned or wasn't.

It's changed. They used to let you have a say, and they'd give you some back. Then these young guys started coming into the game, and you can't say anything to them. When you go up to them, they are defensive immediately: "I didn't miss it."

The best thing the umpire can say to me is, "I may have missed it." Now what can I say to that? We're all human.

But if you say you're right all the time, we know that's not the truth, because nobody is. So if you have that attitude, now it just tells me you have no flexibility and it's probably going to get ugly.

I had one ejection in Yankee Stadium, on April 25, 2013. Runners were on first and second in the bottom of the 7th inning. Robinson Canó, who'd already hurt us with a three-run homer, was on deck, and Ben Francisco hits a swinging bunt type ball to third baseman Brett Lawrie. Brett comes in and makes a low throw to Eddie Encarnacion at first, who kind of traps it. The first-base umpire calls Francisco out. Too close to see from any angle. The Yankee dugout is right there by first base, and they're not complaining one bit. Both runners advanced, and Canó was coming up, and we were going to walk him, load the bases, because he was the best at the time.

All of a sudden, the second base umpire — Jeff Kellogg — who wasn't even involved, calls a timeout. He's the crew chief and he gets the umpires together. He says from what he saw, Encarnacion didn't catch the ball, he trapped it. They changed the call. I'd never seen that, where somebody got overruled from a different umpire spot.

I snapped at Kellogg and threw my hat and was ejected. His decision, and one that was not even questioned by the Yankees. Brutal. In today's game, you could review it to see what you got, but that was before replay. It definitely wasn't obvious, but I couldn't understand how he stuck it to his partner that made the call, and, remember, the Yankees didn't complain about the call from the beginning. We got out of the inning, but I wasn't there to see it, as we lost 5-3.

Sometimes I'd go out there, and if it was an umpire I liked, he'd laugh at me. But the really good ones warn you, "Okay, I've given you your say. Keep going, and I'll have to kick you out."

The more times you get chucked, the more the fines increase. But I had a deal with the Blue Jays that if I got ejected, they'd pay the fine. If I had to pay it myself, I might not have gone out there as much.

I'm currently sitting at 53 lifetime ejections. That's not bad, but a long way from the top: Bobby Cox is at 161, but percentage-wise for number of games managed, it's close.

I've been tossed for arguing balls and strikes more than anything else, but also over checked swings, balk calls, plays at first base and home, an obstruction call, a non-call of a hit by pitch and, once that came along, just for arguing about a replay. In my best (read: worst) year, I was chucked eight times.

Getting ejected in 2004 was different than 2018.

There were more microphones around later, so there were times I was embarrassed by my language, and I regretted it. So much for being a class act; I was not setting a very good example, especially to my kids. Mom would have washed my mouth out with soap if she'd been there.

Social media had arrived too. "Here comes Gibby!" became a meme or whatever the kids call it. The dude who ran the Twitter feed @GibbyGIFS had plenty of fodder. The page says I am "the gift that keeps on GIFing." He made clips of all my best moments: seemingly asleep in the dugout; watching the game with my arms draped over the railing; waving; ranting; raving; laughing. There're clips of me coming out to make a pitching change, and someone's doctored the video so I have a beer mug.

Someone also put together a video on YouTube of every single ejection. I have yet to watch the whole thing — that would take too much time.

The players roll with it all. Again, baseball is a game, and we are having fun — supposed to be anyway. My guys might mock me a little bit, some of the things I might do. Fans think I walk and talk funny anyway. I call that bad genetics and blame my mom and dad. But if you've ever heard Farmer Fran from Adam Sandler's movie, *The Waterboy*, you'll understand.

I had that kind of relationship with a couple of umps, especially Joe

West, who was one of the game's greatest characters. I'd always give him a little wave. One of my coaches usually took the lineup card out, and he'd come back to the dugout with some one-liner Joe had about me.

Joe was a big guy, and one hot day, I said something like, "You know who's got the worst job in this place? The clubhouse guy who's got to wash your underwear after this game!" I think he laughed. One game in Minnesota, the homeplate umpire thought Donaldson said something to him when he was actually screaming at the Twins bench. So he ejected Josh, and I came out. Joe West came in from first to defend his guy. I said, "You guys don't know what you're doing." Joe said, "What are you talking about?" So I repeated it. Joe said, "So you're saying we don't know what the hell we're doing?" "That's exactly what I'm saying!" He replied, "You don't think *I* know what I'm doing?" (Yes, we went from "we" to "I".) I said, "You don't." I was gone.

Joe went on to set the record for most games ever umpired — pretty amazing.

Every year the Blue Jays would have a weekend where they'd let some country bands play during the game. My daughter had a band, Southtown, and they were invited up to play Country Weekend in 2017. So they'd be playing on Sunday at the game, but they got a gig Saturday playing at Toronto's famed Horseshoe Tavern. Turned out Joe West was in town umpiring this series, and he sings and writes country music himself. He's actually really good. Saturday he was umpiring home plate and I go tell him about my daughter's band and ask him if he wants to go. He said yes, but he's not paying for a ticket. I told him I'd leave his name on the guest list. When I got there later, Joe was at the bar with another ump, and he picked up our tab. Love that guy.

Never forget, umpires have a tough, thankless job and hardly ever get home. If I was one, I would probably stick it to a few guys myself. But most of them are damn good. I just hope we don't go to electronic strike zones. The human element is what makes the game so great. But I guess with the okay for sports betting, they might want it exact. Since analytics removes the human element, might as well get rid of the umpires too.

Since I just mentioned music, let me tell you just how lucky I've been. I love country and rock 'n' roll but grew up a rocker. San Antonio is a huge rockin' town. Two of my favorite bands growing up were Rush and Triumph, both having Toronto roots. They were both hugely popular in South Texas. You think managing has its perks? You bet it does.

I got a chance to meet members of both bands.

Baseball has made me somewhat famous, but meeting them is all my homeboys care about.

Rik Emmett of Triumph has come to games and brought his son, who was a good little player. The band's drummer, Gil Moore, let my daughter record a couple of songs at his recording studio in suburban Toronto. Talk about good, generous people.

Then there's Geddy Lee of Rush, maybe the biggest Blue Jays fan there is (other than Paul Beeston). He still goes to a lot of games and we've talked baseball, and he really knows what's going on. You can't fool him. He may like baseball more than he likes music. Well, maybe not. Never hurts to be a manager and a rock 'n' roller.

13.

ON A MISSION

There's something to be said about sleeping in your own bed, especially during baseball season. I hadn't done it since I was in high school. From that perspective alone, my year with the AA San Antonio Missions was incredible.

I can't remember how I caught word that the managing job for the San Diego Padres AA team in the Texas League was open. Doug Dascenzo had managed the Missions in the 2011 season, and they were good and won the Texas League championship. After two years in San Antonio, Doug took a job with Atlanta as their minor league baserunning and outfield coordinator.

Since I was at loose ends, having been let go from the Royals, I had nothing to lose. I contacted the Padres, and they gave me an interview and hired me. If it sounds simple, it was. We did the interview over the phone. They hired me because I had pretty good experience managing already, and I lived there.

I know I've said before how interconnected baseball is. Working in the Padres front office were a couple of guys I knew, both former catchers, A.J. Hinch and Brad Ausmus, so I'm sure they had something to say about me getting hired. (Of course, Hinchy ended up having all that success managing the Astros to the 2017 World Series, and Brad got the manager's job in Detroit in 2014.) Fred Uhlman Jr. was the assistant GM in San Diego, and my main point of contact. The VP of player development, Randy Smith, told the media that hiring me was a "no-brainer" and that when he asked around, people gave "nothing put positive reviews" of me.

As with the Royals, the Padres had their spring training in Arizona, so I drove out there. I'd picked up a lot of lessons along the way, at various camps, but the fact is there are far more similarities than differences between organizations. That's kind of the beauty of baseball; everybody tries to reinvent it, everybody tries to come up with new gimmicks or whatever, but basically, it's still all the same when it comes down to it. They are still running the basic drills that we were doing when I was in high school. The hitting side of it has gotten a little more technical, to say the least, but even some of the hitting drills are the same.

Some places modify things a bit. You always get coaches who want to make a name for themselves, and they'll try something new. But mostly it's basic baseball. The best way to improve your swing is to go out there and take BP, or do some flip drills, all the tried-and-true stuff. The best way to improve your defense if you're an infielder is to take ground ball after ground ball.

You can go to these baseball websites and they try to sell all these products for different things, and I'm sure there's value in some of them, but you can probably still accomplish the same thing without spending any money. There're certain basics — and you stick with the basics, you don't need to reinvent it. There are always new ideas and new drills, but a lot of times, what was good a hundred years ago is still pretty good today.

Dascenzo's team had won it all, but this was a new crop of players, as most of the champs had moved up to AAA. We just weren't very good. People can tell you all they want, "This guy's a great manager" or "This guy's a bad manager," but in the end, if you've got the horses, you've got a shot . . . and we didn't. That's not what minor league baseball's about anyway.

My Missions were a great bunch of kids.

The brand of baseball in AA is good, but they're not all going to make it either. Now you're getting the cream of the crop, players with talent.

With good instruction, you're hoping it will pay off and you'll see your guys fulfill their dream.

As we started the season, they had a little meet-the-manager event at the ballpark, and it was strange because I'd been in the game so long, but I was never known in my hometown. When I was introduced, I quipped, "It's going to be like working from home." Compared to Toronto, with all the media attention, San Antonio was dead simple. There might be a reporter at a game, there might not, and they'd ask a question or two and be done. No big press conferences, ever . . . which was refreshing.

The ballpark itself, Nelson W. Wolff Municipal Stadium, was about a 20- to 30-minute drive from my house, depending on traffic, but a crappy location for such a big city. It was a dump, easily the worst in the league and for the AA level. If it rained — which wasn't often — everything would flood.

But I was living the dream. I'd get up, mow my yard and go to the ballpark. The next day, I'd lay by my pool and then go to the ballpark. There was no complicated planning if my kids wanted to come to a game, and when they did, it was often with friends in tow. I'd see my kids before they left for school, before summer break anyway. Kyle was playing ball, so I was able to see a couple of his games.

Even though there were some long bus trips, I didn't mind; I'd done them in the minors as a player and coach, so I was back at it. It was nice not to have to race to get a 6 a.m. flight. But man, is it hot in the Texas League, which sprawls from Corpus Christi up into Arkansas, Kansas, Missouri and Oklahoma. Those 140 games or so take a toll. The Missions was a really refreshing group of kids, and my year with them re-energized me.

Holdovers from Dascenzo's team were pitching coach Jimmy Jones and Tom Tornincasa, who looked after hitting, and they were invaluable since they knew some of the talent in the Padres system and were really good coaches.

There were a few guys that made it to the bigs, though I can't take any credit for development of a few of them, like Jason Marquis, who'd already been to the bigs and was assigned to AA for a single game by the Padres before being called up to San Diego. Miles Mikolas was our closer, and he wasn't there long, getting into 12 games before jumping right up to the Padres; then he went to Japan for a couple of years and came back and signed a nice contract with the Cardinals. I love those stories. Robbie Erlin is still out there, after 11 games with the Missions when I was there. Jedd Gyorko also went on to have a nice career.

Tommy Layne was a left-handed pitcher, and he was bounced around, sent down to us from AAA because they didn't have any room up there. The feeling was that he was on his way out, but then he came to me and Jimmy one day and asked about becoming a reliever. Teams are always looking for lefties, especially left-handed reliever specialists. We called the Padres, and they agreed. This guy figured it out. He ended up in the big leagues with the Red Sox and the Yankees. I kept in touch with him. He was one of the guys that I was always rooting for, because it was a great story, a guy on his way out who reinvented himself.

One thing that stood out from that year was the Texas League All-Star Game on June 28. I'd seen it on the calendar, and my family and I started planning a short adventure, as we'd done during the MLB All-Star Game break for years. Players and coaches both cherish those days off; while it's an honor to be an All-Star, the time off is great too.

Then I learned that the team that won the championship the year before, their manager serves as the manager in the All-Star Game. The other skipper is whoever is leading the other division. There are stupid rules and things that make no sense, and this was one of them. I can see if the guy that won the championship the year before was still around, yeah, let him manage. But why the guy that comes after him?

The game was in Tulsa, Oklahoma, and I fought them on that. I told them I didn't want to do it, and that I valued my time off — and more importantly, I'd had nothing to do with the championship. The league called the Padres, and the Padres asked me nicely, and I relented.

I hopped in my truck and drove to Tulsa on the day of the game. As soon as the game was over — my team, the South, lost 3–1 to the North, with Nolan Arenado standing out — I quickly changed out of my uniform and drove back to San Antonio. I was exhausted when I got home, but there was still another day off at least.

Going back to AA, I definitely softened up a little bit. You've got to have more patience because you're used to watching the guys in the big leagues — and they're good, the elite. As a kid, my father would take me to a big-league game. I'd watch these guys and go, "Wow, these guys never screw up." They still make mistakes, of course, just not as many. Or it's not as obvious. And, finishing 60-80, there were plenty of mistakes with the Missions.

At the AA level, I had to shake myself sometimes to remind myself that they weren't big-league players yet, that I needed to be patient. I tried to remember what I was like at that level.

When I first got into coaching, I told myself, "Hey, remember one thing, don't forget how tough it was to play the game." Now that I'm on the other side, coaching, it looks a heck of a lot easier than it does when you're out there. And the farther you get from the field, from that front row at the stadium, all the way back to the nosebleeds, the easier it looks still.

I didn't know what the future held for me as far as getting back to the big leagues, if that would ever even happen again. But I was satisfied if it didn't.

Then Alex Anthopoulos called.

Gibby's Greats: Nate Freiman

Standing above everybody on the Missions was Nate Freiman, a six-foot-eight giant out of Duke. The big sucker played first base and got into more games than anyone else on the team that year, and he was an All-Star. He finished the year leading the Texas League in RBIs (105) and hits (154), and was top five in extra-base hits, total bases, home runs, doubles and slugging percentage.

And, more importantly, he was a real gentleman, as good as it gets.

He ended up getting picked up by the Astros through the Rule 5 Draft, but Houston couldn't find a place for him, so the A's grabbed him and, finally, he was a major leaguer. His career wasn't epic, and some of his highest profile games were playing for Israel in two World Baseball Classic tournaments. Nate's a hitting coach in the Cleveland Guardians organization now. Cleveland is lucky to have him.

But I want to talk about his wife and golf.

Now, I am hardly an avid golfer. I got decent at it, but I didn't have the patience — and a round could go on for hours. My swing wasn't consistent enough to really get that much enjoyment. I'd rather go fishing.

Most minor league teams will host a golf tournament for sponsors, and the coaching staff and players are required to be a part of it. It was the same in San Antonio. The Missions didn't have many golfers, and the Latino players had no interest.

Enter Nate's wife, Amanda Blumenherst, who he met at Duke, and was playing on the LPGA tour. I'd met Amanda, in between her tour stops, when she came through town. So I asked Nate if Amanda was around, and whether she'd give a little lesson to his teammates.

The home field in San Antonio is located on a flat piece of land, so there's always wind coming in from right field.

We set up a piece of AstroTurf at home plate and had three players in the outfield. Amanda stepped up to the makeshift tee — I think she was hitting a 9-iron — and without even getting loose, she could place the ball wherever we asked, leftfield, rightfield, center. And this was in the wind. It was truly amazing and humbling. What a pro. It was kind of like watching a good major league player up close — they stand out for a reason.

14.

BACK IN THE SADDLE AGAIN

When I was fired from Toronto in 2008, I didn't exactly cut all ties. I'd made friends, whether it was the coaching staff, the trainers, the people running the stadium or even in the media. A text here, a call there, or, when I swung through town with the Royals, plenty of little chats.

Baseball is a fraternity (though it's slowly losing its boys club nature, with women rising in the ranks everywhere), and you keep tabs on your friends, your foes and everyone in between. We all love the game and love to sit around and talk about different players. Everyone evaluates: who can do what, who is improving, who's almost finished.

As the new general manager of the Jays, taking over for J.P. in October 2009, Alex Anthopoulos had done the same thing. Like all GMs, he worked the phones, talking to others around the league. We'd kept in touch as friends. It never went into the tampering area where I was selling state secrets. It was just a couple of guys chatting, bullshitting about baseball. "How's the family?" "Where are you off to next?" "Hey, I heard so-and-so was really starting to develop. If you get a chance, let me know what you think of him." Billy Beane, running the A's, would do the same thing when he was advance scouting before becoming GM. That's the way the game works.

So when Alex called me in early November 2012, that itself wasn't a surprise.

What was a surprise was being asked to come back to manage the Blue Jays.

But first we need to walk back a bit. John Farrell had been managing the Jays, and he left to take his "dream job" running the Red Sox. I'd only met Farrell in passing and didn't know him. I'd read about his idea of the dream job and blah, blah, blah. I thought, *That's never gonna go over good, especially when you're a first-timer.* If I'm the boss or the owner, and someone was talking about another team, saying, "That's my dream job," then I'd be saying, "Take a hike. Beat it. We gave you an opportunity." Officially, he was released from his last year of his contract on October 21 and traded to Boston.

I don't remember exactly when, but Alex called, and we started talking about what was going on up in Toronto. He told me he'd started interviewing people for Farrell's managing job, but he never really came right out and said to me, "Come interview." I think he was feeling me out a little bit.

Eventually, he said, "Why don't you come up here and we'll talk about a job?" or something like that. I was set to return to manage in San Antonio, but I was open to a visit.

Alex did stress to keep it low key. We met in Midtown Toronto, at one of the nice hotels in Yorkville. "Do you want to come back and manage?" is basically what he said.

"What, are you nuts? You trying to ruin your own career?"

I warned Alex that I wasn't very popular the first go-round and things weren't really that good. But I also told him I'd love to manage for him, if he could pull it off.

He said, "Yeah, I think I can pull this off."

I said, "You may want to, but there's no way in hell Beeston will sign off on this."

"Why not?"

"I don't think he will."

He told me that he'd worry about that.

Paul Beeston was smart enough to know that it is human nature to want people around them that they like and can trust. It also makes you accountable. Beest signed off on it.

I thought, *You're nuts, Alex, but let's go!*

Now, "Mr. Blue Jay" Paul Beeston was a legendary figure in Toronto. He was a day-one employee of the Jays and rose to become the team's president during its World Series years of 1992 and 1993. Then he was president and chief operating officer of Major League Baseball from 1997 to 2002. Beeston was brought back into the Jays fold during my first run in Toronto, but I never dealt with him much. While I was gone, he had once again become team president. This go-round, we became friends, and it started with me being a smart-ass. After I'd been fired in 2008, I can't remember what position had opened up in management, but I left a message with the Beest saying I wanted the job, which was way above my payscale. He got a kick out of it.

We quickly put together a coaching staff. My old pal Brian Butterfield left with Farrell. I kept my word to DeMarlo Hale over the pact we'd made coaching together in the Hawaiian winter league, and brought him in as my bench coach. It was an easy call since D is as good as it gets in both baseball and life. Another great baseball man that deserves a shot managing. It took longer than either of us thought it would (and he'd interviewed for the Toronto managing job they gave Farrell). Chad Mottola was the hitting coach and was rewarded for the work he'd done with our AAA team in Las Vegas; Dwayne Murphy, on first base, was someone the players loved; Luis Rivera, a holdover from Farrell, was on third; and Pat Hentgen came on as the bullpen coach. I've said this often: Hentgen is the best there is. He's a longtime Blue Jay. It was just a matter of whether he wanted to do that job or not. He had so much to offer. Pete Walker was my pitching coach, and he had been one of my pitchers down in the bullpen when I was last in Toronto. He was a holdover, too, as the bullpen coach under Farrell. Unfortunately, I made the call to promote

Petey by letting an old friend, Pappy Walton, go. I've been fortunate to have had the best coaching staffs around. These guys were not only great coaches and instructors but just good human beings. It's very difficult to have to make changes to your group, because it's not always fair and you're dealing with people's careers and lives. Plus, they almost all have families to worry about, which is not as frequently the case with players. But they sure made my life easier.

Media doesn't always pay much attention to the announcement of coaching hires, but everyone paid attention to the massive deal that Alex pulled off with the Marlins. On November 14, we got pitcher Josh Johnson, pitcher Mark Buehrle, shortstop Jose Reyes, utility man Emilio Bonifacio and catcher John Buck — and $8 million in cash — in exchange for some young prospects. It was a salary dump by the Marlins, no question, and I was about to find out what these guys were made of . . .

Alex was still at it, and he got 2012 National League Cy Young Award–winner R.A. Dickey in a trade with the Mets that sent prospects Travis d'Arnaud, Noah Syndergaard, minor leaguer Wuilmer Becerra and the just-acquired Buck the other way. Fortunately, Alex got knuckleball catching specialist Josh Thole included in the deal coming back. A decade out, the Mets came out ahead, didn't they? d'Arnaud and Syndergaard were both solid players and are still playing. Alex, Perry Minasian and I went to Nashville to meet with Dickey and his agent. We were courting R.A., and eventually he signed a $29-million three-year deal, with an option for a fourth at $12 million.

As a former catcher, I'd always been apprehensive about a knuckle-baller. I'd seen a few pitch — guys like Charlie Hough, Tom Candiotti and even the Niekros, Phil and Joe — but there's just something about a knuckleball. I wasn't familiar with it. I haven't seen many do it. I'd tried to catch it but couldn't. It just never really seemed like real baseball to me.

All this new blood in Toronto, and they're basically crowning us world champs already. One thing I've learned in this game is you can't get too far ahead of yourself. You can look great on paper, but you still have to play 162. You always like your team, you always think it's good, but you never know how good. Sometimes individual players get traded somewhere or go somewhere as a free agent, and it takes a little time to settle in. Sometimes they try too hard to justify things, or it takes a while to get comfortable. It's pretty common in baseball.

I always viewed it this way — it's better to have expectations than not. It means the baseball world thinks you're good. It's better than having the baseball world think you're crap, isn't it? Sometimes you learn over time that you don't squelch it, but you always want the hype to slow down a bit — 162 games will tell.

It all started out bad. Dickey threw opening night, and our catcher J.P. Arencibia couldn't catch him. The ball was going everywhere: oh, shit.

Josh Johnson wasn't quite where we thought he would be. Buerhle was old reliable. But you could see that Reyes had slowed down. Then the question mark about how effective the knuckleball is going to be in the American League, and in our division.

We were 10-17 at end of April, and with an 11-game winning streak in June, we finally got back to par. It just took too much to get back to the .500 level. We had expended it all just to get there. It was a merciless division.

A small highlight was getting invited to coach in the All-Star Game. Tigers skipper Jimmy Leyland was the manager for the American League for the game at New York's Citi Field. He said something like, "Anybody that managed in the big leagues and goes back down to AA to manage, I want that guy on my team or he deserves to go to the All-Star Game." Jays Jose Bautista, Edwin Encarnacion and Brett Cecil were named to the team, and the Toronto faithful worked together and got reliever Steve Delabar voted in at the finish line.

I'm missing from the team photo, though, if you're looking for proof.

It was the day before the game, before the home run hitting contest and all that hoopla. You go out early and there's a media frenzy. I sat in the dugout and watched as the National League team was taking BP.

I knew a lot of reporters from my time in New York and Toronto, and a number from around the league. Reporters gathered in the dugout, and we were bullshitting. I got warning from someone that the team picture would be in 20 minutes, and I said great. From where I was in the dugout, with reporters all around me, talking to me and having their own conversations, I couldn't see the bleachers out in centerfield for the photo. We're just talking and talking. I saw players come and go, and I didn't think anything of it. Finally, the scene clears a bit, and I can see everyone from the American League All-Star Team is out on the bleachers for the photo. I said, "Shit, I can either run out there and look like an idiot" — and I didn't have the right jersey on either — "or maybe they can superimpose me in there. It'll be a talking point for me. Nobody will believe I was there, because I missed the team picture."

Jimmy and the other coaches ragged my ass.

As for the rest of the season, the less said the better. We were last in the division. I remember thinking to myself, *Alex, I told you so.*

It didn't mean I couldn't do the job.

I still held on to the fact that it sometimes takes a year for these guys to settle in — I don't care how good a player's been, when they're traded or go to a new team as a free agent, it's tough and takes time to get comfortable.

I had to get comfortable with Dickey too. I told him, "I can't tell when you're running out of gas. Do you run out of gas? You've got to tell us." You'd see one inning where he was really good, then the next it would flatten out and he'd get hit. Then all of a sudden, the knuckler comes back. He said, "Okay, I'll keep you guys abreast."

R.A. and I never really meshed over our years together. We had some talks, but it never seemed like legit communication. And I don't think he was real fond of me either. It's no secret. He'd tell us it was time to come out, and then the media would talk to him after the game and he would say he was fine. That bothered me. Wait a minute, we're relying on you and trusting you to tell us what's what — don't play the hero when the media comes to you. Let's be fair, because in the end, you don't want me telling my side of it. You probably want me covering for you a little bit.

But I'm telling you, a big part of this racket is the division you play in. The AL East is a beast. I'm not crying, but it matters. Some teams might win in another division, but they're not winning in the AL East. Not after 162.

Coming back to Toronto, especially after having spent those years in KC, was a reminder how tough the AL East was. It wasn't going to be any easier in 2014.

I'm always optimistic, but I'm a realist too. The AL East is just a different animal, because you had to face the two powerhouses, Boston and New York, at least 18 times. They both have unlimited resources. Their fanbases expect to win, and they force them to do things. They spend a lot of money. Generally, spending money doesn't guarantee you're going to win anything, but it gives you a better shot than the guys that don't spend. That is what you're up against.

Going into that 2014 season, I had my typical optimism but was a little bit guarded. I always believe in my guys. Publicly I'm always optimistic, but I also understand how the game works. You've got to remain healthy; usually teams that remain healthy have a big advantage. I liked our team, it was solid. I thought we were going to be better than the year before when everybody crowned us champs before the season began.

What hurts a lot of teams is that they have to stretch their budget as far as it can go and simply hope like hell you stay healthy because if key guys go down, you don't have the money to replace them. Some of the bigger outfits, the Yankees, Red Sox, Dodgers, they can go out and get somebody and take on their money and not think twice about it.

On December 9, Roy Halladay signed a one-day contract to retire as a Blue Jay. It was an honor to have watched him pitch. He threw out the first pitch in our home opener, a double distraction. As the manager, those events are fun because, usually, when they do it during the season, the guy throws out the first pitch after being put up in the Hall of Fame. But this was Opening Day. For those who say that Opening Day is the greatest, well . . . it is and it isn't. The excitement is unmatched, but other than that, it's a pain in the ass if you're on the team. You get dragged everywhere for interviews and your routine can get thrown out of whack. Plus, the players have just gotten into town and are trying to get situated. They may have their family with them, so they have to move them into their home away from home. Tough life to bitch about in reality, but let's get the game started already! Next day, it's back to normal, or what we call the grind. I will, however, celebrate Roy Halladay any day of the year. We all loved that guy.

I didn't love the start to our year; it was a mediocre April. Certain players are slow starters and others are fast starters. And if you watch a guy's career, it's almost automatic how it happens. I don't know if that becomes a mental thing or what, but you can count on the speed with which guys will come out of the gates. The old saying is that the flower that blooms in spring wilts in summer, and there's a lot of truth to that. You can't win the league in April, but you can sure lose it if you bury yourself too deep. So much goes back to the division we're in, because you knew one thing: that one or both of the Yankees and Red Sox were going to come out of the gate hot — usually both.

May was something else, and we won 21 games, including a nine-game winning streak. Eddie Encarnacion was a big part of it. He smacked 16 homers, tying Mickey Mantle for most dingers in the month of May in AL history. Eddie was a special guy and could get hot. Generally, most guys are streaky in one way or the other: streaky good or streaky bad. With the great players, the bad streaks aren't as long, and the good streaks happen more often and last longer. And everyone will have their slumps. Eddie could get on those rolls, where you just got out of the way. Other teams had to be careful with him. Eddie would be smoking hot, and they'd take the chance to throw to him, and he'd burn them. He just kept doing it.

He was a great hitter and a slugger. He's a great example of a late bloomer, as he never really got it going in Cincinnati, but in Toronto he did. Jose Bautista was a journeyman till he got to Toronto and figured it out.

But it's still only May. It's a cliché, you've got to take it day by day, but it is so true in baseball — every frickin' day. You got beat or you won a game yesterday, it doesn't matter, it's over. The steady, consistent teams win. You've got to stay loose, calm and relaxed. The harder you try in baseball, the worse you get, as bad as that sounds. Baseball is a game where you've got to be able to relax and slow the game down. In other sports, if you get pissed off, you can hit somebody harder, you can run harder, you can do all those things. In baseball, often, when you try harder, it backfires on you.

We were in it as we neared the end of July and the trade deadline, only a game out of the Wild Card, even with all the ups and downs. We were playing in Houston on the day of the trade deadline, and we didn't do anything because there was no money and we couldn't.

In the end, Bautista and Casey Janssen, our closer, did interviews in Houston and were complaining that we didn't make any moves. And I totally understood it. We were right in the Wild Card hunt. But I also knew Alex couldn't do anything because there was no money. Lesson learned.

We finished 83-79, out of the playoffs.

Gibby's Greats: Mark Buehrle

Mark Buehrle has to be in my Top Three Players list. He had such great drive. Cut from his high school team twice, he finally went out one more time because his dad wanted him to try. So he makes the team, goes on to college and has an unbelievable pitching career.

When we picked up Mark in the trade with the Marlins, somebody told me, "He never shakes off a catcher." I said, "What? That's impossible." And he'd had a lot of catchers, with the White Sox, the Marlins.

I asked him about it. "No, I never have." I told him, "You're so full of shit." He said, "Why would I?" His explanation was the very heart of pitching. "I don't care what he calls, if I put it in the right spot, they're probably not going to do much with it. They may get a hit, but they're not going to do a lot of damage." That was his way of thinking.

By God, if you think about it, guys get hits off good pitches, but they don't usually crush them, right? It's usually the mistakes, the breaking ball that hangs there or the fastball in a bad spot or the changeup that is belt-high. That's when you get whacked. But if the pitcher is on, and he's locating the ball, then usually it doesn't matter what you throw.

Then I watched Buehrle, and he never shook off a catcher. It was the damnedest thing I ever saw.

The key to pitching is right there: put it in the right spot and you're going to be successful. Now when they game plan, with analytics, they'll give you these charts of the hotspots — this hitter hits pitches in a certain area of the strike zone. Now the pitcher knows that if he puts it in the other part of the strike zone, he's probably going to be more successful.

Buehrle wasn't using analytics by any means, but it was the same thing. If you make a pretty good pitch in the right spot, you're probably going to be very successful. Still, they're going to get you sometimes.

Just don't ask him to talk about it. Mark hated doing interviews. He tried to get interviews in the can, one where he pitched well, and one to be on file if he pitched badly. "If I pitch well, play the good version; if I pitch badly, play the other one."

Mark is number two all-time in pick-offs by a left-handed pitcher, finishing with 100 in his 16-year career. Steve Carlton had 146, though they only started officially counting when he was in mid-career.

Most left-handed pitchers, they've got that little hang move because they're looking at the runner as they lift their leg. A lot of them bring it up slowly, they might change their timing, and if they see the base runner at first flinch or take-off, then they just step towards first base and throw over there to pick him off. Or the first baseman catches it and throws the guy out at second. There's no excuse for a left-hander not to have a good move.

I was talking to Mark one day, and he said he never threw over on his own. In our case, the bench coach controlled the running game when there was a guy on first. You'd always see the catcher looking over to the dugout to the bench coach — DeMarlo was giving the signs, and then the pitcher would throw over, to try to control that part of the game. Not only did Mark never shake the catcher off, he never threw to first base unless the coach told him to.

Buehrle would have been perfect for the analytics world, because you tell him to do something, he does it. He never was the hardest thrower, but man could he put it in the right spot.

Mark is not only one of the best pitchers ever, but he's one of the best human beings you will ever meet. One of my greatest disappointments in my managing career was when he didn't reach 200 innings pitched in 2015, his last year. He finished with 198.2. It would have been 15 straight years, an incredible feat. That's select company in MLB history. He's had a no-hitter, a perfect game, he's a World Series champ. We tried to get those two innings in on the last Sunday of the season in Tampa. What a workhorse and true professional, but an even better person, husband and father.

But the lasting memory with Buehrle is wilder.

He and his two kids were driving around before a game in Toronto, and they came across a traveling zoo. The guy had little tiger cubs, and Mark asked the guy whether, for a few bucks, he'd bring them to the ballpark. I got to the Rogers Centre, and I walked in, and there were three tiger cubs running around in the clubhouse. First I thought, *What the heck is going on?* Then, *This is awesome.* The players started filtering in, and everybody was taking pictures with these cubs and shooting it out on social media. It was a cool thing, the guys loved it, and it was a bit of an unplanned team bonding moment. And then my phone starts buzzing: *What are you doing?* PETA this, PETA that. Of course I wouldn't apologize, what was I going to apologize for?

The game needs more Buehrles, and managers do too.

15.

THE PROMISED LAND

Jerry Howarth has said it often, that the real competition in baseball is among the general managers. Alex had a couple of years' experience under his belt, ownership willing to spend (some) money and a great core.

Then, before the season even started, he went out and added two superstars in Josh Donaldson and Russell Martin, both who became not only great Jays but great friends.

Russell, a catcher, was signed as a free agent on November 18, 2014, out of Pittsburgh. He got a five-year deal. I'd seen Russell play; I didn't know him, but I knew he played on winners and was one tough, hard-nosed Canadian.

Ten days after signing Russell, Alex swung for the fences, sending Brett Lawrie, Kendall Graveman, Sean Nolin and Franklin Barreto to Oakland for third baseman Josh Donaldson. I knew Josh was a great player, intense, emotional, and I knew he could be a pain in the ass — I'd called A's manager Bob Melvin for the lowdown on Josh. He's another example of a guy who didn't figure it out till he got a little bit older. Josh was a Cubs first-round pick as a catcher. He struggled in Oakland for a while in the minor leagues until he figured out his swing. Kudos to Alex for the pursuit — he stayed on A's GM Billy Beane until finally Beane relented and traded Donaldson. I think Beaner traded him just to stop Alex from calling any more.

Josh and Russ not only added great production to our team but also added some much-needed toughness as well. They were different personalities, but both laid it on the line every night and played with great emotion. Josh could fly off the handle with the best of them, where Russ held his temper in check most of the time. They played to win and kick your ass, which is evident from all their postseason appearances. A few times when Josh snapped, I can remember looking at Russ, and we would both shake our heads and laugh. *Here we go again.* Great players can be emotional.

Bautista was always one of the most disliked guys in the game by players on the other team — but you loved him when he was on your own team. He was emotional, he bitched and moaned at the umpires . . . and he was good, so other players resented that. So now we were bringing in Donaldson, one of the other guys that is disliked throughout the game for basically the same thing. Jose and Josh: two passionate guys. The key to their success is their emotion and their drive to be the best. Neither guy worried about a popularity contest, they wanted to be recognized for the great baseball they played.

The best did not describe the Blue Jays facilities in Dunedin. At the time, the Jays were the only team out there that didn't have one of those big, new spring training facilities, though they have one now. We were at a disadvantage back then, and we didn't have as many fields there to get ready on. On the minor league side there were four fields, and most spring training sites have at least six or seven. You can only be there a certain number of days anyway because the minor leaguers come in and you've got to let them get to work. Then we'd go back to Dunedin, to our stadium where we played games, and all we had there was one regular field and two half-fields, where the infields were cut out. All the other teams had six, seven fields at their disposal. We really only had one and a half since one of the half-fields was used for pictures and promotional stuff most of the spring.

I only bring it up because Marcus Stroman got hurt at spring training — a major setback. It was a problem with the facility, the poor backfield turf. Certain drills you should do on grass. We're doing these bunt plays, and Stro and Donaldson collided; it was one of those in-between balls that the third baseman's got to come get, and the pitcher's got a line to cover. There was contact, Stroman stumbled, his cleats caught on some rough turf, and grabbed his knee. The trainers came out and put him on the cart. Stro was a guy we were counting on. The diagnosis was a torn ACL, done for the year.

The accident reminded me of a drill we used to do when I was a catcher with the Mets, called the "passed ball wild pitch" drill. The catcher would get down in a squat behind the plate, and a coach would roll a ball to the side, and the catcher slides on the ground, gets the ball and flips it to the plate to a pitcher, just so you get used to making that throw from an awkward position. So we're doing that, and Gary Carter tweaked his knee. Damn. We never did that drill again.

For every setback, there are opportunities. Going into spring training, I don't think anyone saw pitchers Roberto Osuna and Miguel Castro making the big-league team, but there they were. Drew Hutchison got to throw Opening Day at Yankee Stadium, and a rookie I'd come to love, Devon Travis, helped lead us to a 6–1 win.

Let the grind begin.

We had a good mix of veterans and youth, and something just felt different. But you can't help but fret with injuries. Jose Reyes hurt his ribs, Bautista strained a shoulder, and it seemed there was a non-stop shuttle of players to and from Buffalo and our AAA club.

I didn't mention it earlier, but having the team's top prospects 90 minutes down the road in Buffalo was a major change in the organization. Prior to affiliating with the Bisons just across the border in 2013, the Jays were partnered with the Las Vegas 51s. It was a logistics nightmare when they were out in Vegas. A lot of moves are made spur-of-the-moment, or somebody gets injured late in the game and you've got to figure out who's coming up. Then there are the complications with the contracts, where some guys have options, some guys don't, so you can't send this guy down, or you can send this guy down as many times as you want. You may have to make room for somebody on the roster and you're hoping that if you bring a young, inexperienced guy, he's ready. It can be a pain and a juggling act, but you have to take all those things into account.

Sometimes there're some obvious choices about who you can bring up, but it's not always that easy. If it's a pitcher, it may be that he pitched that night in AAA or the night before, so he's not available. It's not just, "Let's grab anybody." Now if you add in the time change, it's even more complicated. Yeah, there were lots of flights in and out of Vegas, but the team could be on the road. In a lot of the airports, you couldn't always get flights. So when they moved to Buffalo, a car service would drive them up. It made a huge difference.

By mid-May, Josh had become comfortable enough in his surroundings to make a play as alpha, and he called out his teammates: "This isn't the 'try' league, this is the 'get it done' league. And, you know, eventually they're gonna find people who are going to get it done." Damn, a manager loves that.

Just as Josh was getting to know the other Jays, I was getting to know him. Are kid gloves going to work on Josh Donaldson? Hell no. Josh is like a racehorse, man. You've got to put that switch to his ass to let him know you're around. But like all of them, if they know you're on their side, not just in it for yourself, things go fine.

There's no need to detail every time that Josh and I had a run-in, because every time we did, we came out of it better. They were harmless. It was like getting in an argument with your kid. There usually was something that led up to it, contributed to the friction. But I love the kid to death.

And the beauty of Josh was you always knew where you stood, you always knew what he was thinking — he was easy to read. Compete hard. Win. What more can you ask for?

By June, things started coming together. We had an 11-game win streak and some great individual efforts. And surprise addition Chris Colabello had an 18-game hitting streak. Awesome, especially for a guy who wasn't fast, so he wasn't getting any infield hits. We were also starting to win the close games, the ones we weren't winning earlier. Josh was named to the AL All-Star team, and Russell and Jose were All-Star reserves, though Joey Bats stayed home to get treatment for his shoulder.

Things were good, not great, as the trade deadline approached. Our record was almost identical to the year before, but in 2014, Alex had no money left to spend. Everyone figured he'd be able to ask for a few extra million, that it could do wonders for the team, and he'd get it. On privately owned teams, you might have a better shot of doing that. A corporate-owned team — like the Jays or the Braves, the two out of 30 that are corporate — sets a budget and sticks to it. There's nothing worse than hearing players bitch about management not doing anything when they don't understand all the circumstances.

But Alex had set aside some cash, and it was his genius that took us from competitors to division champions.

On July 28, a trade was made with Colorado, where shortstop Troy Tulowitzki and veteran pitcher LaTroy Hawkins came to Toronto in exchange for Jose Reyes, Miguel Castro, Jeff Hoffman and Jesus Tinoco. When things were heating up with Tulo, Alex was calling me all the time, that it was on, it was off, it was on. When he finally pulled it off, he called me late. The way Beeston tells the story, he was already in bed when he gave his okay, since it was his call on anything that added money to the payroll. Alex told me to get over to the stadium. "Damn, do you know what time it is? It's frickin' late." I lived close, so I walked over. Reyes actually lived closer to the stadium than I did, and somebody went and got him. So it was me, Alex and Jose late at night, sitting in the manager's office. Reyes was disappointed, he liked it in Toronto and he didn't want to leave — but he took it like a champ. Reyes, God bless him, he busted his butt for us, but his legs weren't the same and some balls were sneaking through the infield, the kind that need to be caught in the big leagues.

Then two days later, Alex gets us an ace, David Price, from the Tigers, for prospects Daniel Norris, Matt Boyd and Jairo Labourt. With far less fanfare but still very important were the separate trades for pitcher

Mark Lowe and outfielder Ben Revere, and, of course, the old reliable workhorse LaTroy Hawkins. You want to talk about an incredible career, check LaTroy's out. Dependable is an understatement.

The clubhouse was the opposite of the previous year. We went from players bitching, "They don't care. They don't want to do anything," to "Damn, we're all in."

Veterans like Tulo, Price and Hawkins had been there, done that in crunch time, which is big. Even if it's unspoken, their teammates *know* and it's a boost.

Tulo fit in. A real pro. When he first came over, though, he didn't seem too happy; I think he was under the impression that he was staying in Colorado, or that they would consult with him before they did anything, which I don't think they did — at least, that was my impression. But then I think he grew to like Toronto, like everybody else does.

Price bought everybody these cool blue bathrobes as a way of saying hello. He was a big giver, which helps unify a clubhouse too. To get to the training room, you would have to walk by Price's locker. That first day, I was heading to talk to the trainers and I saw a sign on David's locker that read: "If you don't like it, pitch better." Wow, that's Halladay stuff. There are things that make the great ones different, and mentality is a big one. Price came as advertised: no excuses and a winner.

We caught fire, and it wasn't a gradual thing.

Our hitters kept pounding the ball around, and we had some big bats and we could score runs with the best of them. It was our improved defense that made the difference.

I think Tulo was the biggest pickup in 2015 because he solidified our defense. David Price was unbelievable too, it's neck and neck. But our defense had been holding us back. No pitchers can overcome a bad defense.

One of the big reasons we couldn't get going is we weren't making enough plays on balls hit to short. Jose Reyes did the best he could, but he was getting older and losing his range. He was one of the most dynamic shortstops in his day, but Father Time gets to all of us. Tulo coming in just solidified our infield, and we became so much better. There's no better shortstop. He's probably the most fundamentally sound guy you'll ever see, that's his trademark.

But we knew the injury bug had hit him. Each time he was injured, it made our team weaker because he wasn't on the field. Not only that, Tulo was a leader on the field, taking charge, and his ability to communicate with teammates was unbelievable. That was the frustrating part, the fact that if he's not out there, we're not as good. And you know what he's been through, so no use trying to pump him up — nobody feels worse than he does.

We better give a little love to Chad Pennington, who we also picked up. He really did a great job for us filling in and actually made a game-saving diving stab in Yankee Stadium when the race was still close. He even helped us on the mound.

Of course, we had the issue in left field, too, where we were playing infielders Colabello and Danny Valencia out there. In all fairness to them, they aren't outfielders, so that was a hole for us. Even that cost us. Then when Revere came along and we put him out there, his defense changed us a ton. There's a trickle down effect. When the pitcher knows the defense is better, he throws with a bit more confidence, knowing if there's contact, the team's got his back.

There was just a different vibe. We had been a tight team before, but now it was like family — protect each other at all costs. After we acquired those guys, we had a series against Kansas City that was very intense. We played them at home, and they were leading their division. We didn't know that would be the matchup that mattered. They threw at a couple of our hitters, and I was ejected for arguing with home plate umpire Jim Wolf after Tulo was nailed by Royals reliever Ryan Madson, who wasn't tossed. Aaron Sanchez drilled Alcides Escobar, and the benches cleared, and bench coach DeMarlo got ejected too. But we won 5–2, and took three of four games in that series.

Every few days we were told about some new record or stat, from Price tying the best-ever debut by a new Jay with 11 strikeouts over 8 innings, to another 11-game win streak, to records for hits (48) and runs

(36) in a three-game series (against Anaheim). Eddie hit his third grand slam of the season too. We fought when necessary and stood up for each other. I'd seen this before — the team had come together and was firing on all cylinders. It felt a little like the '86 Mets.

Oddly, it was an announcement at the end of August that would have the biggest effect on the Jays and me: Mark Shapiro was named the team's new president. It wasn't like Mark came in and met people and threw his weight around. Beeston was still on the job where he belonged.

It was a good time for anyone to be with the Jays. Rogers Centre started selling out regularly, fans coming out in droves. People had always told me, "Hey, if you're competitive late in the year, or look like you've got a shot, this place will come alive." They were right. So now every night, we were playing in a full house, probably like when they first opened that place, the first team to draw four million. And Jays fans are loud! Everywhere we go, the city's abuzz. We overtook the Yankees.

Dickey got his 100th career win, as we beat the Rays 5–3 on the Friday night; technically we clinched a playoff spot after the result of late games. We celebrated the playoff berth after Saturday's 10-9 win. This team was solidified at the deadline. Now we're acting like the Yankees and Red Sox. Time to play with the big boys.

I was so happy for the fans. The team hadn't been in the playoffs since 1993, and we were well aware of that.

The best moment from clinching a playoff berth was Munenori Kawasaki's postgame interview where he said he was going to a "bush party." I don't know where that all came from. But what a character. Kawa was such a team player. If he wasn't in the game, he'd go out to the bullpen and help warm up the pitchers — and the fans nearby would see him and erupt. There was a time earlier in the season when Kawa got a walk-off hit. He got on the plane and was dancing, and somebody videoed it. His parents ended up seeing it, and they apparently got all over him — do not embarrass our family. He was like a comedian, a clown, so unlike other Japanese players. But he was perfect for us.

What a beautiful individual. After batting practice, I'd always walk down to the lunchroom to get something to eat, and he'd be sitting at the table with the two big white rice balls that his wife would make him for dinner. "Hey, Kawa, what are you eating?" "Oh, rice balls, John. Rice balls. My wife make rice balls." "Is that all you eat? No wonder you're skin and bones!"

But the season wasn't done, and we wanted the division title. We had three to play in Baltimore and three in Tampa to finish off.

Everybody was talking about the home-field advantage: if we win against the Orioles, we clinch. But it got rained out. So the next day, we've got to play a doubleheader, probably the worst case scenario even if we win the first game and clinch. My thinking was, *Okay, if we win that first game, which I figure we're going to, now we've got to play that second game, and then a day game on the Thursday, early afternoon, before we go to Tampa for the final three of the season.* We want home-field advantage. Here's my dilemma: We win the first game and the players will be celebrating and on cloud nine, exhaling after the long, victorious grind. I would too. It's hard enough already to play a major league doubleheader, 18 innings, let alone on a crappy, rainy night after clinching the team's first division crown in 22 years. The players were exhausted. I'm going to do what I always do, take care of the players that got us there.

So, it's a wet, rainy day, but we win the first one and clinch. In the second game, Dickey is pitching and he goes five shutout innings and then tells me he's had enough. They beat us that second game, but we got our regulars some much needed rest.

I started hearing, "Why aren't these guys playing this game?" Well, you know why. Obviously some don't. I deal with my guys every day, I know their mentality, but more importantly, I know the grind of the season and the mental and physical effort these guys have to give. I know how they think and what they deserve, as I was once one of them, just not on their level. If I had tried to play some of them in that second game, they would have looked at me like, "Gib, do you realize what we just did and the effort we expended for you these last six months?" No need to explain to me, I knew it, and they deserved a little break. What we really needed was a complete game pitching victory that second game. We ruled no champagne until after the second game, but I can't guarantee that was followed. We had a big, well-earned celebration.

All I knew was we had more games to play. One game would have been ideal.

The next day, we had a day game scheduled and it rained all frickin' morning. I don't know how we played it, or why we played it, but we played. After a night of celebration, the regulars weren't going to be worth a damn anyway. This hearkens back to me catching after the Mets celebration in 1986 — it was against a young Greg Maddux, when he was pitching for the Cubbies, and he threw about 95 back then, before he became a control specialist. Nobody played, it was all of us call-ups. Some of the regulars didn't even put their uniforms on. Anyway, there was no way our regular top guys were going to play, especially in the bad weather. We were neck and neck with Kansas City. I was doing what was right for the players in my eyes, and I have no regrets.

Then we were off to Tampa for the final three. Price would have pitched if we still hadn't clinched, but he needed a breather. Dave had thrown his usual 200 plus innings again, and we acquired him for the playoffs. So catch your breath and get ready for the postseason.

Buehrle throws a gem the first night, like he always does, so we're still sitting pretty. Either way, though, we don't have a starter for the final game of the year. It is going to be a bullpen day, like teams do all the time now, no big deal. An analtyics dream game. Mark was set to finish the year one and two-thirds innings shy of his annual 200 innings guarantee. Think about that: 14 straight years of 200 innings, and this possibly being his last hurrah, and he only needs less than two innings to make it a 15-year run. There have only been a handful of guys in baseball history that have done it, so we think, *Let's do it, let's figure out a way*, especially since we don't have a starter Sunday anyway.

I go to Mark: "Listen, you want to start, and go two innings on that Sunday day game, get your two hundred innings?" "Yeah, I'd like to. I can do that." He knew how to get the most out of what he had. Pete Walker and I talked to the front office, and it was a go, since it was a bullpen day anyway. Mark was on fumes and hanging a little bit, but he's the poster boy for efficiency. He thought it was a great idea. Everybody was on board, let's have some fun. We blew a 9th inning lead Saturday night and lost, so now we're in trouble.

On Sunday, Buehrle was excited he was going to pitch two innings. I actually told manager Kevin Cash of the Rays our plan, that Buehrle would go two innings and the other four starters would go out to take him out in the 3rd inning after facing a batter. He agreed it was a nice gesture. I did the same with the umpires, and the umpires loved Buehrle because he worked fast, he threw strikes and he never complained. He was like the umpire's dream. I asked if the other pitchers on the staff could take him out, and they said sure. It was all set up, everyone was in agreement. If Bautista was one of the most disliked guys in the game, Buehrle was one of the most loved. It was a crazy, hectic morning because we had to do a *Sports Illustrated* shoot. I somehow got in there as the leader of the pack, "The New Jacks." I was on there with Eddie, Tulo, Price, Russell, Jose and Josh. I'm the little guy.

We finally start the game and have the bullpen all lined up. A lot of times I ask the pitcher how they feel when they come into the dugout after warming up. Buehrle said he felt great, even better than he did warming up Friday night.

Ryan Goins was playing second, one of the most sure-handed defenders in all of baseball. Groundball to him, doink, he whiffed it. (That never happens to Rhyno, I mean never.) A couple more hits. A soft line drive to Eddie at first base, *clank*, bounces out. It should have been two outs, and I'm going, *You've got to be kidding me!* Why are the baseball gods sticking it to us? Maybe they don't like Mark. No chance, as he was one of the top five most respected and loved guys in baseball. Maybe it's me since I didn't play our main guys in Baltimore. We'll never know.

Bases loaded, and up stepped the one guy in their lineup that hit Mark really well, Mikie Mahtook, a right-handed hitter. A 2-2 pitch, inside corner, and Alfonso Márquez — the umpire behind home plate — called it a ball. We're screaming at him. Now 3-2, and, *wham*, grand slam. So maybe there's one guy that doesn't like Mark and he umpired that day. Finally, I had to take him out and that screwed up our plan, and he didn't get his 200 innings because of two dropped balls and a horseshit call on a crucial pitch. That's baseball.

Buehrle ended up with 14 consecutive seasons of 200 innings, on a list that includes Christy Mathewson, Warren Spahn, Don Sutton, Gaylord Perry, Phil Niekro and Greg Maddux. Perry and Sutton are the only two that got to 15. Nobody's ever going to do that again, so Buehrle probably would have been the last. That still haunts me to this day, not only because it's historic, but because it was Mark.

I can remember sitting back and reviewing games from that year and wondering where I could have gotten Mark two more innings. It could have been easy, but you don't realize or even think about that during those times. Though I do remember that for the first time in his career, his arm started bothering him a little and we skipped one of his starts. Otherwise, it would have been a lock. Mark never got hurt and was the perfect pitcher.

People were bitching and moaning that we lost the home-field advantage, but there was method to the madness. And there were certain things we could do and certain things we couldn't do anyway.

Bring on Texas.

Like us, the Rangers were heavy on offense. They had some good pitching and were a real good all-round team. We were confident, though maybe that wasn't obvious at the start, as we dropped the first two games of the ALDS at home. David Price against Yovani Gallardo in the first game was a battle, but they won 5–3. In Game 2, Stroman was out there for us, having come back at the end of the season after recovering from his torn ACL. Stro duelled with Rangers ace Cole Hamels for a while, but when a game goes 14 innings, it's about the bullpen, and we lost 6–4. It was also a big deal to lose Brett Cecil, who blew out his calf covering first base. And Brett, at the time, was arguably the hottest reliever in the game — or definitely in the top two or three; right-handed or left-handed, it didn't matter, he was our go-to guy. He was also our set-up guy or that swing guy that could come in any time.

Then we had Aaron Loup as our other lefty. Loupie had been a workhorse for us the last couple years but it had been an up and down year for him. After Cecil got hurt, Price came to me and said, "Listen, if you need a lefty, I'll help you out of the bullpen." Here's a guy, you know he's a free agent at the end of the season, and he's already over the 200-inning mark — and he's volunteering to help the team. That's pretty freakin' good. Everyone was on board with it, our backs were against the wall, down two games. Told you Price was the real deal.

There was no panic. They knew they were good. I knew they were good. I got a message from Joe Torre, and he said, "Hang in there, man. You guys can do this." He'd been there before. I had always liked and admired Joe, and for him to tell me that only confirmed my feeling.

We went down to Texas, and it was a big weekend in Dallas. There was the Oklahoma vs. Texas football. Then we played Game 3 after the Dallas Cowboys–New England Patriots game, which was right next door at Jerry World.

We got to our off-day workout and found out Loupie was going to probably miss a couple of games to help his pregnant wife. Everything went fine, but now we were missing another valuable piece. So we went from having two good lefties to zero. Price had to be our guy.

There was always a meeting with the umpires and the managers of each team before the first playoff game. In Texas, we were finishing up the meeting, and there was a knock on the door. Everyone is wondering who it could be when this head pops in — it's George W. Bush. He asked if he could come in for a minute. It was really cool. On the way out, I got a photo with him. I was always a George Bush fan, and I still am — he owned the Rangers at one time.

Just like on Opening Day, you take the field for introductions in each team's home opener. After meeting Bush, I was in the line near home plate and I look over near the Rangers dugout where Bush always sits with his Secret Service. I got his attention and gave him a salute, and he gave me one back.

Marco Estrada was pitching Game 3, and he threw a gem against Martín Pérez. There came a turning point, where maybe it could have gone one way or the other, so I started getting Price loose. Texas had a heavy left-handed hitting lineup, and the ball jumps to right field in Arlington, at the old park, so you better have your left-handed reliever ready — or your left-handed starter turned reliever, I should say. Estrada got out of it, so we didn't need Price. Here's a guy who's going to make a boatload of loonies and toonies in the offseason as a free agent and I just dry humped him in the bullpen. (For those who are wondering, the term "dry hump" refers to getting a pitcher warmed up in the pen and then not using him.) We won 5-1. I must have known we weren't going to re-sign him.

The next morning, I saw Price in the clubhouse. I asked him if he got hot in the bullpen the night before. He said, "Yeah, close to it." I said, "Okay, here's the deal. If you get up today, you're in the game. I ain't gonna do that to you, I ain't gonna watch you get hurt." He agreed and said thanks.

For Game 4, Derek Holland was the Rangers starter against Dickey, and they had some guys in that Ranger lineup that hit Dickey very well. The thing about that knuckleball that you learn after watching over time, is that it can be really good and then it can flatten out — and when it flattens out, it usually goes for homers, not for singles or doubles. It's unpredictable, so you'd better keep an eye on the pitcher. And if it's a do-or-die game, you'd better not wait too long.

Dickey goes four and two-thirds. We get a nice little lead, and Dickey's pitching pretty good, but I know the guys that hit him well are coming up. (Third time through the lineup, heck I was analytics before analytics.) The crowd's dead, wondering what's hit them, so keep them quiet, and Dickey probably doesn't have a whole lot left anyway. He goes out there, and it's the bottom of the lineup, Shin-Soo Choo, Rougned Odor, all those guys coming. So I get Price going. I can't wait around and let him cough it up if the pitch quits dancing. Remember, it's a do-or-die game, so I'm doing it my way, which was the smart way.

Dickey gets a couple outs, then a couple guys get on and I take him out. I said to myself, *Screw it, I don't give a shit what Dickey thinks.* I told him, "This ain't about who gets credit for the win. It's about shutting this game down right here, and let's go home and play Game Five." (Today's game says wins don't matter, as there are too many variables; on that day, I agreed.) He doesn't say a word, but glares at me.

Donaldson and I had a good relationship, but I always knew he was going to say something when he didn't agree with whatever it was. This time, he muttered, "This is bullshit." I told him to shut it.

After Price shut them down that inning, in the dugout, right in the hallway to the back, Donaldson repeated it. We went at it, yelling at each other, but it was good for both of us, therapeutic even, in a stressful situation.

Price threw a couple more innings, and we closed it out and evened the series. It worked out perfectly: we were going home.

And I know people didn't understand the reasoning, whether it was Price in the bullpen or Dickey getting pulled. The media asked questions after the game, and I explained things, stressing that it's about the team, not individuals. Many thought I had planned to have Stroman pitch Game 5 and this was my way of getting Price out of it. No, if this hadn't happened, Price was going to pitch Game 5 with Stro close behind if needed. You know what this was about? Winning the game and not abusing a great trade acquisition who stood to make mega-millions in the offseason and who put his team first. You bet I'll protect him.

Then came Game 5, back in Toronto on October 14. Now, I was there for Game 6 of the World Series in '86, and this one was right up there as far as crazy games go.

It's Hamels against Stro to start, and it's a good, even battle, tied at 2 heading into the 7th ... which proceeds to run 53 minutes and is etched in Blue Jays lore. Odor's on third base, and Choo's hitting. Choo always held his hands out over the plate, so when Russell throws the ball back to our pitcher, Aaron Sanchez, the ball hits the bat and deflects down the third baseline, and Odor comes in to score the go-ahead run.

I'm thinking, *That's a dead ball.* I can't remember ever seeing that happen before; it never happened to me as a catcher. Home-plate umpire Dale Scott called it a dead ball, sending Odor back to third, and then Rangers manager Jeff Banister went out to argue. They changed the ruling and gave them the run. So I go out to argue, too, and it's chaos. Finally, they got it right, run scores.

Fans are impatient, loud and start chucking things like beer cans. Walking back to the dugout, a can near hit me right in front of the dugout. I made the joke after the game that it couldn't have been Beeston throwing it, because the can was full and his would have been empty. Beest loved it. We shared many a beer together.

But now the baseball gods decide to get involved, and rightfully so. Now I know why they didn't help us out down in Tampa during Buehrle's last game — they were saving it for this game and didn't want to show bias towards Canada's team.

The Rangers had one of the best defensive teams in the game, easily, with Adrián Beltré at third, Elvis Andrus at short and Mitch Moreland at first, all Gold Glove winners, and even our archenemy, second baseman Rougned Odor, who was pretty good himself, as hard as that is for me to say. Things just happened that shouldn't happen at the major league level, especially on that team — booted balls, dropped balls, then the bungled bunt play they'd have made 99 times out of 100. Josh hit a little gork over the second baseman's head, and Odor's a good athlete, but the way he went back for it, his feet got tangled up — normally he would've caught that ball, but it fell. Everything was going our way. Moreland bounced the ball to second, Andrus dropped it. Sitting there in the dugout, I thought, *What is going on here? This stuff isn't supposed to happen.*

Then, of course, the big moment as Jose steps to the plate against Sam Dyson. Perfect guy, Mr. Blue Jay, the face of the franchise . . . and then, bam. I'm watching the ball, so I didn't see the bat flip. Everything happened in slow motion. There was 22 years of frustration in that bat flip. Besides Jose, Vernon Wells and Carlos Delgado would have been the other two who truly understood what it meant.

Dyson thought Big Eddie was popping off to him, but E was just trying to calm things down. The benches cleared. When that was over, next thing you know, Tulo and Dyson were back at it again, so here come the benches. Wild.

It was hard to think, there was so much noise, and it made it so hard for me to concentrate as the manager, mapping out how to do things. It's tough not to get caught up in the emotion. To keep it together, knowing there's still some game left to play. This ain't over yet and they've got a powerful quick-strike offense over there just like we do.

The intensity and the anger was incredible. There we were, at home in that dome — it was so loud you could feel that concrete mass shake — and now the historic home run. Winning that game wouldn't have been the same without the bat flip, well maybe or maybe not. Baseball fans will be watching that long after we're dead and gone.

A lot of it's a blur. Our bullpen shut them down, Sanchez and Osuna, our two young studs, finished things off. That place was rocking. Boom, boom, boom. We won 6–3. Down two games to love and then won three straight. They were equally as talented as us, but we thought we were the better team. We thought we should win. I can't try to describe it. I'll just say that the baseball gods got involved because we deserved it.

In reality, the game was over with the bat flip — I don't see how anybody comes back from that.

After we won, Jon Daniels, the Rangers general manager, came into our clubhouse and congratulated Alex and me, which was classy. I've always been a big fan of that guy. It's not like other sports, where they meet on the field and hug and switch jerseys.

The clubhouse was nuts. I said a couple short, simple things during the celebration. "Congrats, two more battles to go," or something like that. They definitely didn't want to hear a speech at that moment. They wanted to party. We felt we could win it all, but I'd have to try to outsmart some old crafty friends to do so.

Up next were the Kansas City Royals. From my time there as bench coach, I knew everybody on the coaching staff and most of their players. I loved Kauffman Stadium.

I was excited. We'd had some pretty good battles with them during the regular season, and I thought we matched up really well if we're swinging the bats. We were basically a home-run hitting team, and that was the beauty of playing in our dome. But then you go to Kansas City, which is probably the hardest place to hit a home run. They played a totally different game, a perfect fit for their ballpark. Everybody could run on their team, they had good hitters and the Royals were by far the best defensive team in the league. Put it this way: they could manufacture runs better than any team in the league. At least the way I was thinking, we were going to have to score because they also had very good pitching and a really good bullpen. In close games, we needed to out-slug them. They were awfully tough to beat in low-scoring old-time baseball–type games.

Our staff put together its usual details on how to play against their team. Really, it wasn't much different than a regular season series, just that the stakes were much higher.

We presented their lineup to our team in the usual way: "This is who we're playing; this is how we're going to position these guys." Then the hitting coach gave an overview of their pitching staff, highlighting what they do and how they throw. If anybody wanted to add in their own observations, the floor was always open. The infield coach would run his part, positioning the infielders, then the outfield coach talked about his guys. The hitting coach would always go up to each individual hitter before a game and maybe talk about that guy's approach, but each hitter is different. Both the hitting and the pitching coach spend so much time looking at video that they put their own game plan together. They'd take the info that scouts gave them, but they also probably relied more heavily on what they were looking at. And every team has a couple of invaluable video guys — you tell them what you need, and they put it all together.

Sometimes I think you can get carried away and have too much info, and it paralyzes some players, and they out-think themselves. But it sure as heck helps that we can look at something and see it with our eyes instead of just hearing about it.

Mike Shaw, our traveling secretary, had his work cut out for him, too, in the playoffs. He did all the dirty work. Whenever somebody needed something, we'd ask him, and he'd do it. And most of us — me included — waited until the last minute, which meant he was scrambling. He's actually the most valuable guy in the organization, if you want to know the truth — hands down.

It's become standard that players get to bring their families to the away playoff games, so that means organizing a second plane. You need to celebrate the family, since they put up with a lot of crap. Without a good family, without that support system, you're not going to succeed. So the families need to be rewarded as well. And they love it. It's a chance for them to fly first class, they get great accommodations, all that. The players all know what it means, though, and remind their families that they are there to play baseball.

The first game in KC was on October 16, and I spent a little time chatting with former colleagues, including manager Ned Yost and his staff. Our bats just never got in that one, with their starter, Edinson Vólquez, throwing great; the Royals just kept poking at Marco Estrada and his successors. We lost 5–0, only the sixth time all season we didn't score a run.

In Game 2, Price was just mowing them down — he gave up a single to the leadoff hitter then retired 18 straight. The Royals had a very balanced lineup, but a lot of their top hitters were left-handed. Price was rolling along until the 7th inning, when things imploded. I later heard that the Royals had figured out when he was throwing a changeup, and that turned the tide. We think it had something to do with Price's breathing. It wasn't all Price — David was great. Things started to unravel when that little turd-ball fell in between Ryan Goins and Bautista in short right field. That's all it takes sometimes to get things rolling or to sabotage a team. Where did those baseball gods go that helped us against Texas? Someone must have pissed them off. We went from a 3–0 lead to being down 5–3, and we lost 6–3.

After we dropped the second game, I told them, "We've been here before, boys." There was never any panic with that group, just confidence. We'd already advanced from the first round, and we knew we had seven games to play now. "Let's go home and win some and get right back into this thing." Disappointment, but no panic. We didn't want to keep making it so damn hard all the time.

Game 3 was all about Marcus Stroman, who had turned into a true big-game pitcher. We won 11–8, and the atmosphere was electric.

The next game? Not so much. Dickey started, and he gave up five runs in the first two innings. He must have still been pissed that I yanked him in that Texas game. Then it got uglier, so bad that I sent in Chad Pennington to throw, making him the first position player to pitch in the playoffs. He went in with two on and two outs in the top of the 9th, and they scored two more. You never want to have to do that, ever, even in the regular season, and it's embarrassing to do in the playoffs. But it's that time of year, everybody's out of gas, and the game was over (a 14–2 loss). At the beginning of the year, you ask a general question: "If we ever need a position player to pitch, would you want to?" They all want to throw. There are certain guys you're not going to put in there, put it that way. Like in 1993 when Jose Canseco of the Rangers blew his elbow out — you don't put your stars in.

Game 5 was a rematch from the first game, and Estrada came out big. He did not get the credit he deserved. He threw some gems for us, none bigger than that 7–1 win that sent us back to KC. You're not going to find a better guy, a better team player. He really came into his own with Toronto. He didn't pitch as well in Milwaukee. But what a changeup; at the time it was the best in the game.

With it all on the line, we sent Price up. People kept reminding us that Dave hadn't been very good as a playoff starter, but any time you have Price out there, you have confidence. You felt good any time he took the mound, and you always got his best effort. Plus, he was overdue. He didn't get that monkey off his back until a World Series game for the Red Sox in 2018.

There was so much in Game 6. Ben Zobrist homered in the first inning. In the next inning, a fan grabbed a ball in right-centerfield hit by Mike Moustakas; it was ruled a homer, and I challenged it. That delayed things, but the play stood.

Price lasted until the 7th, when I sent in Aaron Sanchez, and it was 3–1 Royals as a rain delay arrived in the next inning. A rain delay doesn't ever help you, but it's equal for both teams at least. The worst part about it is you worry about who's pitching for you. The length of the rain delay determines whether you can leave that guy in there or not. We had an unwritten rule where we'd wait about 45 minutes, but beyond that, we'd go with another pitcher. When a pitcher gets all tight and stiff, there is a far better chance of injury. I'm reminded of a World Series from 1982, St. Louis against Milwaukee, and John Stuper of the Cards kept going out after all these rain delays, and he was never the same after that.

Osuna came out for us after the rain delay. It was do-or-die — time to shut them down. Again, remember we didn't have Cecil. He could dominate left-handers and right-handers with all the strikeouts. Would it have made a difference? I don't know, but I would have liked to try.

They were up by two runs. But we rallied. We ended up tying it in the top of the 8th on a home run by, you guessed it, Bautista, his second of the game. For his first postseason, he really showed the world how good he was. They had to bring in their closer Wade Davis to bail them out in the 8th. Now it's essential to hold them down since Davis can't pitch forever. But the tie didn't last. Now the Royals were a great baserunning team, probably the best in baseball, and that's how they went ahead in the bottom half. They scored the go-ahead run on that ball down the right field line, when Bautista came up and threw it to second base. Lorenzo Cain was on first, and the third-base coach kept wheeling him, and he ended up scoring. Normally, any time you've got a guy on first base and the ball's considered a sure double, you line up and throw it home. It wasn't quite deep enough for a guaranteed double, and I'm sure nobody thought he could score, so we came up gunning for second. That run scored because of the great third-base coaching from my old friend Mike Jirschele and the all-out hustle from Cain.

Top of the 9th, here we go. Russell Martin led off with a single and we put Dalton Pompey in to run. Not a tough decision. Dalton was on the team because he could fly, and he greatly increased our chance of scoring. But if we don't, it's over. Pomp stole second and third. The way he ran, we just made contact, there's a good chance we score. Pillar gets on with a walk. Now, Kev was one of the most aggressive hitters I've ever seen, so to get on via walk in that situation was the last thing we expected. Then he steals second, and we have men on second and third with no outs and two of our best contact hitters coming up, Navarro and Revere. I would have bet everything that one of those two would have made contact and we'd score. Thank God I don't gamble. Navarro is just a good hitter and Revere is a contact machine. Davis struck them both out. Don't ever blame an umpire, especially when one of the game's best is on the mound, but damn, there were a couple of calls that seemed wrong in our eyes and there's a big difference between a 2-1 count and a 1-2. At 2-1, the hitter's in the driver's seat. Davis strikes them both out and if you can do that, I tip my hat to you. He was one of the best closers in the game for a reason. We still had one more shot, and it's the league MVP. I'd bet here again. Josh grounded out and it was over.

It's hard to describe the feeling when everything suddenly stops. A lot of great teams have experienced it, but it still knocks you back.

You never like to lose but if you're going to lose . . . the fact that I respected and liked that group so much, it was probably the least painful way to go. KC deserved the win, they had a great team. They were an old classic major league baseball team. They had no weaknesses, they played the game the right way fundamentals-wise. They deserved to win the championship by beating us, and they did, beating the Mets, who were run by one of my old managers, Terry Collins.

It was quiet in our clubhouse. Everybody was exhausted, emotionally drained from the long season and the ups and downs. I went out into the room, thanked them for the effort and the year, wished them well and a good offseason, and said I was looking forward to seeing everybody next year. I left it at that. I was proud of them.

There was the usual media, but I don't recall much about it. I do remember sitting in the coach's office with Alex and Beeston for a while.

Bottom line, we just got outplayed. It was a whirlwind. We felt we should've won it all. I still feel that way, more so than in 2016. When I look back on Game 6, I can't help but think that that was the way it was meant to be. Somebody's going to put that ball in play, it might sneak through, now we got the lead, Osuna shuts them down, we go to Game 7 — and everything swings back in our favor because we've got the momentum now.

It usually comes down to pitching, and they out-pitched us. Baseball has changed quite a bit since then, and 2015's not that long ago. In today's game, everyone strikes out or hits a home run. But in the end, it's good old-fashioned fundamental baseball that still wins. Game 6 is a perfect example. You strike out, you've got no shot at scoring. We had two of the best opportunities to take our shot, but it didn't happen. I would bet on my guys in that spot every time.

It's frustrating to watch all the strikeouts now. But hitting's not easy either. The game used to frown on players that struck out a lot . . . I know because I was one of them. But now there's no emphasis on just putting the ball in play, and it's hurt the game. Yeah, home runs are great, and you score a lot of runs on dingers — the 2015 Jays were a perfect example of that — but there are other ways you have to be able to score runs, and we were pretty good at that too. It just didn't happen that night.

It felt like we got beat by a 1970s- or '80s-style team. Fundamentals galore. But it was two very good teams that were built for their own specific ballparks and divisions, and they both worked. I'll take our guys any day.

I stayed a couple extra days in KC to decompress and then flew home.

Gibby's Greats: Devon Travis

When I hear the term "unsung hero," I think of Devon Travis.

There's no doubt in my mind, he'd have been an All-Star someday, but Devon's knee problems killed him. He was always banged up, but this sucker could hit.

Drafted by the Tigers in 2012 out of Florida State University, the Jays got him in November 2014. The knock on him was he wasn't very good defensively, but he could hit. It turned out he did a very good job for us defensively at second base as well. And he really hit.

The first year we got him, by the middle or end of May, he was leading our team in everything — home runs, driving in runs. Dev had such a short, sweet, compact swing and could throw line drives all over the park, which is a rarity today. I think he could have been an All-Star. But he couldn't avoid the injury bug.

In the 2016 playoffs, in the series against Cleveland, he started on the active roster, but his knee gave out again. And so we bagged him and put Justin Smoak back on the active roster. Injuries prevented him from reaching his own expectations and what he was capable of, but he was still a damn good big leaguer. Dev was one of those guys that did everything quietly and everybody loved him. And he was one of the finest young men you will ever meet. I tell you, his parents couldn't have done a better job raising him. Great job, Mom and Dad!

16.

COMING UP SHORT AGAIN

The Blue Jays went from the disappointment of the loss to the Royals to major changes behind the scenes — the kind that don't normally happen after a successful playoff run.

We all knew that Mark Shapiro was taking over for Paul Beeston as president, but it was unexpected for Alex Anthopoulos to reject a five-year contract extension as GM. From a PR standpoint, it didn't go real well when Alex left. He was the homegrown boy that the ownership kept raising the ante to keep around, but he chose to leave and went out to LA for a job with the Dodgers. That didn't settle well with Toronto baseball fans. A lot of people were disappointed, but in the end it proved to be a great move, for him anyway.

Beeston became a very good friend and confidant. Being the president, he wasn't around the clubhouse much, but when he was, everyone knew he was the big cheese. Beest was one of a kind. Nobody cares about the Blue Jays more than Paul does. He's still at most of the ball games and maintains an office at the stadium. One of my greatest memories in my waning time in Toronto was when Beest would come down to my office around 6:30 p.m. and sit down and talk. We had some great laughs. I also learned the extent of Paul's great career in and out of baseball. He truly is a Toronto icon.

Alex was different, he was around all the time and became very friendly with the players and got to know them personally. It wasn't like the days of Frank Cashen anymore, where you would never see the GM. If the GM showed up in the clubhouse, something was going down. But Alex genuinely cared about the players, and they appreciated that. The modern GM.

I knew I'd miss him. My relationship with him was similar to the one I had with J.P. We could laugh and joke and tease. I was lucky that these relationships were more than business, they were friendships. That doesn't mean we agreed on everything and didn't fight some things out, but that's old-time baseball, and it's healthy. If you don't argue and disagree over players, something's wrong. But at the end of the day, the GM has the final say, he was hired to make personnel decisions. I was hired to get the most out of their guys. And when you trust each other, everything is good and healthy.

There's always apprehension when new people come in because they generally bring their own crew along with them. I know that was on everybody's mind. But for me, we were so successful in 2015 that it would have been a bad PR move, especially after losing Alex. Well, they could have, but it wouldn't have been smart.

Tony LaCava was assigned as the interim general manager. We knew that wasn't going to be permanent. I was tight with Tony, and I still talk to him. He is one of the best baseball guys I've ever met. Tony was always the stabilizer around there, the voice of reason. He never got too emotional or overdid it or got too revved up. He'd sit back and watch. He was always the guy that talked you down: "Wait a minute, think about it this way." Of late, he's interviewed for a couple GM jobs, and he was a finalist, and didn't get those jobs. The baseball world's missing out when this guy isn't running a team — that's all I have to say. He's probably the guy I respect most in the game.

On December 3, Ross Atkins was named the new general manager, with LaCava remaining as his assistant. Atkins had been with Shapiro in Cleveland.

Even before we took off in 2015, the talk was Shapiro was coming in to rebuild the team. That was just the word on the street. Then we took off, and Alex made some great moves, and now you can't make major changes. After 22 seasons, the team's back in the postseason, and your core guys are back … a teardown would have been a nightmare to explain to the fans. And the money was pouring in because of the success.

The coaching staff all felt that we had to try to keep it rolling as long as we could. *If we spring a leak, they're gonna tear it apart.*

As for the team, we knew David Price was likely leaving, and sure enough he did, but it was to Boston, so we knew we'd face him often. J.A. Happ was brought back to fill out the rotation; Happy had been here before, so we knew him, and we were excited.

It was also Bautista's contract year. There was talk about that with the coaches, that we didn't want it to become a distraction. It never really was. Jose threw some figures around and got shot down, jeered at a little bit because of his age. But honestly, it was never really a distraction. It could have been. It goes back to the belief that they were going to break down the team once it started going the other direction, so we all thought maybe he'd be part of the cuts if it did get to that point.

At the Rogers Centre, they put in a full dirt infield, which was great, but did require a little adjustment, learning how the ball bounced.

So all this is going on around us, and yet we still put together a great season.

Marcus Stroman pitched Opening Day 2016. There's something about Opening Day, and they all want to be out there. When we had an ace, like Roy Halladay, it was an easier decision. But Stro was a good guy for it. Happ was just coming back. Dickey was the Opening Day guy when we first picked him up. Stro had made it back the year before and helped us tremendously at the end of 2015. It was a nice little honor for him. He was coming into his own. Stro was always the guy that would let you know that he wanted to be the Opening Day guy, that's his personality. I loved that confidence. Stro was a showman, he always liked to be in that big moment. He's going to get the most out of his career, not just on the field — his HDMH Apparel line stands for Height Doesn't Measure Heart. So, he had that chip on his shoulder. But the counter is that sometimes you've got to pin Stro's ears back a little bit to keep him grounded; he was like a racehorse, strong and ready to go. The most important thing was he thought he was good, and he was right.

Heading into the season, we were feeling really good about ourselves. We'd conquered that division for the first time in forever. We thought we had the team that could do it. That sense that teams were gunning for you was real. All those years we played the Yankees or the Red Sox when they were on top of the world, we loved beating them. There's always something to that. In the brief time I spent with those Mets teams, they were really hated in baseball because they were as arrogant as can be — but they could back it up. They got into a lot of brawls. They were cocky and confident — you can be cocky all you want, but if you're not any good, they'll laugh at you.

While the '16 Jays weren't the '86 Mets, we were disliked. We had some guys that were cocky, who wore their emotions on their sleeve, who weren't afraid to complain and bitch at umpires or to fight. As a team, we weren't afraid to stick our chest out, because we were coming off a good year and we were good.

Right off the bat, I was in trouble with the PC police.

The commissioner was at it again. He had already changed the collision rule at home plate because one guy got hurt, and now he's changed the sliding rule at second base because someone else got hurt. Now, occasionally over the years, guys got hurt on these plays — it's part of it — but come on, they are two of the most exciting plays in baseball.

Our game has been good for so long — leave it alone. Get out of the way, and let the boys play. I guess they'll even move second base in a little closer soon.

Back to the sliding rule: it's sometimes called the Chase Utley Rule, because he's the one who took out Mets shortstop Ruben Tejada at second base. It wasn't a normal play, Tejada was spinning off the bag and Utley slid in after him. Tejada fractured his fibula. It wasn't intentional, and there's no comparison to the way they slid in the '70s and '80s and before that. They would try to knock you into left field, or at least put you on your ass.

They'd already made the Buster Posey Rule, where you couldn't take out the catcher and the catcher couldn't block the plate. The worst part of that is there are a lot of catchers that aren't great hitters, but if they can do those little things behind the plate — block balls, block the plate — that's what keeps them in the big leagues. That was me when I was playing!

What's the goal in baseball, and any sport? To score. If you can keep the other team from scoring, you've got a chance to win. Why do we need to change the way the game is played behind the plate? Because Posey got hurt? Yeah, guys have gotten hurt in the past, and it was a shame when they did, but did it happen all the time? No.

I also thought, if you don't want your catcher getting hurt, tell him not to block the plate, ever — give the other team the run. Problem solved.

I guess it's accepted now and nobody thinks anything of it, but at the time, everybody was going, "What are we doing?" If you have the ball, you can take the plate away — what good's that? What's the difference? Now I see games all the time where the catcher is forced to make a sweep tag, when in the past he would have caught the ball and the runner never would have made it to the plate. Now guys slide headfirst, but they never would have or could have in the past because they'd have gotten hurt.

Okay, those are the rules, we get it. Plus, I am a law-abiding citizen.

Back to second base sliding rule for the second time. One of the coolest plays in baseball was breaking up double plays — fun to watch, fun to do. There's an art to being a shortstop or second baseman and pivoting on a double play. The shortstop used to throw from low and down under to make the baserunner get down — that was their protection. Tony Fernandez was one of the best at this. The runners knew that if they didn't get down, they would get hit right between the eyes. Players knew how to take care of things and protect each other back then, and they would today, too, if we let them. But these days, they don't have to do it. Players don't have to be acrobatic at all. That's why you see guys playing up the middle who couldn't have played there before. Maybe they instituted the rule because of the shift, players are running all over just to get to the bag and cover, so they'd be very vulnerable. Who knows. The spring they passed the sliding rule, a couple of umpires and a rep from the commissioner's office hit all the camps to explain it. Everyone's thinking, *What are we doing?* The umpires didn't like it either. As coaches, we sat around and bitched — we figured it would burn a team and possibly cost them a playoff spot.

Sure enough, in our second game of the season, in Tampa, going into the 9th inning, we're down a run and we get the bases loaded, and Encarnacion is hitting, Bautista's on first. Eddie hits a chopper down the third-base line. Evan Longoria throws to second. Bautista goes into the bag, but he puts his arm out and clips the second baseman, Logan Forsythe, coming across the bag on the leg. Forsythe throws it wide, past first baseman Steve Pearce, into the dugout, and we score two runs and have the lead.

A light goes on in the Tampa dugout, "Hey, wait a minute. We have a new rule about that. Let's check it." Manager Kevin Cash goes out there, and the umpires meet up to watch the video in front of the visiting dugout. I could sense we were about to get screwed.

After 90 seconds, the umpires announce that Bautista's out and the game's over — we lose 3–2.

So you're going to end the game on a new, passive, controversial play? That's a problem.

I was furious, and in a postgame interview, I vented, "I guess we'll come out wearing dresses tomorrow, maybe that's what everybody's looking for."

That didn't go over well. Now, everybody's commenting on it, even some of the news channels. I was actually trying to be a little light — I was joking and I wasn't. That blew up and both the front office and our PR team were in a panic.

I started getting emails from women's groups. Really? Did I say anything that bad? The women's baseball league played in skirts — what am I missing here?

Atkins told me I should apologize. I said, "For what? I don't apologize unless I'm wrong." Ross didn't know me that well and didn't really know how to take me. He and Shapiro are both as politically correct as it gets, and I'm just the opposite. No wonder I got into the old University of Texas and not Stanford.

I talked to my wife, my daughter and my mom. "You've got to help me out here. Did I say anything wrong? Were you offended by this?"

The next day was a firestorm, and Jay Stenhouse, our PR guy, said I had to address it. Essentially, I said, if it's okay with my mother, my wife and my daughter, it's okay by me. The world needs to lighten up a little bit.

People want their pound of flesh. Even if you apologize, regardless, they'd still come at you. If you say, "No, I'm not going to apologize, I didn't say anything wrong," and it dies. It goes away. When you feed some of the people, the professional protesters, and you give them an apology, they keep coming at you, thinking that they've got you and you're vulnerable. If there's something you have to apologize for, of course you do. That one died because I didn't play into the drama. A few days later, I got a nice fine and a memo from the commissioner saying I'm alienating half our fanbase. I didn't see a drop in our attendance. Now, if I truly and legitimately offended you, I apologize.

When the schedule was released, the dates against the Rangers were circled. We had developed a rivalry, and a really big deal was made out of Bautista's bat flip, with so many people calling it disrespectful. I did talk to Jose before we played the Rangers. He expected to get drilled or something and just accepted it. He knew it might happen and said he'd just go to first base. We'd played them four games at home in the beginning of May and nothing happened. Then we were in Texas for three more a week later. It wasn't until his final at-bat of the final game that they plunked Bautista. That's the part that bothered me. I've been in the game for 40 years, I understand it, I get it. I've also seen other teams throw at Jose. But when you wait till the last at-bat of the last game that year, I have a problem with that. To me, it's gutless, and I think the baseball gods feel the same way, judging from that season's postseason outcome. We all expected it, but when nothing happened to that point, I thought maybe they finally understood that the bat flip was just a release of frustration at the time.

I told you I've been around a long time, and if you're going to do it, do it right away when the world expects it, even if not everyone understands it. But be prepared, because now it's our turn. Fans don't always understand an eye for an eye, and I don't always either, but that's what has kept the game in check forever and helped to create our greatest rivalries. What may be the worst part of it all is that the pitcher that drilled him wasn't even on the 2015 team, and nobody celebrates home runs more enthusiastically than the Rangers did.

Aaron Sanchez was pitching in that infamous game. The Rangers pitcher, César Ramos, balked a couple of times and the umpire didn't call it, and Tim Leiper made a scene and was ejected from his first-base coaching spot by crew chief Dale Scott.

An inning or two later, the home plate umpire, Dan Iassogna, missed a couple calls on Sanchy, at least Aaron and I thought so. I started barking at him and he threw me out.

I go join Leip in my office there in Texas, and we both had our shoes off and feet kicked up. We were having a beer and watching the game on TV when they got Jose, so here we go.

Matt Bush was one of the hardest throwers in baseball, so that added to it. Jose paused but then took his base, like he told me he was going to do. Bush left the game to a huge ovation from the Rangers fans. Jose handled it the way they used to a lot of times in the past. Back then, if your guy got drilled, the middle infielders had better watch out because if there is a ground ball, they're going to get knocked on their ass. That's just the way it was, before the commissioner came up with this sliding rule where you can't make contact because one guy got hurt. Watch the old videos: Guys like Hal McRae slide in to break up double plays at second base. Those middle infielders got smoked. They learned how to play that position and learned how to get out of the way.

The ground ball hit by Justin Smoak was a simple enough ball for a double play, and Bautista goes into second hard, but didn't really get Odor, who leaped in the air. Bautista gets up, looks at Odor and Odor shoves him, Bautista shoves back and then Odor clocks him — but Jose stayed up! He wobbled, but he stayed up. Then all hell broke loose.

Leip and I were chilling in the clubhouse, and neither one of us had shoes on. I throw mine on real quick, he goes out in flip-flops. We head out to the field just to help police it, to break it up. Next thing you know, the brawl is moving towards right centerfield and we're out there trying to break it up. Their manager, Jeff Banister, is a big dude and always in the middle of stuff like that.

Finally, they broke it up, and as we were heading off the field, Banister and I were jawing at each other, and we each had some players around us. I called him gutless. As he was going off the field, he was inciting the crowd like he was at a pro wrestling show. Brutal.

I did *not* go out for the second brawl, where our pitcher, Jesse Chavez, hit Prince Fielder. Jesse got tossed and so did DeMarlo Hale, who'd taken over for me.

The media asked me after the game what I thought of it. I used "gutless" again, said that if you're going to do something, do it early on. Jose had some comments too.

Any time you have a big brawl, it can be a uniting moment, but this team didn't need that, we were close.

What was odd about that brawl was, in baseball, you very rarely see punches thrown. Not like hockey. Usually it starts with the hitter at the plate, depending on whether he really wants to go get the pitcher or not, he'll start jawing at the pitcher and then the benches empty. He waits until everybody grabs him before he goes towards the mound. That's when you know that guy doesn't want any part of that pitcher.

But occasionally, guys will charge right away. There's usually not a whole lot of punches thrown, but a lot of chest-bumping. We had a brawl later that year with the Yankees, and it lost us a pretty good reliever, Joaquín

Benoit, and then we didn't have him in the playoffs that year. Brawls were costly to us.

When we got back to Toronto, they started handing out the fines and suspensions. The rule in baseball is if you're ejected from the game, and if you're in the clubhouse, if something happens on the field, an altercation, you cannot go back out on the field. What I didn't know is that the rule applies to coaches and managers as well. How stupid is that? Don't you want them out there trying to police things and calm things down? They do so many dumb things in the game that make no sense.

I'd actually done the same thing the year before, where I was ejected but came back out. So I got a fine and was suspended for a game in 2015.

After the Rangers brawl, I got a fine of $4,500 and a three-game suspension, which was almost the same thing Odor got for throwing the punch — he was fined $5,000 and got eight games. Banister didn't get fined at all. I'm not even out there, I go to try to break things up, and I get fined almost as much as the guy that threw the punch.

Joe Torre was in charge of the fines at the time, so I called him up, as we'd always gotten along. "Joe, what's this? I didn't throw a punch." I was a peacekeeper.

He reminded me that I'd done the same thing the year before, so they wanted to come down a little harder on me. I argued that you needed the coaches and managers out there helping to control things.

I noted how Banister was inciting the crowd, and he didn't get fined. Joe said, "Don't you worry about who I fine. Just take care of your own."

Jim Leyland was working for the league as an advisor. I'd gotten to know Jimmy over the years, and we became friends. He was the best manager in the game when he was active, hands down. I would pick his brain every chance I could, and I learned a lot. He looks like this mean ol' guy, but he's the funniest — boy, can he tell some jokes!

I told Jimmy about my penalty, and he couldn't believe it either. "It seems a little stiff to me," he said, and noted that he was going to New York the next day anyway for some meetings. "Let me see what I can do."

The following day, I was at my desk in my office in Toronto, and the phone rang. It was Torre.

He goes, "We're going to cut your fine in half."

"So, I'm half guilty, huh?"

He laughed, and said, "Hold on a minute."

He put it on speakerphone, and in the background Leyland was laughing. Jimmy went to work for me and got my fine cut in half. The game misses guys like Leyland, another one of the true characters of baseball.

I was still suspended three games, and Leip got a single game. The rule is that you can go to the ballpark, but you can't be down by the field or in the clubhouse at game time. I was out there for BP. No interactions during the game. Instead of managing and coaching, Leip and I got to sit in the President's suite at the Rogers Centre during the game. The team president and the GM have it made. We sat out on the balcony and watched our game and the Raptors game on TV. They brought us food, drinks, everything. I lived like a king for three days. Heck, I want to be the team president, not the manager.

In the end, we expected to see the Rangers again — likely in the playoffs.

We were playing good solid baseball, but the offense wasn't as dominating as it was in 2015. In 2016, it was our pitching that was holding us together.

The Canada Day Weekends in Toronto were always fun affairs. It's a day game, since it's a national holiday, and there's a big, patriotic crowd. It's always a great day. But one Canada Day game stands out for me, and it was this year's. The game went 19 long-ass innings, and I watched 18 of them from the clubhouse.

Big Eddie very rarely complained to the umpires. Josh and Jose did that for him. They kept the umps on their toes and were right a lot of the time but not always. But if Eddie was complaining, you knew something was definitely missed.

I don't think home plate umpire Vic Carapazza ever really liked us — we pissed him off or something. Cleveland had Josh Tomlin on the mound; he had great control, but Carapazza was giving him every pitch you could imagine off the plate. He called strike three on Eddie, and Eddie just snapped. I went out there and he chucked me and Eddie. Son of a bitch, 1st inning. I went into the clubhouse, kicked back and watched it on TV — and Carapazza kept up the terrible calls. He tossed Russell Martin in the 13th for arguing with him. How can you toss a Canadian on Canada Day? It ended after 19 innings, a 2-1 loss.

DeMarlo took over as the manager, and he had to pitch two of our position players, Ryan Goins and Darwin Barney. There are times you'll see one position player throw in a game, but very rarely do you ever see two. That was a long-ass day. I was the luckiest guy there, being able to watch it from the couch. And to be honest, I may have taken a couple cat naps.

I made DeMarlo talk to the media. He resisted at first, but that was my rule on the days I got ejected. "No, you're going down to that media room. They're going to interview you. You were out there. I saw it on TV." And I argued that he deserved to be a major league manager and it was good practice for him.

As the season progressed, I tried to look out for my players, to see who was really feeling the grind. A veteran is going to be different than a young kid. I always checked with the veterans and said, "Listen, if you're a little banged up, and you need a day, you need to tell me. I've got no problem giving you a day off." If I asked them the day before, they'd let me know the following morning.

On August 17, we were in Yankee Stadium, and CC Sabathia was pitching for them.

This particular day, Josh was a little banged up and I suggested taking a day off, but he said, "I'll be all right." I told him he'd be the DH then. Sabathia was always tough on Josh, and it was a day game after a night game, and everybody was tired. It was the dog days of August and obviously I should have given him the day off.

In Josh's first at-bat, he goes up there and strikes out. You can see that he's pissing and moaning. Ah, great. While he's complaining in the dugout, I'm thinking to myself that I'd told him to take a day off and now he's acting like this.

That second at-bat, he strikes out again. I'd always stand by the railing where they go down the stairs at Yankee Stadium. He went by me, almost foaming at the mouth in anger. He took the bat and whammed it against the bar I was leaning on, right next to me. I followed him down, thinking, "This ain't happening."

We met by the bat rack. I called him on his bullshit, told him never again, and where to stick his bat.

Tulo was always the guy to keep the peace, and he'd be willing to get in the middle of stuff for the good of the team. Josh and I jawed back and forth, and Tulo pulled us apart.

After the game I explained to the media my side of having to get up close to him, but Josh delivered a beauty: "I was just coming back to the dugout and hit my bat against the [wall], and Gibby asked me what kind of cologne I was wearing," Donaldson told reporters. "I said, 'It's this new cologne called Tom Ford, I just got it.'"

We moved on from that. I love the kid to death, one of my all-time favorites, but he was a handful.

August itself was a good month, as we went 17-11, and in September, things slowed down a little. What was interesting and cool about the 2016 Jays is there wasn't a lot of rah, rah. They rooted for each other, they were very intense, but when they were playing the games, they were locked in. A lot of times when the team's not very good, you get that vocal "rah, rah" stuff, and it ain't working.

But there's something different when a team's really, really pulling for each other and truly cares about each other. You see it, and it's just a different feeling. We had a lot of big characters on our team too. It's easy to go the other direction, some high-maintenance guys. But they could focus when they needed to.

Now we were competing for that Wild Card spot. We knew it was going to go down to the end, that final series in Boston, who took the AL East. We had to win in Boston to even get in the playoffs. Boston has always been a tough place to play. They've always had such a good team, and it's tough to win there and the crowd's always into it. But I felt good, I believed in our team, our guys were ready and they knew it. We knew it was going to go down to the wire, but they rose to the occasion, with Sanchez carrying a no-hitter into the 7th inning in a 2–1 win.

We finished tied with Baltimore, but took home field since we won the season series, 10 games to 9. Playing at home on October 4 is a big deal. Home field gives you the crazy home crowd and the last at-bat. Plus we were really tough at home and our dome could be suffocating to the other team . . . just ask the Rangers after Game 5 in 2015.

I'm not a traditionalist when it comes to playoffs, and I love it with more teams — as long as winning the division means the most. If you prevail through 162 games, that says something. It's hard to do.

Now, for true fairness, there should be a more balanced schedule. In the AL East, like it or not, the Red Sox and Yankees have the most resources. They always have the largest payrolls, they sign the top free agents and more of them, and their fanbases make them do it. Without crying, I'll say it makes it tough when you play them so often. So instead of playing them 18 times a year, cut that in half and play the teams in the other divisions more often. I think that's how they used to do it. It's the only way to get a true Wild Card winner.

If there are more teams in the playoffs — and there're more now than when I last managed — there should be more do-or-die games for anybody who didn't win their division. It's the luck of the draw or a roll of the dice, you get a one-game playoff — and maybe the best team doesn't always win, but that's why it's so important to win the division outright. There's something about that one-game playoff — 2016 against Baltimore was the first time I was in one — but it was like, damn, this is intense. There's no tomorrow. I loved it. It's like Game 7, or even Game 5.

We knew Baltimore as well as anybody, and they knew us. You see the guys in your own division so often (as we talked about earlier) that there are no secrets any longer. We've both seen everything and everybody, so now it's who plays better on that particular day. In a normal length series, where you've got a few games to play with, you might go with your starter a little bit longer, and you still have some strategy with your bullpen. But not in a do-or-die game. You'd better not wait too long or it's over.

The big thing was, going into that game, I can remember talking with the coaching staff and the front office, saying, "Who are we going to pitch?" If Stroman was available, he was probably going to be our guy. But we also threw Francisco Liriano's name in there because he'd been so tough on Baltimore. They had more trouble against lefties than righties, and Liri seemed to own them. There was a little bit of debate there, but Stro was our guy: He rose to the occasion the year before. He was a big-game guy. You wanted him out there. But I can even remember going to Russell Martin to get his thoughts — that shows you how savvy Russ was and how much we leaned on him. Stro pitched very well and so did Chris Tillman, Baltimore's starter. Now it's a bullpen game and one that is still talked about and probably always will be. Both bullpens held each team in check until the 11th inning. Not only was this a winner-take-all-game, but it went into extra innings. Talk about tension and drama. With the score tied 2-2 in the 11th, Orioles manager Buck Showalter brought in Ubaldo Jiménez, and that's where the major second-guessing started. Now, when I say Ubaldo was tough, I mean he was tough. This ought to tell you something: I think Bautista was something like 2 for 40-something life-time against him, and our other guys weren't a whole lot better. Now that's crazy, considering how many good hitters we had. But he had our number. That's how baseball works sometimes. There's always a pitcher or a hitter that owns you or it may be a team that gets you all the time, and vice versa. Makes no sense, that's just the way it is. Then it probably becomes mental or maybe it's just the baseball gods again.

I knew exactly what Buck was doing — at least I think I did — putting Ubaldo in there instead of Zack Britton. He obviously knew what Ubaldo had done against us in the past, so that made sense, and then Britton was available for the save. I'm telling you, when Ubaldo came into the game, I went, "Ah, crap."

Then Eddie hit the big walk-off homer. I told you I missed the bat flip in '15. I also missed Eddie's blast this time around since I was looking at some stats. But I sure heard it.

I had some sympathy for Buck and all the people questioning his call. In fact, I have a lot of sympathy and understanding for every guy that has managed in major league baseball. There's all the scrutiny. You have a lot of control, but you have no control.

It's easy after the fact to say, "You should have done this, you should have done that," but people don't always understand what led into the decision. Now it's different in the postseason, winner-take-all. No doubt about it.

After the Wild Card Game, Buck went in for the media stuff first, and we shook hands when he was on his way out, and he wished us luck. Classy guy.

It was a quick turnaround, but up next were those Rangers.

I was short on words before we started the ALDS. I've never liked managers or coaches that talked a lot in those settings. The players are champing at the bit — they know what they've got to do. They're already really good to have gotten to this point. The time for talking is over.

Before the games, we'd have our meetings, going over the teams, the players, how we're going to position them and all that kind of stuff. But as far as motivational type talk, I just wished them luck.

I always said, "Have some fun with this, boys. It's hard getting here. No doubt it's pressure, but have some fun with it."

And the series against Texas, which started on October 6, was going to be fun and very intense. Neither team liked each other but did respect each other. And now is not the time to get even, unless maybe we're gasping for air and desperate. Just kidding.

You're only as good as that day's pitcher is. If your guy's good, you've got a shot; if he's not, you're probably in trouble.

Estrada was awesome, going eight and one-third innings, giving up only one run to Elvis Andrus in the 9th; but we had scored five in the 3rd and never looked back, winning 10-1. The next night, both teams sent out two tough veterans, Yu Darvish and J.A. Happ. It was a unique game in the fact that they had 13 hits and scored three runs, while we only had six hits but four of them were big flies accounting for all of our five runs. I guess the phrase "home runs win" is true.

Now it's back home. We were feeling really good, but I wasn't about to forget 2015. Remember, they took the first two at our place, then we dropped that bomb on them, winning three straight. Game 3 was a tight one, going to extras. They weren't going down without a fight. This one was back and forth and ended the best way it possibly could. In the bottom of the 10th, we have first and second, Donaldson on second, with Russell Martin hitting. It was one of the best at-bats you will ever see, especially since the ball didn't leave the infield. Russ kept battling and finally hit one into the 5-6 hole, as we refer to it (between shortstop and third base). If he doesn't put it in play, something great can't happen. Nowadays, nobody cares about strikeouts, but I did, Russell did, and the 2015 Royals sure as heck did. Ball goes to Andrus at shortstop and he throws it to Odor covering second base, trying to complete a double play. The throw to first is low and wide. Donaldson is flying around third (I don't think I ever saw him move so fast) and scores the series-winning run. Unbelievable. At this point, nobody cared about the Bautista-Odor dust-up earlier in the year, except maybe those ol' baseball gods. But we got the last laugh again.

The champagne was flowing in the dressing room. You have to win 11 or 12 games to become World Series champions, so when we did the toast, I reminded them how many more to go: "Great job, eight more!" Everyone cheered, and we celebrated the moment. I sure was proud of those guys.

Up next was the Cleveland team now known as the Guardians.

We knew they were good. What was interesting was that Shapiro and Atkins had just come over from Cleveland. It might have been a mixed kind of series for them, their new team against their old team, and they still had a lot of connections there. They were always winning that division. We knew they had good pitching with Corey Kluber and a couple other guys, and that's the name of the game, but they also had some pretty good hitters.

We started on October 14, at Progressive Field. It was a pitchers duel, with Estrada tossing a complete game, and Kluber getting six and one-third shutout innings until their bullpen took over. We just couldn't score, and we lost 2–0.

Game 2 was almost the same. Happ and Tomlin were both really on, with Cleveland winning 2–1. They had four hits to our three. One thing I knew for sure about my team, was if we didn't hit, we were in trouble. We hit home runs. Live by the sword, die by the sword. But Cleveland could really pitch. We headed home down 0–2.

Trevor Bauer had been originally scheduled to start Game 2 for Cleveland, but he cut a finger while fixing a toy drone. Instead, he was sent up for Game 3 in Toronto.

In our pre-series meeting with the managers, umpires and GMs from each team, it was noted that Bauer had cut his hand. They were going over possibilities. At first they said they didn't even know if they were going to keep him on the roster. The league gave them 30 minutes to decide. The umpires said that if he did pitch, and the finger bled, they would have to remove him from the game.

He started the first game in Toronto, and that finger began bleeding, you could see it. I knew how good he was, but the umpires weren't doing anything. This was early in the game, and my thinking was, if we get to their bullpen early in the game, we might have a better shot at them, and maybe it will affect them the rest of the series if we wear the pen out a little bit.

I finally went up to the umpire and said, "Hey, we had this meeting about blood on the ball — check it out." So they went out there to see, and they took him out of the game after 21 pitches. Whether that mattered or not, who knows. Their bullpen was not lights-out. Still, we lost 4–2, and again, our offense just never got rolling.

In Game 4, we prevented the sweep, winning 5–1. Not much more to say about it.

Bautista had told a reporter that Ryan Merritt, a new guy called up from AAA, who wasn't part of their normal rotation, should be shaking in his boots. Oh no! Never do that, especially when we're staring down elimination. Merritt went out there and shut us down big-time. The baseball gods must have heard it too and they didn't like it either. Merritt's pitching style was the perfect style against us, a soft-tossing finesse pitcher that changed speeds and located very well. We were a unique team, we had very good plate discipline, and yet we were a free-swinging team, and usually those two things don't go together. We had mostly pull-hitters, so the soft throws were usually our kryptonite. Pitchers who were stealth (threw below radar) gave us the most trouble because they kept us off balance. We'd hammer the hard throwers. But if some guy had a really good breaking ball or changeup, those are the guys that year that gave us trouble for some reason. And so this guy just fed right into that, he'd change speeds and get us out front, and he shut us down. Merritt rose to the occasion and never rattled.

Jose made those comments, and I was hoping he was right. Thinking, *Maybe in the moment we'll get to this kid, and he won't be real sharp,* that we'll hit around early and if we win this game, we're right back in this thing. But the kid was dynamite. I tip my hat to him. He was fantastic — in control that game. Merritt didn't last long in the majors though. Our 3–0 loss was a disappointing end, doubly so because Game 5 was at the Rogers Centre. Cleveland always had pitching that was tough on us anyway. They had some of the best in the game at that time. So the fact that we didn't score, I mean, it wasn't like, gosh, we're supposed to score off these guys. No, I mean, they were pretty damn good. They shut a lot of good hitters down all year long. Then the Guardians had that historic World Series against the Cubs in 2016, both teams trying to end long droughts. Cleveland had a 3–1 game lead against Chicago, and the Cubbies came back. Crazy things happen. You think you've got it right there and all of a sudden it evaporates. That's the beauty of baseball: you never know.

I said it earlier, but I really thought we were going to win it all in 2015. In 2016, I didn't know because it was a different type of team, basically the same guys, but things weren't clicking as easily as they did in '15. We had to scratch and claw just to get in. That 2016 team was always a mystery. We never really got going offensively like we thought we would, but we were still good, don't get me wrong, but we weren't as dominating as the year before.

Baseball is such a streaky game. You get on these rolls, good or bad, and the worst thing you can do is try to overanalyze things. What am I doing right here? Or, what am I doing wrong?

If you're on a roll as a hitter, two or three hits a night, I always tell the guys, "Don't think about it, man. Just roll with it. If you start analyzing it now, you'll overthink things and screw it up."

Same way with a pitcher, it's just baseball. When things are going well, ride the wave but know that it won't last. And when it changes, don't panic, that wave will be back. Same way with teams, you get on these nice streaks, but you also know it's never that easy. That's why baseball is so tough, so many ups and downs. But one thing is for sure, the good players and the good teams don't stay in the lows quite as long. And never forget, you need a little luck too.

In the clubhouse after Game 5, I didn't say much. I knew they were all feeling down and exhausted. We all replay things over and over in our minds, the what ifs, but they needed to know that they did one hell of a job, and that not only did I enjoy the ride, but so did all of Canada. Short and quick. I owe those guys, they made my career.

Gibby's Greats: Chris Colabello

One bat we missed in 2016 was that of Chris Colabello.

Coming out of Division II Assumption University, in Worcester, Massachusetts, Chris Colabello wasn't drafted and is Exhibit A when it comes to the term journeyman in baseball. From the Independent League to the minors, he'd been good, but not dominating. The

Twins finally gave him a shot in 2013 and '14 but never made him their guy.

In December 2014, the Jays claimed Chris off waivers. With us, he did some amazing things.

He was such a good hitter, that's where we benefited the most. He could give the team a lift when we needed it. He played some first base, and he was good over there, but we were forced to play him some in the outfield, and that didn't work out well. He wasn't suited for outfield.

Colabello was just such a good guy; he fit in, he mixed with everybody. Everybody loved him — and the sucker could hit. He got some big hits in the 2015 playoffs.

We had him penciled in for much of the same in 2016, and then in April, MLB announced that Chris had been suspended for 80 games after testing positive for performance-enhancing drugs in March. What, he's on the juice? Look at him!

I talked to Chris a couple of times when he was in the middle of that, because you care about the kid. But we all learn the hard way, like it or not, that the game goes on with or without us. Selfishly, we think it won't, but it does. He got nailed, right or wrong, but it doesn't diminish some of the great things he did for us.

17.

FAMILY

Players often mentioned that I was a family-first manager, which included both my family and theirs. I tried to make an effort to learn about their kids and wives not only because it interested me but because I knew it was the most important thing in their lives. This job is tough enough as it is, and if things aren't good at home, it's even harder.

I don't think all clubs or even managers allow kids in the clubhouse, but I felt it was important the kids could hang out with Dad and see what he did all day. Plus, I wanted mine in there, so what's good for one is good for all.

Today, I still keep in touch with many people from baseball, and it's nice to hear when everything in their lives is great, especially with their families. I have to talk about my number one fan, other than my mother: my grandmother, Mary Boyson, who we called Nana. She was a huge Red Sox fan, having lived her whole life in Boston. My grandfather, who had also been a semi-pro catcher, died when he was 62, before I got into pro ball. I reminded her of Grampy, so I think my career helped her reminisce about earlier days.

Nana made this beautiful scrapbook from newspaper articles she got a hold of and wrote notes around them in really cool block lettering. The ticket stub from a game against the Expos on Thursday, April 19, 1984, is in there, and she noted how I'd gotten "Charlie Hustle" out: "Took good care of super star Pete Rose." You know she remembers the 1975 World Series when Rose's Cincinnati Reds beat the Red Sox.

I made sure she got to see me play, and she wrote: "I finally got to Shea as John said I would. One of the biggest thrills of my life. Had a great time with John after game & next A.M. He is the best & I am so proud. Good luck John & keep it up. I will always admire you on or off the field. Your most fantastic fan, Love Nana."

When I was in AAA in Tidewater, we played some games on the East Coast, up to Rhode Island and Maine. My cousins and my Aunt Mary would always bring Nana out to the games, and I'd get a chance to see all of them. I have such a great extended family throughout New England that will do anything for you. Hard to believe that's where my roots are, huh? Especially the way I promote Texas.

So when I was hired as a coach and then manager of the Blue Jays, we'd go play at Fenway, and they'd all come out. It must have been tough switching allegiances from the Red Sox, but she did, wearing her Jays hat and shirt. The great local sports writer Rob Bradford kept up with us and wrote some neat stuff about our relationship.

As she got older and couldn't get to the games, I would rent a car and drive up to Beverly, on the North Shore, to visit her. Nana lived to age 99. My last visit is burned in my memory. As I drove up, I had been feeling sick, like I had the flu. She was living on her own, but in a retirement complex. We waved at each other, blew each other a kiss when she stuck her head out the window. That was the last time I saw her.

I always wanted kids and thought three would be a good number — probably because of growing up with my own brother and sister. I met Julie MacFarlane during the offseason in San Antonio, where she was attending Texas State just up the road. We dated, got married in 1987, had our kids: Jordan in 1992; Troy in 1994; Kyle in 1999.

Jordan was born just as I started coaching, and I wasn't making a lot of money. It didn't cross my mind whether we could afford a family. Looking back, I do wonder how we managed without quitting or hitting a breaking point. It was always in the back of my mind: *I've got a family now. I've got to provide, I've got to do whatever it takes, I've got to make something out of this.* My father set a great example.

I'm very family oriented. Family is important to me. But so is baseball. I was always excited for spring training and a new season, but I hated leaving my kids. When I first started managing, I would always head to spring training at least a week or 10 days before it started to give me extra time to set up and acclimate. But as I got older and missed my kids so much, I would do the same but would intentionally get a refundable ticket and inevitably cancel it to stay a couple extra days at home.

There was separation anxiety, no doubt, especially when I got to the airport. Kyle always had a tougher time with me leaving, since he was the youngest and hadn't lived through it like Jordan and Troy. Kyle would cry, and that would make me break down. They all learned to deal with it in their own way. Their dad just had a different job than the dads of their friends. But it didn't affect them too much, since they've all grown up and are wonderful adults.

I was always conscious of and wondered how the amount of time I was gone would affect them. Calling home every day wasn't just routine — I needed it.

Then when I was home in the offseason, after a little time to decompress, I was involved. I loved taking them to school. When they got a little bit older and played sports, I helped where I could. Troy got into tennis, so I took him to the courts; Kyle got into baseball, basketball and football; and Jordan and I kicked the soccer ball around.

I don't remember what year it was, but the day after I got home from the season, Troy wanted to go play catch in the backyard. We hadn't played in a while, and he was still young and had a little bit of fear of the ball. He'd have his glove off to the side, so if he missed it, the ball wouldn't hit him. So I gave him a bit of a demo: "Alright kid, this is what you've got to do. If I throw it right at you, just put your glove up right here," I raised my glove in front of my face, "and catch it. If I throw it over here, just turn your glove and catch it like this." First one I threw went right at him. He put his glove up — Dad knows best, right? — and it went over the top of his glove and hit him right between the eyes. He threw his glove down and started bawling, ran in to mom. The next day, he was black and blue, but still had to go to school. Sorry, kid. Maybe that was when he decided to be a tennis player! I don't blame him.

Kyle is the one who took to baseball, but it wasn't without incident either. The family came up to Toronto, and Kyle was still fairly young but could handle a glove pretty well. Luis Rivera, the third-base coach, had Kyle out fielding ground balls. The second one Rivera hit caught a seam on the carpet, took a bad hop, *wham*, right into Kyle's noggin. Blood running pretty good. I assured Kyle that he'll look as good as new since he's probably in the best country in the world to have your nose fixed — you have to with all the hockey. If not, he can always hide behind a catcher's mask like his old man. They set it and it looked great, and then a month later, when he was back home in San Antonio, he was playing football with his buddies and he took an elbow to the nose and it broke again. He's still as handsome as ever — he'd better be, since everyone says he's my clone, Mini-Me.

My kids got to live a pretty good life, a little bit spoiled as far as big league baseball goes. They would come into the clubhouse — especially Troy and Kyle, Jordan couldn't when the players were around — and my players always looked after them. They'd take them to the cafeteria and load them up with ice cream, cookies, chips, you name it . . . all the good stuff that's bad for you. They still talk about it. Since they basically grew up around big-league ballplayers, it wasn't a big deal to them. They were just friends to my kids, whereas when I was that age, I would die to get a Johnny Bench bubblegum card.

Now, there's some Ba Humbugs out there too. During my first tour of duty, my family met me in New York on a road trip. We were walking around Manhattan on our way to a department store. There are Yankee clothing stores everywhere. Kyle's birthday was coming up, so he said, "Dad, can I get a Jeter jersey for my birthday?" Derek Jeter was his favorite player, like most kids, so I said, "Sure, great idea." He couldn't wait to put it on. We got to the department store and Kyle and I sat on a couch while everybody else did some shopping. While we were sitting there, I guess a fan from Toronto must have noticed us, and apparently they disliked Jeter. Supposedly they notified one of our higher-ups and complained. Really? Were we at the ballpark? Maybe they were jealous that they didn't have one. We were on the plane home the next day and J.P. came up to me and asked, "Did Kyle have a Jeter T-shirt on yesterday?" Not thinking anything was wrong, I said, "Kyle wanted one for his birthday since he loves Jeter." J.P. warned, "You're not going to believe this." "Try me." "Some asshole sent an email to someone with clout and they want me to fire you." "Seriously?" "Yes." "Over a Jeter T-shirt? Go for it. I'll have a field day with this one." J.P. said, "No way, it'll go away." I'm thinking, *If you want me out that bad, I'll quit instead, but at least tell me you hate Texas and not Jeter.*

Then I told J.P., "If I get fired for that, make sure whoever is in charge of our Blue Jays stadium souvenir shop gets fired for selling Red Sox and Yankees stuff in our home stadium. Better yet, whoever is in charge of the tickets for the owner's box right next to our dugout, make sure they get it, too, because there's nights people are sitting there with Red Sox or Yankees stuff on. What's fair is fair." Nothing ever came of it, but it just shows you that if they want your head bad enough, some people will try anything. Just go ahead and do it. I guess I could understand if it had been me wearing it — I loved Jeter too.

Things just happen in New York, the city that never sleeps. As you can tell, my family loved visiting there. After one trip, it was time for them to head home early on a Sunday morning. They had an early flight, so were waiting for a car service in the lobby. In walks two of our players around 6 a.m., and we have a 1 p.m. game. They knew my kids, so they begged them, "You can't tell your dad! Promise us you won't!" What do you think my kids did? Blood is thicker than water. But they didn't tell me until later that night. The evening out didn't hurt our players one bit. One of them had a big game, but I wouldn't recommend that type of training.

My favorite Kyle and New York story happened on another family visit. Julie, Jordan and Troy didn't want to go to the game; they wanted to cruise Manhattan and see *The Lion King*. So Kyle came with me to Yankee Stadium. Now I should get paid for this babysitting duty. He was still young enough that you needed to keep an eye on him, but you could still occupy him with coloring books and cartoons. During BP, I was talking to reporters and Kyle was standing near the batting cage, flipping balls in the air while the Yankees hit. Next thing you know, Jeter finished his round then goes over to Kyle and starts talking with him. Now Kyle's in heaven. You wonder why Jeter is thought of so highly, he has time for everyone. But here's the good part. During the game, Kyle can't be on the bench, obviously, so he's got to stay in the manager's office. Now this is old Yankee Stadium, the Cathedral of Baseball. The visiting manager's office is real small, but it has a TV on the wall, a desk and a couch. The best part is they always kept a full basket of candy handy. I told Kyle to sit at the desk and color in the book we brought, and he could watch cartoons on TV. The great Lou Cucuzza, who ran the visiting clubhouse, said he'd keep a good eye on him. We blew the lead late in the game and suffered a tough loss. I headed to my office all pissed off. I opened the door and there's Kyle coloring and watching SpongeBob with candy wrappers all over the desk and floor. He ate them all! We got on our hands and knees to clean up the wrappers before the reporters arrived. We got done in time, and I told him to go sit on the toilet, right behind the desk, with the door closed. After I finished the media scrum, I opened the door and he had this big ol' grin from ear to ear. The loss wasn't so bad after all. I just laughed and thought, *This is what life's all about*. That's my favorite Kyle baseball story. I still laugh.

My kids got to see how players in the big-time sports world live. It's not the real world, but it sure is nice — but you need to check yourself every now and then and humble yourself.

My three kids were all able to fly on a chartered team flight, which is the ultimate in traveling. Troy even got to sit in the cockpit jump seat for a takeoff. After that, I thought he might try aviation when he got older; instead he got his master's at the University of Texas business school then headed to the Big Apple to start his life.

To show how good we had it, for my first All-Star Game invite to Pittsburgh, Troy Glaus rented a private jet to fly the players selected to the game. Not bad, huh? And the best part was Troy flew with us. For my All-Star Game in New York, Paul Beeston rented us a plane to fly back to Toronto, and this time Kyle got to go. And talk about icing on the cake, when we got back, the team had a suite in the dome for the Jay-Z and Justin Timberlake concert. Doesn't get much better than that, but I might have dozed off a few times. I'm too old for that music.

My mom's three favorite players were Josh Donaldson, Vernon Wells and Colby Rasmus . . . and Jerry Howarth, but he wasn't a player. We were playing in Houston one time, and she came down with my family to see her kid. This was the year Colby was with us. So I go to the park and make out the lineup, and Colby's in it. We start getting near BP time and Colby's not there yet. His family was also in town, so I get it. Finally, it gets to the point where I say, screw it, and put someone else in. Colby gets there and I told him I was sitting him, and he said that was fine. Later that night, I get back to the hotel and see my mom. She was so excited. She said, "Guess who I met today?" It was Colby. Mom was raving about him: "What a beautiful family. They're delightful. He even took some pictures with us." It turned out they were all at a nearby mall. It was probably my mom's fault he was late. Nice going, Mom. The Jays were always wonderful to all our families. They really went out of their way. Marnie Starkman and her crew are unsung heroes of that organization, and every player and their families who spent time there owe them a debt of gratitude. We always had some cool guests throwing out the first pitch. One night, Josh Donaldson's mom got to do it and it was a fun sight to see. The only problem was that my own mother was watching that night on TV. I think she got jealous. Next thing I know, *my* mother is telling me that she wants to do it. Well, a manager has a little pull, so let's see what I can do. I had always told her I would buy her a Corvette if I made it to the big leagues, so if I can get her to throw out the first pitch, maybe she'll forget the 'Vette. She came up with three of her grandkids and just had the greatest time. I did warn her: "Mother, don't do anything to embarrass me." Mom's pitch was a strike, and I should know since I caught it. Then she sat in the dugout and was interviewed by the media. My mom's a hoot and she had a wonderful time, and still talks about it.

Jordan didn't get as much access, being a girl, as her brothers did, but she still did some pretty cool stuff. Every year, there's a Country Weekend at the dome, and on the Sunday a band performs between innings up on the flight deck. Jordan is a very talented musician, and the Blue Jays invited her band, Southtown, to perform. What a thrill for them and her old man. They were awesome. Her band had been playing originals and covers around San Antonio, so this was a big jump, playing to a crowd of 40,000. There goes the Blue Jays entertainment staff again . . . thanks Marnie!

Not only that, they got to perform the night before at the legendary Horseshoe Tavern on May 27, opening up for the Rheostatics and our good friend, Dave Bidini.

So the morning of the big day, we headed down to get the car with all their stuff, and we couldn't find the keys. Everyone was in a panic since we were running late. I'm thinking, great, they're going to blow this great opportunity over lost car keys. But one of them found the keys in the condo. We laugh now, but I was looking around for something to break the window to get their gear out and rush to the ballpark — whatever it took, get 'er done. Southtown's performance couldn't have gone better.

Jordan has since moved to Austin and started a new band called The Barrens. They've made some attempts in Nashville, with the help of an old roommate and co-podcaster, John Arezzi, who was managing country artists.

But my favorite Jordan moment was when she wrote a note on a whiteboard behind my desk when I wasn't around that said, "Go get 'em, Dad. We love you." That stayed on the board and spurred us on to win the division for the first time since 1993. Sounds a lot better than the ship is sinking, play for yourself.

We love music in our family and one of my favorite bands growing up in San Antonio was Rush — they were big down there. Geddy Lee, the lead singer, is also a huge baseball fan and knows the game as much as anybody. Jordan and I were fortunate to have lunch with him, set up by that other great rock 'n' roller who I mentioned earlier, Dave Bidini. Big Dave will do anything for you, and he's another big Blue Jays fan. Geddy is a huge baseball collector and he gave me a Rush Hall of Fame ball signed by all three members. Now that's a keepsake.

Having been around baseball, I can say without question the wives are the heroes. To have a husband in professional sports, and be a wife and take care of a family, that's rough. As the player, not only are you worried about the impact being away will have on your kids over the long run, but you wonder how fair you are being to your spouse. Julie had to be the bad cop, the disciplinarian, so when I was home, whether for a day or for the offseason, I could be Fun Dad. But bottom line, she married me, I've got to make a living. They weren't knocking down my door offering me jobs in the real world.

Julie and I were married 32 years, but if you do the math, I was only there for half of those, total. It was her call to settle in one location so our kids could put down roots and make friends, and it was the right decision. I was a guy that believed you always gut it out. We grew apart, and got divorced. There's a lot that I don't want to get into, but she gave me the three best kids, and I thank her for that. I couldn't be more proud of all three, and I hope they feel the same about ol' Dad.

In the spring of 2020, while in Houston on a scouting trip, I met a wonderful woman named Christi. She's a treasure. Right after meeting, the pandemic hit, so I just stayed in Houston to try and romance her. I guess it worked, we ended up married. She has adult twin boys, Jack and Jake, and has a great family like I do.

Family is the most important thing in my life, like it is for most baseballers. Families sacrifice much more than we players and coaches do. A writer once asked me about the number of games my teams had won in my career, and I told him I was proud of my teams and my baseball career, but that I hoped my life has been more than that. I know for a fact my win-loss record won't be on my tombstone. I hope it reads, "Loving son, husband, father and friend who always gave his best and tried to help make the world a little bit better."

18.

THE INEVITABLE FALL

Since we know what's coming — no manager lasts forever — I want to talk about Toronto itself.

First off, what a way to go out — with my own day . . . dedicated by the mayor himself:

> Whereas today marks the last home game for John Gibbons, who became manager of the Toronto Blue Jays for the second time, on November 20, 2012. He has won 791 games as the Jays manager, achieving his 500th managerial win on June 22, 2015.
>
> Under John's coaching and leadership, the Jays have had two very thrilling and memorable playoff runs, ending their 22-year playoff drought in 2015 when they were crowned American League East Division Champions.
>
> John Gibbons is considered a player's manager who has earned the respect of his colleagues and Blue Jays fans in Toronto and across Canada.
>
> Today on John Gibbons Day, I would like to thank "Gibby" and celebrate his tremendous contributions to the Toronto Blue Jays franchise and to our great city.

Now therefore, I, Mayor John Tory, on behalf of Toronto City Council, do hereby proclaim September 26, 2018, as "John Gibbons Day" in the City of Toronto.

The Jays also presented me with a framed photo of the proclamation with a ticket stub, and it's hanging in my memorabilia room. I really don't have much that I have kept from my lifetime in baseball. There're some photos of myself over the years, shots of family at games or events, a large 1986 Mets reunion photo done at a big autograph show. I've got a spot for some bats; none are game-used, but still, they are special: Albert Pujols' 600th home run, signed to Kyle Gibbons; George Brett, signed to "Kyle a future Hall of Famer on and off the field. Your pal George Brett"; Dustin Pedroia, AL MVP; Josh Donaldson, from when he was MVP, in 2015; and Eric Hosmer, who was Kyle's new favorite player after meeting him during my time in KC (Sorry, Jeter, kids can be fickle.)

Toronto was a pretty special place.

When I first started coaching there, I had the usual worries that being in Canada was going to be a big deal, since it's a different country, the immigration crap, the taxes. Players, who get paid a lot more, think that too. They think it'll all be a big hassle, but it's not. They find that out pretty quickly. I have never spoken with anybody that, after they finished playing in Toronto, did not like it. In fact, they loved it. Zero complaints. Their families enjoyed it there, the people were good to them. The values of the whole country fit most guys. Once they realize, damn, this is really what it's all about, what it's like, they all enjoy it. You might have a couple of disgruntled guys, but they are just pissed off at the world anyway.

It was a rough start for me in Toronto. I had to shack up with the pitching coach, sleep on the couch, but I could walk to the park. Son of a gun, this is not that easy. Quit complaining, I was in the big leagues. After a couple months, I realized that I really liked the city.

I hate to insult the Canadians reading this book, but I'm like you in a lot of ways.

Then I got my first chance to manage, things didn't go particularly well, and the fans didn't take to me. I was thinking, *They just don't care for Americans*, but I knew better. The team stunk and I can't sugarcoat that, and I represented the team. I don't think my boy J.P. Ricciardi was liked any better than I was. I think they tied us together, which is true. He brought me in and hired me. J.P. is one of the best baseball minds I know and a great person. But don't forget, he's from Boston, and Bostonians wear it on their sleeves. They'll tell you what they think whether you like it or not. I tell everybody I'm from Texas, but actually my blood's from Boston, that's the asshole in me.

I said to my wife many times, "I don't think anyone here likes me." She might have replied, "Can you blame them?" It's like all professional sports, it comes down to winning and the production on the field. If the team's playing well, everybody loves you. If it's not, nobody likes you. And I thought it was guilt by association.

Then things slowly turned, I changed my attitude and started enjoying the city more, and I fell in love with it.

My second go-round, I treasured it. It was a unique situation, because very rarely do they bring a manager back unless he's won something. Billy Martin is a great example — heck, he managed the Yankees five times, and then in Toronto, Cito Gaston replaced me my first time.

Things were definitely better early on my second try, but when the team started playing well, and when I let my guard down, that's when I truly started appreciating Toronto. But it's no secret, when you're winning, everybody loves you, so you might as well win.

One thing I learned about Canadians, they're good, hard-working, genuine people — not a lot of B.S. They like beer, and they like to have a good time. Not a whole lot of airs about them. Obviously, you get your odd segments in every country, but I thought they were people to be admired. I would always rent a condo in Toronto, though my first two years as a coach I lived with pitching coach Gil Patterson. He had seniority so I slept on the couch and gave him the bed. We lived near the intersection of Church and Wellesley. We'd talk on our way to the park each day, about 30 minutes.

But when I started managing, I found places closer, as I didn't have the energy any longer to walk that far there and back. I've stayed at the Soho and Icon buildings, but my final and favorite spot was the Rosemont on Wellington at John St.

At the Rosemont, I'd get up every morning and would go get coffee. But the big decision coming out of the condo was whether to go left, where there was a Tim Hortons at the end of the block, or right, where there was a Starbucks 30 feet away. I usually went to Tim's. To show you the difference in my two stints managing there, my first go-round, when things weren't going well, I'd walk down to Tim's and people would spot me and look away, kind of like New York City. They recognized me because I was on the TV every night. The only guys friendly to me were a couple homeless guys hanging on that corner. They would ask how the game went the night before and tell me to hang in there. I'd buy them a donut or coffee and then pass them a loonie or toonie. They were my buddies. The second go-round, when we were winning, people would recognize me and smile and say hello. Everyone loves a winner.

When I could, I'd pop home for a family visit, so I often flew commercial on my own. The occasional passenger would recognize me, want to talk baseball and give me their two cents. That was cool. And then you get in the line to go through customs with everybody else, and some people would recognize you, and you'd make baseball small talk with the customs agent. I didn't expect to be shuttled to the front of the line, and I never was.

One time in my first go-round, we were headed to Texas for a series but were scuffling our asses off, and we might have lost seven or eight in a row. But there was an off-day scheduled after the final game, so I arranged to pop home. The plan was to drive home Sunday with my family after the game, spend Monday at home and Tuesday morning catch a flight — there aren't a lot of flights to Toronto, but this still left plenty of time to get back and do all our work. Because of the losing streak, J.P. let me know that team president Paul Godfrey wanted every-one at Rogers Centre for a meeting in the afternoon. He had never done that before. I told J.P. I was going to be in San Antonio, and that my flight got in after lunch — I'd roll the dice and see what happens. I got into Toronto just a little late. I think I flew American, and my baggage carousel was Dallas, Texas, and the carousel right next to it was for a flight from Karachi, Pakistan — and boy did they have a lot of luggage. I was racing to get through customs, but I got stuck in this long line, and they all must have been moving to Toronto because they seemingly had everything they owned with them. I kept looking at my watch. Godfrey wanted us there in 45 minutes. I think he was ready to get rid of me any-way, and this would have been one more reason. Somehow I got through customs, and the Jays had sent a driver, and I got to the stadium with about five minutes to spare.

Everyone in professional sports has many stories like that, racing to get somewhere, or other travel woes.

When I was a coach with the Jays, one time we were in Texas, coming back to Toronto. We had one of those older, heavier planes that airlines used to fly, with three engines on the back. We were taking off from Dallas, but we turned around. Everyone was wondering what was going on. I was sitting near our hitting coach, Mike Barnett, and he had his pilot's license so he started musing. The pilot got on the intercom and said, "We didn't pressurize, we've got to go back down." We landed, and they did what they had to do. We took off down the runway again, and then the pilot put on the brakes, *hard*. It was something else. Finally, we got up in the air, but we were told that we'd be flying low all the way to Toronto. We could see all these storms off in the distance. Then when we landed, something fell off the wing!

One of the perks of professional sports is the first-class travel. We still bitch and moan sometimes because we've been spoiled rotten. We can lose sight of how good we've got it, there's no doubt about it. We create some prima donnas. I've talked to the flight attendants who've also flown with hockey teams, and they say it's totally different. Team management keeps a pretty good grip on what's going on; they are very structured in everything they do: diet, alcohol, everything. Baseball is different, at least we were. It's more like a smorgasbord; we enjoy our traveling, but it was nothing like the '86 Mets, I can assure you of that.

During my early years in Toronto, we flew some older planes that were heavier, so any time we went out to the Left Coast, we would stop to refuel somewhere. Usually, we'd stop in Kansas City, and we loved that. For some reason, we would clear customs there as well. We'd get off our charter, head inside and when we reboarded, there was always a giant barbecue feast waiting for us. KC has the best barbecue around. Mike Shaw would take care of us, especially me.

You want to talk about being an impatient dude, check this out. We finished a series in Tampa one afternoon and we were headed to Anaheim with a day off the next day. I asked Mike Shaw where we were stopping to refuel and he told me it was El Paso. I asked him if they could switch that to San Antonio, which is closer than El Paso yet on the same route. He said, "Let me see if I can pull some strings." He sure did, they switched it up. Approaching San Antonio, you could see the thunderstorms everywhere, so we circled a few times and had about an hour delay in landing. We finally landed and I hopped off to meet my family while they refuelled. I hightailed it out of there and Mike told me later that they had to wait a couple of hours for the weather to clear before heading to Anaheim. Sorry, boys, but I had a great time at home. I can't say enough about my good friend Mike Shaw. He has a thankless job that's vital to the operation of a major league team. I can't tell you how many times he bailed me out, or the players, or the front office, you name it. Whether it's travel, hotels, tickets, anything, he gets it done. He can also be a psychologist, for me anyway.

That's a good cue to get back to stories about managing.

Our offense carried us in 2015, and in 2016, our pitching got us into the playoffs and a big part of it was because we stayed healthy. In 2017, it all caught up with us. In all fairness, we were getting older.

There was a lot of noise contract-wise, as both Eddie and Jose needed new deals. Jose stayed for another year, but Eddie left. I was sad to see him go. Baseball's a business, but we definitely lost more than we added. This was the first signal that change was on its way. We certainly didn't add any impact players — and he's not a guy you could replace anyway. I never heard the full story, but from what I understand, they offered him good money early, but he naturally rejected it, and moved on instead of negotiating. I also understand management's side since in certain circumstances, you can't wait around or you end up with nothing. We ended up signing Kendrys Morales and he did a solid job for us, but he was getting older as well. Kendrys had a great career coming over from Cuba, and he was one of the best people and teammates I've ever been around. Father Time gets us all. We still had our rock Russell Martin catching and signed veteran Jarrod Saltalamacchia for his bat to backup. He never really got it going so we released him, and Luke Maile took over as backup and did a tremendous job. Luke's still out there playing, helping teams win.

In 2017, the master plan was beginning to happen. When you come off back-to-back final fours and you don't make any impact moves, the writing's on the wall. In all fairness, we were getting older, and you don't want to wait too long as an organization. I get that. I thought we had one more good year in us, but guys like Eddie aren't going to sign one-year deals. I was caught in between.

But our goal was to go out there every day and make the most of it. We all knew what was happening. Remember, our job wasn't to put the team together, but to make it work.

On the coaching side, we let assistant hitting coach Eric Owens go. We replaced him with Derek Shelton, an old confidant of Shapiro and Atkins. People asked me if that made me uncomfortable. I said, "Heck no." I would talk to him all the time in past years and really liked Derek. Plus, if the hatchet was going to fall, so be it. This game is definitely the buddy system, but I benefited from that as well. I do see now that they probably envisioned Shelton taking over the team, but that never developed, and he went on to manage the Pirates.

On April 1, I signed a two-year contract extension, with an option for the 2020 season. They were good to me. In baseball, you hear everything. People just talk. Shapiro had mentioned upon his arrival in '15 — to some pretty good sources that I trusted — that he may get rid of me, that he didn't think I'd be a part of their plans and they'd be going in a different direction. It didn't really bother me hearing that, because I knew how the game worked. If you're a new president, and you've got a new GM coming into a new team, especially a first-time GM, you deserve a manager that you're close with or at least one you know. I wasn't that guy. I get along with everybody for the most part. But I'm probably a little more opinionated than they'd anticipated, or maybe than they liked. They were very politically correct. I'm not, so maybe I shocked them with some stuff — I don't know. But they took care of me. I can't complain about that. They let me do my job.

To actually hang in there as long as I did, with a new regime, is kind of unusual.

Put it this way: Because some guys are very flexible, and they want a job so bad, they'll do anything to appease everybody to save themselves. Not me. I figure bosses should know the real person they're getting, not some phony politician. When I say I'm opinionated, I mean I speak my mind as far as what I think the right way to do things is or how baseball ought to be run or how I run the game. But don't ever forget, everyone has a boss, and I knew my place.

On the field, we fell off right from the start in April, and never ever got it going. At the end, we were fourth in the AL East, 76-86. It was tough after being so competitive for a couple of years.

When things start going bad, frustration sets it. It's not just the coaching staff that reads the writing on the wall, the players feel it too. What was once a great team to be a part of isn't any longer. They also understand that in a rebuild, they're probably not part of the plan either. But that's baseball.

Kevin Pillar directed an anti-gay slur at Braves pitcher Jason Motte on May 17. Motte and catcher Kurt Suzuki immediately confronted

Kevin, and the dugouts cleared. Look, a lot of inexcusable stuff is said on baseball fields in the heat of the moment, and it happens in every sport. But now with all the TV cameras and the microphones everywhere, you're not getting away with anything. Not that you should. Kevin apologized immediately and took his two-day suspension without protest. He slipped up. Nobody felt worse than he did.

The season limped along. It felt a lot like the past did. One thing about coaching staff and players, we're well aware of what's going on, what players are up against, a team's reality at the time . . . it's so hard to win anyway. But you don't change your attitude. You don't accept losing, and you don't accept things the way they are, but you also have to be careful to not let it eat at you as much. Some guys have a hard time doing that, and they destroy themselves. Sometimes it's good to step back and take a realistic view of things.

Everybody starts the season optimistic. Coaches sometimes believe they can produce miracles. Occasionally, you'll have some teams in whatever sport that come out of nowhere, that nobody expected anything from — but that's kind of rare, and it's even more rare in baseball because you play so many damn games. A couple teams overachieve every year, and a couple teams underachieve, but other than that, everybody really finds their level. You never lose your competitive edge, you never lose your desire, your optimism or the thought that if we get on a nice little roll, if something breaks our way, we'll be back in it. But when you've been around the game as long as I had been, and a lot of these guys had, you also understand in the back of your mind, that doesn't happen much. And even if you never lose hope, you don't quit, you don't sulk; that downward trajectory sheds light on what's going to happen in the next year or two, the big changes that are coming. And coaches have families, players have families, so it's not just those in the game who are going to be affected.

When the season ended, it was almost immediately announced that Bautista wouldn't be back. He had a great career that all started in Toronto. Jose threw out some money figure at one point, and you knew he wasn't going to get that. But I thought they still might bring him back because, public relations–wise, you never know when the heat gets put on guys how they'll react, and he had been the face of that franchise. Anyway, I wasn't in the loop, nor did I want to be.

It was truly so different for me than it had been working with J.P. and Alex. Decisions were made, and not only was I not consulted, but they directly changed how I operated.

The coaching staff was retained for 2018, but trainer Mike Frosted and strength coach Chris Joiner were let go. Atkins and Shapiro were making everything more corporate, and now that included how the team tended to the players physically. They brought in this group, they called them high-performance, and it was people with different medical type backgrounds — a lot of them. No longer was it the two trainers, team doctors and an intern. We've gotten smarter health-wise over the years, but it sure seems like more guys get hurt now than ever before.

There was some conflict there with that. I had always relied on my trainers to keep me abreast of how the players were feeling, who was banged up, who could use a day here or there. They'd always tell me that.

When they brought this new staff in, they pushed the trainers to the side a little bit. I was really tight with the trainers professionally, even personally, and so I didn't like that. And it was change, and we're not always good with change. I thought things already ran pretty smooth around here.

Everything was in transition. There was a lot of hiring going on, and every time you turned around, it seemed like you bumped into somebody new. Now I knew why we couldn't sign Eddie or Jose — we had to pay all these new people.

If you talk to a lot of guys my age, they'll say the same thing — the game functions a certain way, and it can be very simple, but we try to complicate it all. There's a certain way to do things, and clubhouses are sacred. That's for the coaches and the players. With all these new people, everybody coming and going, it tears apart a little bit of the closeness, the camaraderie and cohesiveness. People are bumping into each other and they don't know who's who. What it really comes down to is communication. When there are too many people in the communication chain for certain things, it can actually confuse things more, and something's always lost in translation.

Some of the players complained about it, but there was nothing I could do. It fit well for a 2018 season that was going south again pretty quickly. It gave us something else to bitch about.

But there was some light ahead: Vladimir Guerrero Jr. and Bo Bichette; maybe you've heard of them?

When the Jays first signed Vladdy Jr., assistant GM Tony LaCava came to me and told me about his signing, that I'd love him and that he was probably going to be a fast-moving kid. They raved about him, but it's always a gamble when they're that young. They knew there was something different about him. I also heard a lot of good things about Bichette, but Vladdy Jr. was always the talk of the town.

Then I got to see them firsthand at the 2018 spring training, and what stood out was the way they both carried themselves, oozing confidence. I had watched both their dads play and they both could really hit, but I didn't know either one. Bo and Junior came from great bloodlines. I don't think anybody thought Bo would come on as fast as he has. But they all thought Vladdy Jr. would. They should both anchor the Blue Jays for years to come.

The debate with Junior was the same as with every great young player: when do we start his earnings clock? Were they going to keep him down to suppress future earnings or did they really think he wasn't ready? Most teams do it, so Toronto did too. Is that right or wrong? Who knows.

It made me reflect back. I'd been a first-round pick, and I got to the big leagues quick out of AA. I was only 21 — and I wasn't ready. I had a couple of injuries in spring training, so I didn't start the season in '84 on time. As I look back, I think a year of AAA probably would have benefited me. So if you rush somebody, and they're not ready, you may lose them and never see them again — that's kind of what happened to me. But I'm no Vladdy Jr. either.

I have a soft spot for those young kids, knowing both sides. Mentally, if they're not ready, you may never get them back. With Vladdy — well, you saw what happened to him. It wasn't all easy when he first got to the big leagues, he had some growing pains — then, all of a sudden, it clicked. Different kind of player than I was, obviously. Still, you want to make sure that they are all good and ready.

I heard they were trying to make some adjustments with him. This kid did not get to this point with your help, leave him alone. It can be a tough job coaching the can't-miss phenoms. First off, everyone in baseball knows he's good, so there's no debate there. But if you're his coach, he'd better not fail. I did a couple of radio shows, and the people would ask, "What's going on with Vladdy?" I'd say, "Nothing's wrong, leave him alone, keep running him out there and get out of his way. He didn't get here with your coaching or my coaching. Throw him BP or do his drills, then sit back and watch. He's not only going to make a lot of money, but he'll make you some too." Certain guys are destined. Pat them on the butt and say, "Go get 'em, kid." Then say your prayers every night and be thankful Alex signed him.

While I never managed Vladdy in the big leagues, I did have him on our team when we left spring training for a couple of games in Montreal at Olympic Stadium. Talk about a homecoming . . .

His father was a great player for so many years there in Montreal, and Vladdy Jr. was around to experience so much of that time. He basically was channelling his dad when he hit that walk-off homer on March 27, against the Cardinals at the Big O.

Before that game, we were laughing in the clubhouse because there was an ice cream machine in there. Through an interpreter, we learned that Vladdy used to come into the clubhouse as a little kid, but he couldn't reach the ice cream. The players would see him and lift him up to get some. Vladdy had a big grin as the story was told. What a great kid.

That was my fourth trip to Montreal for our last preseason games. It actually mirrors my initial perceptions of Toronto — at first, we all thought it was going to be a hassle. I think it was early on, we flew up to play those two games from the Tampa-St. Pete area, and then back to Tampa to play the Rays in the season opener. Then, the schedulers came to their senses and changed it so we'd go to Toronto after Montreal.

It turned out to be quite fun and enjoyable because we had huge crowds. It had that feeling of the season starting. Spring training can be fun, but it's also dull at times since there's no pressure, no enthusiasm, and it lacks atmosphere. So you go in to play those games, and Olympic Stadium is rocking, there's lots of media to do and it's a good preparation for the start of the season.

We all ended up enjoying it because Montreal did a great job hosting. It's similar to those players who said they didn't want to play in Canada, but ended up loving it once they got here. People's thoughts changed from *What an inconvenience* to *Damn, that was pretty cool.*

Heading into 2018, we'd added some quality people. Curtis Granderson had seemingly always hurt us when we played against him, and now he was on our side. Grandy came as advertised: another player whose parents did everything right, who was very respectful, a great citizen and cared about his teammates, the staff, the fans. We also brought on John Axford, who I loved, a big ol' strong, strapping Canadian boy who could throw hard.

It was a good group. We just didn't do enough to be competitive. The injury bug was starting to flare a little more often. It's tough to compete every year; the teams that do it, you've got to tip your hat to them. Once again, we finished fourth in our division, with a 73-89 record.

The darkest time in that season was learning of Roberto Osuna's domestic violence charge in May. It came as a complete shock. I was fairly close with Roberto, I was his first manager when he became a great major league closer at an incredibly young age. He was always special and very respectful to me, but I couldn't defend this, if true.

Domestic violence is unacceptable — there's no excuse. You don't want to believe it, but usually when the cops are called, there's a reason. That was a lot more important than anything baseball-related. The allegations weren't good, and his life and the young woman's life would be changed forever. It's a heck of a lot more important than someone striking out with the bases loaded or blowing a lead in the 9th.

It was uncomfortable in the locker room at first, that's for sure. His teammates were talking about it, but nobody knew the facts. The front office may have known more, but it's best to stay quiet and let justice take its course. Players have an ability to compartmentalize and move on. Roberto was there one day, and then gone the next — not all that different than when a guy's sent to the minors.

Ross had really no choice but to ship him out. While he was suspended, Osuna was sent to Houston on July 30, for former Astros closer Ken Giles and two prospects, Héctor Pérez and David Paulino.

Though it was nothing compared to what Roberto was carrying, Giles came with some baggage too. He got into a shouting match with A.J. Hinch, the Astros manager, and apparently told him off. I knew A.J. from my time with the Padres in 2012, so I called him when the trade was made. I told him from a baseball standpoint, Osuna would help them if he's mentally okay. In return, A.J. told me Giles was fine, that things got overblown and that I'd really like him. Giles ended up pitching great for us.

Houston got raked over the coals in the media for bringing in Osuna; many teams, I'm sure, wouldn't touch him because of the potential PR hit. In the end, the woman Roberto allegedly assaulted was the mother of his then-three-year-old child and she returned to Mexico; she declined to testify and the charges were dropped. Roberto got a 75-game suspension. Another out-of-the-ordinary moment stuck out in 2018.

That was the year a big chunk of ice fell off the CN Tower and punctured the roof of the Rogers Centre. My first thought was, *What if that ice falls and hits somebody on the street?* I went up the CN Tower once with my family, so I'd seen the view and got a good impression of how high up it is. For a Texas boy, it took me a little getting used to the signs in the spring all around downtown Toronto warning you about ice falling from the high-rises. I'm actually surprised damage doesn't happen more often.

They cancelled one game, and then we did a doubleheader.

Nobody wants to play doubleheaders, I don't care what time of year it is, because in the big leagues they're nine innings. In the minor leagues, it's better because they're only seven innings. But that's a long, long night. The doubleheader throws your team out of whack as far as setting up your pitching, using your bullpen, because you don't want guys throwing both games — and occasionally some of them do, and then that screws them for the next two days.

The strategy of baseball is really what you do with that pitching staff. The on-the-field play, the position players, you've got your lineup and it just kind of rolls, with guys out there damn near every day if they're healthy. The biggest decision you can make is to adjust the batting order . . . and then they go out there and do their thing.

The pitching staff, you've got to worry about the number of pitches they throw or keeping them healthy and not overthrowing them. They're all different; you get some guys who get a little older, and they can't throw as often as the younger guys. There're guys on the pitching staff that we say are "Taking it for the team." They have to throw more innings to get us through the game. Usually, it's a younger guy with less mileage on his arm, or the pitcher without a late-inning role. You don't want to abuse anyone, but sometimes it happens. Where today's game is so different, in the past the whole bullpen could throw multiple innings, even the closer. Nowadays, hardly anyone throws more than one inning.

They used to play doubleheaders every Sunday in the major leagues years ago, and I think Monday was off or something like that. But back then pitchers threw more. You might have a doubleheader, but there was a good chance both of those starting pitchers would be throwing nine innings.

That's unbelievable nowadays, and they wouldn't even let them if they could. In today's game, the best you can hope is to get six out of your starter. And if you can only get five or six innings out of your starter, you've got four innings or more to fill. The relievers only go one inning, most of them. They come in, air it out, throw it as hard as they can — that's the way they're groomed.

There's a lot of strategy that goes into it, and you've always got to keep in the back of your mind that you'd better keep these guys healthy because it's a long year. So a doubleheader that early in the season can really mess things up.

You'll hear that working with the bullpen was one of my strengths as a manager, and I'll agree with that. I'd sure spent enough time in the pens myself, so I should know how to run one.

The August 31 trade of Josh Donaldson to Cleveland was the final signal that it was all coming down. Josh epitomized playoff baseball for us those two years.

Did I know I wasn't coming back either? Yes and no. But it was inevitable.

As the season went on, I felt further and further away. Atkins and Shapiro had their plans in place.

It was a far cry from J.P., who I could tease. One time, he started the analytics-talk about how Josh Towers never had any success against the Red Sox, and that I shouldn't use him. Well, during the game, I got Josh up in the pen *only* to annoy J.P. It worked.

Baseball is a billion-dollar industry, but if people only knew some of the crazy stuff that goes on, how simplistic it is for the money they spend ... I've said it often — I can be very immature. If you're in baseball your whole life, you never have to grow up because you're with kids all the time.

At the beginning of August, we were out in Seattle and won three out of four, so we're feeling good, but we're going nowhere. Then somebody floated a trial balloon in the news back in Toronto that upon returning from this trip, Gibbons would be fired.

I'm going, *Really? This late in the season?*

That chapped me, nobody knew for sure who said it. Obviously, it's somebody in the front office putting it out there, seeing the response they'd get from it. It's like politics. Politicians float these ideas to gauge the public's response because they can't make decisions on their own or have no core principles. It's like flipping coins. If you're going to do something, just do it and own it.

And that bothered me because of where we were in the season. Was it going to make any difference? Things got tense between me and Ross. I knew I was done after the season, I was ready, but if we're going to do this before the season's over, how about a little respect? I'm not looking for a lot, just a little. Now, one thing you should know about me by now is, if I'm going down, I'm going down fighting.

It made me think back to a phrase that Paul Beeston taught me: "screw you money." I asked him what that meant. He said, "Well, you're guaranteed that money, so you can always say, 'Screw you. That's money coming to me anyway. Get rid of me.'" Since I had a year left on my contract, that "screw you money" ended up coming in handy. Plus, sometimes they do you a favor firing you.

News broke on September 26, before our final home game of the season, that I wasn't being brought back for 2019. Ross and I had a joint news conference announcing it — hey, just like J.P. did with Carlos Tosca, though not quite the same drama.

"We kept that secret pretty good, didn't we?" I joked to start, and I explained the deal. "We had been talking, obviously, the last couple of months. Ross and I are on good terms. It's just one of those things that happens in baseball. It's not surprising, it's pretty common. And we've come to the conclusion that it's best for both sides if we go in a different direction."

That was a tough day for me, since I knew this was it. I'd never manage another game in a city and country I'd grown to love. Plus, I was leaving behind many good friends. From my friends in the media, to the stadium workers I saw all the time, to our baseball people who I worked closely with for so many years — I'd spent more time with them than with my own family. And especially the ones who gave me the opportunity to manage the team — not once, but twice. From J.P. and Alex to Beeston and Godfrey. I feel my greatest trait is loyalty, they know they can all count on me if needed. But it'd better go both ways.

For the final game of the season, in Tampa, I stepped aside and let Russell Martin be the manager, just for fun. From one catcher to another. I watched from my office. "Gibby was nowhere to be seen today. I told him today was my day," Russ told the media. "It was fun, I didn't realize how much went into it, how much preparation, how much you have to think ahead. It was a cool experience. It's tougher than it looks."

Amen. If Russ ever wants to manage, he'll be an instant success.

Gibby's Greats: Jon Berti

Jon Berti finally made it to the big leagues during my last few days as Jays manager. A kid of out Troy, Michigan, he'd gone to Bowling Green State. He'd been in the minor leagues since being drafted by the Jays in 2011, and even played in Australia for a time. But he'd had a few concussions. Always a very productive player, but he was an older kid. Every manager who ever had him on their team in the minor leagues loved him, and he always produced.

Then he got the dreaded label of filler player on a team, but every manager still played him — he was a true utility guy. Medical issues stalled him a little bit. There were a number of times we tried to get him up to Toronto, but it just didn't line up. This is *the* ideal guy that you want in your organization. But not only that, he's good.

We had about a week left in the season, and even with the expanded September rosters, something happened and we needed a body. I lobbied: "For crying out loud, finally, bring this kid up here!" They did. I don't think the front office thought he would play much, but I said screw it, I'm playing him every game, let him get his day in the sun. I figured, by God, if anybody's earned this, it's Jon, and he may never get another opportunity. He's been busting his butt, been loyal to the organization — even if the Jays traded and reacquired him earlier that season. If he gets up there for one day, a week, one month, he can go home and say, "I got to the big leagues." Now he could turn it into something much better. And heck, he played great, like he belonged. He's been in the big leagues with the Marlins ever since. Now he can say that his dream came true, he's capitalized on it.

So if he didn't get that opportunity, who knows, he may have been out of the game right now.

My point is, you do what's right.

Take care of your loyal guys. You can't always do it, but when you can, you should. You don't play favorites; if the guy is not deserving, you don't do it. But Jon was deserving because he was a good player, too, and he filled a need. This also does wonders for team morale. Not only did most of the players on the team know this guy, whether through being in the system or from spring training, but they all loved him. So now they're excited that this guy got to the big leagues. They all figured he wasn't ever going to make it. Hell, even Jon probably figured he'd never get there.

19.

PATHS NOT TAKEN,
STILL TO COME

I f I'd done my schooling like my dad had wanted, I could probably pull out some deep quote from my memory about paths not taken, walking in the woods or other nonsense.

The only paths I ever saw were basepaths. I'm a baseball lifer. I love the game, and I want to be a part of it. But I don't want to overdo it. I love the managing aspect of it. I would love to have one more shot at that.

I may not be able to quote poets, but I know my classic clichés, and baseball's been *berry berry* good to me. I've got two World Series rings for being a very small part on two championship teams.

Oh, I haven't told you about the second one. Right.

It's from the 2021 Atlanta Braves. Officially, I was a special assignment scout, but with two years of a global pandemic, there wasn't always a lot to scout. Jonathan Schuerholz (son of the Hall of Fame Braves executive) and I were dispatched to watch the Astros and Red Sox battle it out in the ALCS — ironically, I'd been interviewed about managing both teams after leaving the Jays, which I'll tell you about in a bit. We went to the ballpark in Houston to check out the action and realized we were greatly outnumbered — the Dodgers had sent five or six scouts and Atlanta had sent just us two. But Schuerholz is really good and thorough, so I helped him the best I could. I watched the pitchers and catchers, and he locked in on position players and pitchers. Was our contribution crucial to the Braves winning? We'll never know, but they sure got hot.

The Braves got in the playoffs with the least number of wins, and it wasn't till the end of the year they took off. They were smoking hot when that thing started and they rolled through it, against some pretty good teams. Alex Anthopoulos, the Braves GM, once again worked his magic at the trade deadline and acquired some difference-makers.

Baseball is such a streaky game. And sometimes the good guys win.

When Alex left the Jays, he went to the Dodgers. I tip my hat to him — he looked at things realistically for his own career. The way it was structured with Beeston as the president, Alex got free rein and a lot of autonomy, but Beeston had to sign off on moves. Beeston trusted him. Beeston believed that you are accountable for what you do, and you'll be held accountable. I think that's all anybody ever wants — let me do my job. How can you fairly hold someone accountable if you're always looking over their shoulder and micromanaging everything? It never works.

What happened to Alex, with a new boss coming in, he wasn't going to have that anymore. On the baseball end of it, I think Shapiro would have been more hands-on; he would oversee things and also be very active, but that's his style. Alex obviously made the right move.

Alex got a job out in LA with the Dodgers and teamed up with some really good baseball guys. We kept in touch, and there were a couple of times he called me with an update on a job here or there. He was always my guy, someone I wanted to end up working with again. We all missed him when he left, but that's baseball.

Then he got the job as the Atlanta GM. They already had a great manager in Brian Snitker, who took a very similar route to the one I had taken. He's a great dude, older guy — a little bit older than me anyway. He was a fixture in that organization. The only way Alex ever would have made changes with the Braves coaching staff would have been if things went south, and they never really did over there.

When Alex and I talked, I told him that I'd love to do some kind of special assignment. It's similar to what a lot of ex-managers did. Cito Gaston stuck around behind the scenes with the Jays after his first run, and then he replaced me. Later, his role was almost that of an ambassador, he'd come around spring training, shake a lot of hands. That happens a lot of times with ex-managers, they stay in contact with their ex-clubs, or the ex-GM that hired them. It's an extra voice of experience that you already trust. There's no denying it's a sweetheart job to many as well, that never hurts. (Incidentally, when Cito was inducted into the San Antonio Sports Hall of Fame, they had me do a little video for it because I'd known him from the Blue Jays.)

Alex offered me a scouting role, which got me excited. I would scout some amateur stuff, have a look at some of our minor league teams and possibly go look at some major league players.

I'd sat out a year collecting my "screw you money," not going to baseball games. So when my new job started, Dana Brown, the Braves scouting director and ex–Blue Jay also, sent me out to watch some high school and college players. Then, boom, COVID hits.

There's no question that a baseball scout is not an essential worker in a global pandemic, because there were no games. Spring training was out of the question, as they wanted to limit the numbers. I get it. My hat's off to the real heroes — doctors, nurses, scientists, first responders — that helped pave a way out of the pandemic.

I barely got to know any of my colleagues in Atlanta. The only chance you really get to know these guys is when you get together in groups for meetings. We only had one of those in Atlanta before COVID hit. With a lot of them, you could tell me their name, I couldn't tell you what they look like.

Scouts all sit in their section; at whatever ballpark you're at, they have a certain area, usually right behind home plate, so all the scouts are lumped together. If I didn't know them, I got to a little bit. We bullshit about the players we're watching, but there's lots of reminiscing too. Inevitably, you'll share connections somewhere, whether you played together or managed against him. People said to me, "It must be tough scouting after managing in the majors." It was definitely different, but scouts have the toughest job in baseball. I admire them all. The thing about managing in the big leagues, you're going to get whacked — it's just part of it. There are very few Walter Alstons and Tommy Lasordas that stay with one organization for a long, long time. It's a business. Everybody wants instant results. Never overvalue yourself — that's in baseball and in life. There are only 30 of those jobs out there, so if you don't have one of them, and you want to stay in the game, sometimes you take jobs that outsiders may view as a step down. But if you love the game, it's a pretty good gig at any level. Plus, I loved getting back to the game's foundation and roots.

Eventually, I got back on the road. Scouting for a team is just a little more formal version of what we do, as baseball lifers, every day. You can be a player, coach, manager, whatever it is, in professional baseball, and you're always a scout, because everybody watches other players, measuring up competition, whether one guy has more talent than another, different swings, things like that. So you're actually scouting then. When analytics came along, it was the kiss of death for a lot of scouts. I always thought scouts were the unsung heroes because they'd be out there on the road all by themselves. When they'd come to town, we'd talk about baseball in my office. I enjoyed having them come around. With analytics, they don't come around as much any more, not as many have jobs.

I did have a couple of other potential jobs come along at various times.

Trey Hillman, my pal from the Royals, called me after I was axed in Toronto and said his old team in Korea was looking for a manager, and he had talked to them and he brought up my name. He was calling to see if I had any interest in doing it, because if I did, he was going to push me. But I told him that as much as I missed the game, I'd rather keep my feet grounded in the good ol' USA or Canada.

The fallout from the 2017 Astros cheating scandal got me two other interviews; completely different ones.

When news broke that Houston manager A.J. Hinch was suspended for a year, I was in a Braves scouting meeting. So I texted him to wish him luck and to hang in there. An hour later, the Houston owner announced that they had fired him.

That night, Hinchy called me and said, "Hey, you want this job down here in Houston?" I said, "I've always wanted to work in Texas — Dallas or Houston — but not under these circumstances. You're my buddy."

"Don't worry about it. I know the owner really well, and I'm gonna throw your name in there."

The next day, we were sitting in the scouting meetings, and I got a call from owner Jim Crane asking me to come down for an interview. Naturally, he had to ask the Braves for permission, and Alex was not going to stand in my way. They let me leave the scouting meetings a couple days early, and I flew to Houston to interview with Jim. They didn't have a GM either since he was dismissed as well, so I sat there with Jim for about four hours and talked about everything. I was impressed, apparently more than he was, but I'll tell you one thing — he wants to win.

Then the league was investigating Alex Cora, who Boston had hired away from Houston, where he'd been the bench coach. Chaim Bloom was in his first year as the GM of the Red Sox, and he'd just left Tampa. He called me in for an interview, almost as a backup, depending on what came out of the investigation. They knew Cora was suspended for a season, and they were leaning towards going with Ron Roenicke, the bench coach, as manager to keep as much continuity as possible if the investigation turned out fine.

The idea was if they found something in that investigation that they didn't like and was too egregious to ignore, then they were going to clean house and have a new manager. I must have interviewed with half the people in Boston, it was that thorough, and some very impressive people at that. One of the groups were three guys from their analytics department. I think I have the reputation of being anti-analytics, which is wrong. I know there is a lot of value in it, and it's made a lot of things better in the game. I just don't take it to the extreme. I still recognize the human element.

They asked me if I had any questions. I said, "There's something I'm curious about. You guys and the Yankees have the most resources available in the game" — well, you can add the Dodgers to that group — "so you two can hire as many analysts as you want, no limits. Can the Yankees figure out something that you can't or vice-versa?" I don't remember the response. When it gets down to it, like always, the team who has the most talented players wins in the end. My point was that the two analytic departments should balance each other out, so how do you outdo other teams when it's so saturated?

Big Frank Howard, known as the Gentle Giant, was a Mets coach back in the 1990s. Another true character of the game. He could tell the best stories and really made you laugh. One day, we were talking about teams that win, and he said, "Son, when you look in your dugout and see two or three cannons, then you look in the opponent's dugout, and you see five or six cannons, you may win a battle, but you ain't winning no war." That's my point. Now, if you have a bad general in charge, you may be in trouble regardless.

The Red Sox ended up staying with Roenicke.

I'll regularly drop a text to an old pal. It's working my connections, staying in touch. That could be media — Bob Elliott broke news of this book before ECW Press announced it. My connections have led to a podcast, *The Gibby Show*, though I had to give up my scouting job with the Braves to do it, an occasional promotional deal and even a test for a TV commentator gig — I can hear you laughing, but maybe with a little practice, I can lose the mumble-mouth! In 2019, I headed back north and did a few fundraising banquets. I didn't know what kind of reception I was going to get as one of the guests, but it was incredible. I went from Moose Jaw in Saskatchewan out to one in Halifax, Nova Scotia, and another two were in Toronto. It was the coolest, so uplifting, and it made me miss being with the Jays even more. I met some of the great sports stars like hockey legends Darryl Sittler, Ray Bourque, Chris

Pronger and a few more, race car driver Amber Balcaen and legendary figure skaters Tessa Virtue and Scott Moir. You talk about a lucky guy. As for what's next? Whatever happens, happens. Heck, I've gotten this far unexpectedly. The thing about baseball is there's nothing to complain about or fret over, and remember, there's no crying in baseball. There's pressure, but it's a different kind of pressure. We're in the entertainment business, we're not solving any of the world's problems. But the best thing of all is you never have to grow up. You can't, since you're hanging out with kids all the time.

But the toll it takes on you is real. Traveling all the time is hard on a body. It's even tougher on your family, when you're gone eight months of the year.

When I got a chance to manage with the Jays, it was a major boost in pay, and my MLB pension is there for me, too, scraping and clawing as I did to get my 10 years in. Having started when I did, I knew those guys who truly gave up something so that the game could grow. I can remember when I first started in 1980, my scout telling me that you used to have to work 20 years in the big leagues to receive a full pension; now it's 10. And you had to have four years in the bigs before you even got on the pension plan; now it's one day. I would have been in big trouble back then.

All those guys who went on strike and sacrificed greatly, the old-time players, I don't think guys today truly appreciate what they did for them. They are reaping the benefits now because of what those guys did.

The lockout before the 2022 season was inevitable, but it was also ridiculous. So little information was coming out — and I worked in the game!

But you can't kill baseball. It's going to survive.

I've got a handful of years left, and it's all I want to do, in whatever role in the game. I don't want to die in my uniform. Eventually, I don't want to answer to anyone else but God.

Those baseball gods have been tough on me, but they've also watched over me.

ACKNOWLEDGMENTS

John

My last few days in Toronto in 2018, a couple of my favorite writers and reporters approached me and said, "Hey, if you ever write a book, keep me in mind." I said, "A book? Nobody wants to read about me — even I wouldn't!"

But things change, and here it is.

Hopefully, you've enjoyed it and it confirmed how you felt about me, good or bad. It's been fun looking back at a lot of great memories that have made me who I am today.

This is the tough part, to recognize and thank all the people along the way.

I have been blessed to have had so many great people in my life. I can honestly say I can't recall anyone who has been a thorn in my side for any length of time. I've had the best friends you could ever want. I've coached not only the greatest players on earth, but some of the best people on top of that. I've had a few run-ins, but that doesn't change my thankful attitude towards those guys. Remember, it takes two to tango.

As I get ready to sign off, there are some more people I must recognize. They were instrumental to our success, otherwise I'm just a footnote in Blue Jays managing history. Jeff Ross, Kevin Malloy and all their cronies running the clubhouse; they make it a home away from home but often get overlooked. Our trainers and doctors; Glenn Copeland (Dr. Foot) has been a wonderful friend and is part of a terrific medical staff. Mike Frostad and Jeff Stevenson are two of the best trainers around and great friends. Then there's George Poulis, my trainer and confidant. I have never known a person more willing to help anyone, anywhere, at any time. Thanks, George. Marnie Starkman's staff always came through when I was there, and with this book, Sherry Oosterhuis sourced the great Jays photos.

Our coaching staff. DeMarlo Hale, Pete Walker, Luis Rivera, Tim Leiper, Brook Jacoby, Eric Owens, Dane Johnson and Alex Andreopoulos (not Alex Anthopoulos, but another Greek). These guys were an All-Star staff and even better guys, who I miss every day. Plus, they did all the work.

Then there are the boys in the trenches doing all the heavy lifting. This group made it fun going to the ballpark and kicking back and watching them do their thing. Not an easy group, but they sure were fun. Good players make managers successful, don't let anyone tell you otherwise. Thanks to Josh Donaldson for the honest foreword, and for being the very first guest on my podcast!

And last, but not least, Blue Jays fans. Toronto, and Canada as a whole, is a special place. A bunch of genuine, hard-working, fun-loving and appreciative people who like to keep it simple. Without you, who's gonna read my book? Keep in touch, *eh*? It really is me answering the tweets! https://linktr.ee/thegibbyshow

I have three great kids and a large, wonderful family across the U.S. I wish I could mention everyone, but I'd need another book. But I have to recognize my immediate family. Mom and Dad instilled in me values and love, and the importance of always trying to do the right thing. My brother and sister, Bill and Kris, always supported me, even in tough times. I had it good.

To my three kids, Jordan, Troy and Kyle, who always make me proud and make me smile a lot even during trying times. I thank their mother,

Julie, for bringing them into this world and helping raise them while I was gone too long.

And now to my new wife, Christi, who has really lightened my life. She's been a blessing and a real gem, and her boys, Jake and Jack.

As I look back on my life and career, I say thanks to everyone who knows me and has made me a better person. Thanks!

Oops! I can't forget ol' Greg Oliver, the author who became a great friend and did a terrific job leading the way, and John Arezzi, who put all this in motion.

Till we meet again.

Greg

I first talked with John Gibbons to write a foreword for John Arezzi's memoir *Mat Memories: My Wild Life in Pro Wrestling, Country Music, and with the Mets*. I remember joking with Arezzi that I should do Gibby's book next. Well, it wasn't next, but it *did* happen. Thanks to "Big John" for putting me over (to use a wrestling term), and to Wayne Halper, the lawyer who figured out all the paperwork.

It was an easy sell to Michael Holmes, senior editor at ECW Press, as he had once sat with Gibby at a sports dinner and was transfixed just hearing tales. The great staff at ECW Press put the book together like magic.

Thanks to all those who shared memories of Gibby. From his family, it was: his mother, Sallie; his children, Jordan, Troy and Kyle. From the world of baseball, it was: Josh Donaldson, Steve Springer, J.P. Ricciardi, Syl Perez, Brian Butterfield, Justin Speier, Jerry Howarth.

In November 2021, John's wife, Christi, and her son Jack were wonderful hosts as I acted as Gibby's shrink, asking him questions for three days as he lay on the couch (Kyle later told me "the couch is his favorite spot"). Gibby mentioned how he was always recognized walking the streets in Toronto, because he was on TV so often, but never in San Antonio. At breakfast, John signed two cards from his managing days; our waitress saw the cards and told a story about finding some baseball cards hidden in the wall of her place, but never put two and two together, that they were cards of Gibby who was sitting *right there*. We reviewed a collection of his ejections when arguing with umpires; watching these on Gibby's big screen was surreal.

Closer to home, to use a baseball analogy, Dominic Jones was my bench coach, someone I could rely on for research, proofing and cleaning up transcripts. The Blue Jays should promote him already! Fellow writers Dan Robson, Eric Zweig, Todd Denault and Bob Elliott, the dean of Canadian baseball journalism, all provided advice. The Toronto Public Library hunted down Mets-related books for me. My son, Quinn, has always loved baseball, and used to try to throw a knuckleball like R.A. Dickey; Quinn's an umpire now, but Gibby never yelled at him on the phone, so John must be mellowing. Much love and appreciation to my wife, Meredith, for the support through the years — finally, a break-through book, Meppie!

SELECTED BIBLIOGRAPHY

Blair, Jeff. *Full Count: Four Decades of Blue Jays Baseball.* Toronto: Random House Canada, 2013.

Davidi, Shi, and John Lott. *Great Expectations: The Lost Toronto Blue Jays Season.* Toronto: ECW Press, 2013.

Dykstra, Lenny. *House of Nails: A Memoir of Life on the Edge.* New York: William Morrow, 2016.

Pearlman, Jeff. *The Bad Guys Won: A Season of Brawling, Boozing, Bimbo Chasing, and Championship Baseball with Straw, Doc, Mookie, Nails, the Kid, and the Rest of the 1986 Mets, the Rowdiest Team to Put on a New York Uniform — and Maybe the Best.* New York: HarperCollins, 2004.

Strawberry, Darryl, with John Strausbaugh. *Straw: Finding My Way.* New York: HarperCollins, 2009.

Wilson, Mookie, with Erik Sherman. *Mookie: Life, Baseball, and the '86 Mets.* New York: Berkeley Publishing Group, 2014.

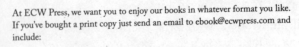